MW00772719

Grass-roots NGOs by
Women for Women

Grass-roots NGOs by Women for Women

The Driving Force of Development in India

Femida Handy
Meenaz Kassam
Suzanne Feeney
Bhagyashree Ranade

SAGE Publications
New Delhi • Thousand Oaks • London

First published in 2006 by

SAGE Publications India Pvt Ltd
B1/I1 Mohan Cooperative Industrial Area
Mathura Road
New Delhi 110 044
www.sagepub.in

SAGE Publications Inc
2455 Teller Road
Thousand Oaks, California 91320

SAGE Publications Ltd
1 Oliver's Yard, 55 City Road
London EC1Y 1SP

Published by Tejeshwar Singh for SAGE Publications India Pvt Ltd, typeset in 10/12 Calisto MT at Excellent Laser Typesetters, New Delhi, and printed at Chaman Enterprises, New Delhi.

Fifth Printing 2009

Library of Congress Cataloging-in-Publication Data

Grass-roots NGOs by women for women: the driving force of development in India / Femida Handy . . . [et al.].
    p. cm.
    Includes bibliographical references and index.
    1. Women in development—India. 2. Women in community organization—India. 3. Non-governmental organizations—India. 4. Women—India—Societies and clubs. 5. Entrepreneurship—India I. Handy, Femida, 1949–

HQ1240.5.I4G73   338'.040820954—dc22   2006   2006014023

ISBN: 10: 0–7619–3500–2 (PB)   10: 81–7829–655–1 (India–PB)
        13: 978–0–7619–3500–1 (PB)   13: 978–81–7829–655–5 (India–PB)

SAGE Production Team: Abantika Banerjee, Anindita Majumdar, Purnendu Ku. Barik and Santosh Rawat

*To our mothers, Zubeida, Parveen, Sue and Manik
who inspired us in many ways so we can be the best we can be
and to the women who founded the NGOs
we portray in the book, who lead and inspire other women
to lead better lives.*

Contents

List of Tables and Figures

Tables

Figures

Preface

The India that is presented in this book is different from that presented in movies or the many profound and ancient philosophies. It is the India of real people, where many women are living life in a society that suffers from scarcity and thousands of years of male domination and authoritarianism. Bringing about change in this society is a long and painful process. It does not come with a single social movement or a national crisis, but it is won one step at a time. It was our aim to follow twenty such efforts at change and to learn from them. We focus on the less glamorous aspect of Indian life, and hope that by doing so many more women will be served and the knowledge presented will be used to help new social entrepreneurs who will follow the footsteps of the twenty women leaders discussed and presented in this book.

India is very complex. To understand the way people live and organize their lives, one needs to have lived in India for many years. When one has lived in India for many years, one may forget the way the rest of the world is organized. As a team of four authors, one of us has lived in India all her life and has the deepest understanding of life on the ground. One of us had never been to India before starting on the book and brings in the Western perspective. Two of us were born and raised in India, but have lived and worked in North America for many years; we provide the balance between the Western view and life in India.

We also come from different disciplines: economics, sociology, public and non-profit administration, and business. This led to interesting conversations, many debates, lots of laughter, and finally, fruitful cooperation. We hope that the resulting book gives our findings a diverse lens for an interpretation that is interdisciplinary in its perspective.

It is our hope that future generations, who may come upon our work, will be genuinely surprised that there was a time when women and men did not live in social equality, and that women were marginalized members of society. We hope that the mission undertaken by the twenty non-governmental organizations (NGOs) we profile, and other similar NGOs, will change the Indian social and political scene sufficiently so that women and men equally share responsibility and power.

Acknowledgements

This book would not have been possible without the help and support of many people. First and foremost, the twenty amazing women who founded the NGOs we have studied in this book. They generously allowed us, over a period of five years, to probe and question them and their staff. With their incredibly busy lives, they were gracious each and every time we approached them for information. We hope our words accurately reflect their work, but no amount of words can capture their commitment and dedication to issues of social justice. We dedicate all the royalties from this book to their NGOs to help them achieve their missions of social justice and empowerment for women in India.

We owe a debt of gratitude to the anonymous referee who gave us excellent suggestions and helped shaped this book into what it is. Our various editors at Sage, Mimi Choudhury, Anamika Mukherji, Abantika Banerjee, and Anindita Majumdar who wisely steered us when we most needed it, we are indeed thankful. We are also grateful to Rochelle R. Côté, a doctoral student at the University of Toronto, who helped us with a careful and most intelligent review of our work—taking care of the many details involved in writing this manuscript.

Our husbands, Ram, Mohammed, Patrick, and Ajit and our children provided the moral and emotional support which helped us persevere. They believed in this project and encouraged us from the very beginning and tolerated our long absences as we conducted our research.

We gratefully acknowledge the various grants received from the Faculty of Environmental Studies at York University, Social Sciences and Humanities Research Council, Small Grants Program at York University, Hatfield School of Government and the Mini Grant Program of the Office of International Affairs at Portland State University and the Shastri Institute that helped fund the research at different times.

Introduction

This book is a result of a five-year study of small NGOs that were started by women at the grass-roots level in and around the city of Pune in Maharashtra, India. What started as a study of the women-founded NGOs, mushroomed into an analysis of the social impact and organizational structures of these NGOs. As women social scientists, we pay close attention to how these NGOs function through a gendered perspective and use aggregate data to find patterns and insights.

To capture the important realities of the lives of women, we couple the conceptual and empirical studies presented in this book with individual stories of the women leaders and their NGOs. These stories chronicle in detail the experiences of these incredible women. Our project culminated with two further visits to India in order to meet again with the founders and staff of six (of the twenty) NGOs who agreed to participate in the narrative part of the study and share their journey with us.

This book reflects our various interests in the non-profit sector and a growing commitment to empowering the lives of women in India. One of us started a small NGO in India to provide vocational training to poor women and the others engage in the academic study of NGOs. We all work with and support many NGOs dealing with women's empowerment by serving on boards of directors, donors, and volunteers. Hence, a natural choice for this study were NGOs founded and led by women that dealt with the empowerment of women.

The developing world has increasingly come to look at NGOs as a conduit for financial aid and assistance. The for-profit sector cannot be relied on to put aside their profit-making instincts to look after the poor. Development projects for intervention taken on by the government have often been sidelined by a failure to capture the heart and spirit of those involved in the implementation. Non-governmental organizations are increasingly important vehicles used by many governments, the United Nations (UN), and other non-profit organizations, to foster development around the world, as well as provide urgent humanitarian relief. It has become crucial to understand the entrepreneurial spirit of the people who start and lead NGOs locally and who are able to tap into local resources and comprehend the problems at a local level. Many of these organizations efficiently use resources through management strategies based on indigenous knowledge at the grass-roots level. They can also act as effective conduits (or nodal agencies) for aid received from other domestic and foreign donors, making NGOs increasingly important players in the field of development.

In the last few decades, there has been a proliferation of NGOs in India. The *Johns Hopkins Comparative Study of the Third Sector* found more than one million NGOs in India representing various sectors, ranging from the environmental to social development sectors (Salamon and Anheier, 1997). Indeed, the 1985–90 five-year plan of the Indian government included NGOs explicitly in its plan for the first time and integrated them in the development process. The vast numbers of NGOs in India have varying tasks and purposes. They come in all sizes and have differing structures with differing approaches. They range from large well-known national organizations like SEWA (Self-Employed Women's Association), with as many as 220,000 members and a large budget, to small, virtually unknown, rural organizations with few members operating on shoestring budgets (Crowell, 2003: 10). These NGOs have proliferated in Maharashtra where we locate our study, and are often 'grass roots, community-based organizations, where women are organized as collectives towards the overall goal of achieving sustainable, comprehensive community development.' (Purushothaman and Purohit, 2001: ix).

The popularity of NGOs has generated considerable literature. However, attention often centers on the larger, well-known NGOs such as SEWA, Asha, Aware, Sadguru, and CRY, who are recognized leaders in the field, just as in the for-profit sector where attention is often focused on large multinational corporations. It has long been recognized, however, that small businesses are the engine for economic vitality (Viswanath, 1991). In the same vein, we believe small NGOs are the engines behind development efforts around the world. National development policies cannot be effective or relevant without stimulus from grass-roots and local organizers.

Small NGOs have attributes that make them effective agents of change. They are flexible, localized, and encourage the use of indigenous solutions. Grass-roots groups, the very foundation of civil society, need to be studied and documented, in terms of their formation and impact on development. Non-governmental organizations, domestic and international, have long attempted to alleviate poverty in India in numerous ways. Initially, this aid was to assist with local relief of the poor, education, and help in times of crises. Over the years, aid has been redirected to diverse areas, from technical assistance to self-help strategies, and from neutrality to advocacy with multiple constituents with pluralistic orientations.

There are several important reasons to study small grass-roots NGOs. Indeed one might argue that all NGOs start small. Indeed, it is the initiation of NGOs and the entrepreneurial spirit of the leadership of such NGOs that this book focuses on. Little is known about women's leadership in India apart from the for-profit management literature (see studies by Chandra, 1991; D'Cruz, 2003; Dhillon, 1998; Rani 1996). A gap exists in the literature on the leadership in the non-profit sector, especially of small grass-roots NGOs that are ubiquitous in the Indian landscape (Nanavatty and Kulkarni 1998; Srivastava et al., 2004). Even less is known about the impact of these small NGOs on urban and rural poor women. Accordingly, attention needs to be paid to small organizations that are flexible and that address a multiplicity of issues that are interrelated in the lives of poor women (Purushothaman, 1998).

Our book sets out to study women's organizations that serve poor women and documents the narratives of such efforts. Along the way we study the characteristics of the women who started these organizations, the organizational structures themselves, the multiplicity of activities they are involved in, their holistic approach, and their impact. We pay special attention to social capital used by women, and document narratives on several founders of these NGOs. There is a gap in the literature on leadership, structure, and impact of small women-led NGOs and this book provides an important contribution to correct that.

Not unlike the rest of the world, poor women in India lack the power to control their lives and determine their future. This is in part due to social and religious traditions in India, where the power to control one's life is even less available to women than men. Being women and poor multiplies inequalities. As a result, women who are at the bottom of the economic and social ladder are doubly burdened. Despite constitutional mandates for gender equality in India, women fare worse than men (CIDA, 2005). Many efforts to promote these mandates are either impeded by tradition and custom or are subverted by token representation. For example, the constitutional mandate that provides for one-third of the seats at the local government level to be held by women has, in many cases, resulted in women sitting as fronts for their husbands or other strong male relatives. These women have little knowledge of what it means to be an elected official and often simply function as mouthpieces for the men (Narasimhan, 1996: 45). However in a number of cases, women's participation has made serious differences in their communities, especially where women receive training and capacity-building inputs from local NGOs. In the cases where educated and middle-class women are attracted to join the panchayats, these panchayats operate significantly differently from those where women enter because their male relatives want them to (Batliwala, 1996; Chattopadhyay and Duflo, 2004; Kudva, 2003).

Another example of gender inequality exists in comparing national literacy rates. While men enjoy a literacy rate of 64 per cent, women have a literacy rate of only 39 per cent according to the 1991 Census (Bose, 1991). In the more recent 2001 Census, this difference shrinks slightly from 25 per cent to 22 per cent as men show literacy rates of 76 per cent and women show rates of 54 per cent (Tata, 2002).

In some cases, women are further marginalized when modernization introduces technologies that makes them redundant in the labor force. For example, Aital (2004) relates the story of women in south India who objected to being displaced from their traditional water-bearing tasks when faced with a technological aid to pump water from their local well. They insisted that they, not the men, be trained to maintain and repair the water pumps. Often these disparities are difficult to identify at the macro level where statistics are not compiled by gender. This disparity persists because women are often unaware of their own rights, and do not have faith in the institutions around them to protect them when they perceive injustices. This suggests that without third-party intervention, many poor women remain resigned to their absolute powerlessness.

The disadvantages that women face are embodied in indices of development and socio-economic status. These indices include education, income, employment, health, decision-making authority, status in the family, ownership of property, as well as access to, and control over, resources (United Nations, 2000).

Regardless of region and population strata, women have invariably fared far worse than men. Even when national indices of development show an improvement, the benefits of development often accrue more to men than to women (CIDA, 2005). Some evidence suggests that

Indian women lag behind men in regard to education, literacy, health, and persons living in absolute poverty. Though some women in middle and upper class families have more disposable income due to greater numbers of women in the workforce (women make up 60 per cent of employees in information technology and outsourcing work) by and large, women are often excluded from decision-making structures and processes at all levels: government, corporate, societal, and household (ESCAP, 1997). Although women's work is a vital and productive sector of the Indian economy, and the majority of women work long hours at home and outside the home, they often have to defend their right to paid work in the face of familial and community opposition (UNIFEM, 2000).

It is not surprising that many important transformations in the lives of poor and rural women are often the direct result of the intervention of NGOs. Non-governmental organizations that deal with the reduction of poverty for women have been able to reach many marginalized communities and have empowered women through a variety of programs, the most popular being microfinance. Although legislation in India does, in most instances, protect and promote women's rights, NGO intervention aids in enforcing such rights. As a result of successful intervention by NGOs, their intervention has been credited with transforming the lives of poor and rural women and successfully altering the political context in which women live and function (Fisher, 1993).

India, and particularly Maharashtra, has witnessed a rapid emergence of organizations focused on the empowerment of women as a way to ease rural and urban poverty. For example, NGOs often initiate self-help groups (SHGs) in communities where they act as facilitators rather than leaders and rely on local knowledge to initiate income generation projects as well as community development activities. The increasing number of these types of NGOs are a part of a distinctive community-based movement grounded in local issues where the concerns of local women determine the direction of the movement.

As women associated with such movements are taking charge of development and getting involved in local government, they are addressing multiple issues affecting the daily lives of the women in their communities. They also work to institutionalize women's priorities and make government officials and policies more sensitive to women's issues. This new vision of development is more holistic and heralds a future where women increasingly talk to each other across both national and international borders. Women partner with each other on a global scale and engage with institutional actors such as the UN, the World Health Organization (WHO), and the International Monetary Fund (IMF). They create additional synergies that result in shared strategies despite many cross border differences (Purushothaman and Jaeckel, 2000).

Although statistics on the gender of the founders of NGOs do not exist, the popular literature is replete with examples of those started by women. Women have long attempted to influence the social landscape in India by engaging in large-scale movements such as struggles for national independence and social reform, as well as specific movements including agrarian struggles and revolts (Lingham, 2002). Activism by women in the 1970s to promote equality led to the emergence of NGOs that placed emphasis on women's empowerment. These NGOs carve out particular niches among the disenfranchised urban and rural women and their impact on women's empowerment is significant (Leonard, 1989, 1995; Sebstad, 1982; Viswanath, 1991; Yudelman, 1987). Many of these NGOs are founded and led by women who bring with them experiences in social movements, commitment to the cause, as well as entrepreneurial and leadership skills.

Women helping other women is not at all a surprising phenomenon, given that they best understand the barriers and challenges faced by women. Women clients also tend to be less suspicious of other authority figures if they are women, especially when dealing with issues of domestic violence, health, and child welfare. The single most important force fueling the grass-roots explosion is the empowerment of women through NGO support (Fisher, 1993). This impetus comes from the actions of many women. Who are the women who found NGOs that deal with issues related to women's empowerment? What compels them to helping other women, instead of turning their energies to other causes? Is this an entrepreneurial enterprise? If so, the entrepreneurial forces need to be understood, harnessed, and supported.

The literature on NGOs and development has concentrated on the changes in NGO orientations and outcomes, as well as the factors that influenced such changes, especially in moving towards desirable outcomes (Carrington, 2002; Edwards and Sen, 2002; Lindenberg and Bryant, 2002; Mawdsley et al., 2002; United Way, 1997). This literature revolves around the implications of shifts of power in the North–

South relationship, investors' perspective towards community funds, and the power influence on the choice of NGO agendas and orientations. In this context, the very existence of NGOs has been taken for granted. Other than some anecdotal stories and case studies, the question regarding the founding and existence of NGOs has not been pursued systematically. This question initially motivated the project. We asked other questions such as: What was the origin of these NGOs? How did they come into existence? Who was responsible for their existence? What motivated the founders? What are the barriers to entry?[1] What intrigued us was not their efficiency and impact, but rather their very existence, perseverance, and survival. Hence, we focus not only on questions of impact and efficiency, but begin our study by examining the entrepreneurial spirit behind the founding of NGOs. In our narratives, we document in rich detail the practices and environments that enabled the NGOs to grow from one-person, one-issue enterprises with few or no resources into successful, functioning multi-issue organizations.

This book is based on research[2] that initially focused on the entrepreneurial nature of the women who started small grass-roots NGOs focusing on women's issues and challenges faced by them as well as the resulting organizations. We then turned towards questions of organizational structure and examined the social impact of these NGOs. Due to the various social reform movements including the feminist movement, it was not surprising to find that nearly all of our founders were feminists. This led us to inquire whether their feminist visions manifested themselves in the organizational structures—an egalitarian and flat structure—of the NGOs they lead. We also distilled the successful strategies used by women's NGOs in India for local development. We show how these NGOs use limited resources and provide 'more bang for the buck', as increasing the efficiency is uppermost in the minds of all donors as well as for the managers who run NGOs.

Finally, we were interested in the impact of these organizations on ameliorating women's problems. Scholars, who have studied NGOs focusing on empowerment and change, disagree on how to measure organizational impact. Non-governmental organizations, too busy

---

[1] Numerous case studies do address origin, formation, and motivation of founders of large non-profit organizations. However, there are not very many studies that look at small-scale grass-roots entrepreneurial NGOs formed and run by women.
[2] Most of our field studies were conducted in the year 2003–04.

with their service agenda, do not have detailed statistics on their outcomes and impacts. Consequently, we looked at impact more qualitatively, drawing on measurements such as generational activity, scaling, and organizational evolution as well as the measures of growth and stability. We examined personal networks that generally characterize women's organizations in order to estimate the propensity of social capital[3] to strengthen organizations and increase their impact.

Our Method

As this research was designed to further our understanding of successful NGOs run by women for women in India, we undertook primary research with twenty successful NGOs led by women for women.

We selected one region for our study. We did this to achieve certain uniformity within the context in which our NGOs operate. The choice of Pune, Maharashtra, was one of convenience and was a region about which we had local knowledge. As explained earlier, one of the authors resides in the city of Pune, while two of the other authors have lived significant parts of their lives in this area.

The state of Maharashtra is bustling and prosperous. Its population exceeds 78 million (1991) and accounts for nearly 10 per cent of the population of India. In fact, Maharashtra is the third largest state in the country both in terms of population and land area. Politically, it was carved out of the State of Bombay in 1960, which segregated the area based on a common language (Marathi). In its major cities like Pune, tall buildings coexist comfortably with crowded slums, and the latest models of automobiles jostle with bullock carts, cyclists, pedestrians, and occasional cows.

There is a strong agricultural base in rural Maharashtra, despite the overcrowded cities like Mumbai and Pune, that contribute significantly to the economy of the region. While heavy and light manufacturing industry have moved into the environs of the larger cities and also

---

[3] Social capital refers to the collective value of all 'social networks' and the inclinations that arise from these networks to do things for each other, according to Robert Putnam (1993).

account for the general economic prosperity of the state, agriculture still remains a significant way of life for most people in Maharashtra.

Second to Mumbai, Pune is the most important trade and commercial center within the state. A city of 2.5 million (as per the1991 Census, MASHAL 1996), it is located 115 miles south-east of Mumbai across the Western Ghats. Pune retains its strategic importance as an armed forces base, continuing since the end of British rule. Educational centers are numerous and interspersed throughout the city. In recent years, growth in the number of software firms has made Pune a major hub for the software industry in India.

In order to control for the variance of external circumstances that may arise in studying entrepreneurship, organizational structure and differential impact by sub-sectors, we chose one sub-sector of NGOs dealing with women's issues. As the principal source of satisfaction for NGO entrepreneurs comes from the pursuit of their organization's mission (Young, 1983), this choice also better controls for the differences arising among entrepreneurs attributable to different (or even competing) missions.

We also chose to use the 'learning from success' method by focusing only on successful NGOs. This is a tested method from the field of business (Peters and Waterman, 1985). It is predicated on the assumption that in a random sample of people or organizations, the researcher will encounter a full spectrum of problems and successes. Learning from success is an approach that focuses solely on those who made it as winners or achievers. This starts with identifying those who made it and whose success stories may be generalized. The researcher, therefore, focuses on a number of clients or organizations that are defined as successful and attempts to identify commonalties and themes that can account for successes and that are applicable to others (Rosenfeld, 1997).

We used the 1996 Directory of Organizations (India) to identify NGOs in and around Pune. To include NGOs established after 1996, we used telephone directories and referrals. From this database, we chose organizations whose mission dealt with women's issues, whose founders were women, and who had been around for at least five years. We also identified NGOs with some evidence of continuing success in terms of increasing numbers of women served, increasing programs, or budgets. We arrived at a final list of twenty-six NGOs.

Twenty of the NGOs (77 per cent) agreed to participate in our study, given the usual caveats of confidentiality. Of the six that did not participate, two organizations were no longer led by the women who founded them, and the others did not respond to our letter and telephone calls requesting their participation. The twenty organizations that did participate in this study are involved in providing basic services, mainly for rural women and children. These services include counseling, primary health services, family planning, literacy training, and a variety of legal and administrative services. Many are also involved in advocacy for women's rights with local politicians and within the judicial system.

We conducted in-depth interviews with the founders about the origin of their NGOs and the factors that influenced and motivated their decisions. We used two instruments to ascertain the organizational dimensions and socio-economic characteristics of the founders, including a self-evaluation of personality characteristics and their cultural and family history. We conducted follow-up interviews with their staff to obtain information on programs, check for reliability, and validity of the data, and obtain missing information. The interviews were first conducted in 1995 with follow-up interviews over the next six years to keep up with any changes in the twenty NGOs; that is, staff, programs, organizational culture funding, etc. In 2002 and 2003, all four authors conducted a round of in-depth interviews. We also conducted site visits at seven NGOs for additional stories and material that appear in the nine case studies.

We conducted interviews in the language most familiar to the respondent: Marathi or English. The author most familiar with both languages did the coding of the transcripts of interviews for the open-ended questions. We used a simple tabulation for close-ended data questions.

We realize that the study of twenty NGOs in a particular geographical region will limit any kind of generalization to a country that is as diverse and complex as India. Furthermore, we restricted our study of NGOs to those that deal with women's issues and are led by women. On this point we feel comfortable that the generalizations may be useful, in that women all over the country experience many similar problems, including the influences of religion and caste. Both the founders and staff at the NGOs, as well as the people they serve, are influenced by their roles as women in a patriarchal society. We hope our findings will be relevant to the many women who struggle to serve other women in trying to remedy the effects of poverty, discrimination, and cultural biases in India and elsewhere.

As a result of our focus on women-led NGOs, male-run NGOs were excluded. That was beyond the scope of our book, but we hope that this will serve as an invitation for others to take on this challenge: What kind of issues do male entrepreneurs of NGOs gravitate towards? What kinds of structures do they prefer, how do they make choices of services, and what ideology do they bring to the table?

In addition to focusing on NGOs that only deal with women's issues, we have ignored a gamut of other types of NGOs that deal with issues of importance to women, such as the environment and globalization. This omission allowed us to make organizational comparisons across our twenty NGOs as we have been able to control for the mission of the NGO as well as the cultural and social differences in the environment by restricting our NGOs to one geographic region. However, we believe that the insights may be generalized cautiously to other women-led NGOs dealing with women's issues in other areas of the country to help their effectiveness and reach.

This book is organized into three parts. The first part deals with a study of the women who had the entrepreneurial role in the founding of the NGOs we study. This is followed by detailed narratives and commentaries on two of the entrepreneurs who exemplify different ends of the spectrum of women NGO entrepreneurs. The second part deals with organizational structures of the NGOs in the context of the feminist ideology of the founders. This is also followed by comprehensive narratives and commentaries, which exemplify our aggregate findings in detail. Part three examines the social impact made by these twenty NGOs. The narratives that follow provide in-depth examples of unique, successful projects undertaken by two of the NGOs in order to increase their social impact.

Our narratives in Chapter One are the stories of Sindhutai and Medha Samant. We chose these women entrepreneurial founders because they represent both ends of the spectrum among our female founders. The first story is an example of an uneducated rural woman who has no resources at her command and no support from her family of origin. Her position in society resembles one you would expect of a woman in need; yet, she rose from near starvation, enduring the trials and tribulations of poverty and subjugation to rise to a position of leadership. Sindhutai did this through passion and true grit and she has been recognized nationally for her achievements.

Medha Samant, on the other hand, is an educated, upper-middle class urban professional with plenty of resources at her command.

She deliberately chose to avoid the easy life of a well-to-do professional in order to struggle with the issues of poverty she saw around her. Both women embody strong leadership and entrepreneurial qualities.

In Chapter Two, the narratives explore the influence of feminist ideology on evolving organizational structures, resource mobilization, and management techniques. We follow this study with a narrative on the evolution of two NGOs: Swadhar and the Nari Samata Manch (NSM). Swadhar is a relatively young organization, less than ten-years-old. It went through several interesting organizational transitions. The Nari Samata Manch, on the other hand, is a much older organization, founded more than twenty years ago. Its development trajectory is more traditional and quite different from that of Swadhar. By looking closely at these two organizations, we get insights into the diversity of organizational responses of NGOs to needs in their communities.

We highlight Chaitanya and Susamvad in Chapter Three to explore how choices of adding new services contribute to organizational impact. They illustrate diverse approaches: the organic evolution of programs and building on the successes of previous programs. In each case, we detail their choices of programs, how these choices were made and what difference it makes. We illustrate several programs to examine the synergies between them and their contribution to women's empowerment.

We invite our readers to journey with us as we explore the origins and successes of these twenty NGOs and uncover their experiences in the struggle to serve marginalized Indian women. These NGOs set out to help such women, empower them, bring them into the mainstream of society, and reject their low status attributed solely to the accident of birth. The environment in which these twenty NGOs function demonstrates the long and continuing history of gender and caste subjugation. It took the courageous actions of twenty women founders who set about to change this for many women in and around Pune. Their stories provide a picture of truly remarkable women.

We hope our attempt at outlining the actions and impacts of these women founders contributes to the literature on grass-roots NGOs by demonstrating an effective alternative model of organizational structure and behavior. The collective organizational model described in this book provides a sharp contrast to the more familiar and ubiquitous hierarchical and bureaucratic model of organizations we encounter in both the NGO and for-profit sectors. We anticipate that readers will be able to apply the lessons learned about organizational culture and effectiveness in their own work environments.

Our findings may also provide new strategies for getting work done. Whether an organization chooses to offer services or create products, this book illustrates how to develop a democratic and participatory organizational culture, which can be the most important determinant of an enterprise's success. *Grass-roots NGOs by Women for Women* also highlights specific insights about the values that drive the formation and operation of women-led organizations. We hope that many of these insights will be useful to other NGOs dealing with women's issues in India and help them increase their reach and effectiveness.

The options described in *Grass-roots NGOs by Women for Women* can pave the way for more mainstream organizations in learning that shared ownership of solutions by staff and clients complements and enhances the work of organizational leadership. Employees and clients are ultimately the forerunners of success because they implement solutions and are the beneficiaries of improved services and products.

This culture of participation that empowers both clients and employees may influence other entrepreneurs to look at the benefits of inclusiveness. This book provides specific insights on how woman-led organizations can be efficient even as they grow and assume bureaucratic features. There exists a potential model for mainstream organizations to reorganize themselves, cut down waste typical of large-scale bureaucracies, learn to be more democratic and become more participatory so as to build in ownership and future sustainability.

While some of the ideas and insights presented in this book may be familiar to many leaders and managers in the NGO sector, this study specifies and describes the critical factors for success that characterize democratic collective organizations. We hope this book will encourage others to emulate the practices of these twenty remarkable women entrepreneurs and experience a new brand of organizational effectiveness and success.

Chapter One

Women Entrepreneurs: Who are They?[1]

The best way to find yourself is to lose yourself in the service of others

(*Mohandas Karamchand Gandhi, 1869–1948*).

Introduction

In this chapter we look at the intriguing subject of enterprise in the non-profit sector. The concept of a flourishing non-profit sector is at the heart of all recent scholarship on social capital and development. Yet, the origins of the organizations which make up this sector are rarely studied in any systematic way. Although there are many anecdotal and historical accounts of founders and the founding of successful and usually large NGOs worldwide, little is known about smaller grass-roots NGOs. Yet, these organizations are at the heart of development actions in India, and many other regions around the world. Although there is no official census, scholars have a tentative estimate that the total number of larger NGOs in India is upward of 50,000. However, this number does not include many of the small grass-roots NGOs (Nanavatty and Kulkarni, 1998).

---

[1] Many of the results in this chapter first appeared in 2003 in Handy et al., 'Factors Influencing Women Entrepreneurs of NGOs in India', *Non-profit Management and Leadership*, 13(2): 139–54.

The enormity of the impact on development of grass-roots NGOs is in stark contrast to the dearth of knowledge about how these organizations originate. In response to a social need, one or a few individuals often start these ubiquitous NGOs. However, little is known about what motivates these individuals to start such organizations. Even less is known about those who are at the vanguard struggle to steer these organizations to success. The challenges and opportunities they face are rarely documented. In this chapter, we attempt to fill the gap in the literature. We present twenty women who started grass-roots NGOs in Pune, India.

Women's non-profit organizations have long played an important role in the lives of women in many parts of the world. In India, well-educated and affluent women have traditionally found socially-sanctioned work outside the home in the voluntary sector. Women have worked as volunteers under the aegis of religious organizations and for social service non-profit organizations dedicated to the alleviation of poverty and misery. Not unlike other traditional societies, participation in NGOs in India has given women the opportunity to enter social and political spheres in ways often denied them by the for-profit and public sectors. These volunteer experiences give women the opportunity to develop and practice leadership and organizational skills, as well as to obtain personal fulfillment outside of the limitations of traditional domestic environments.

The number of non-profit organizations has grown dramatically worldwide during the last few decades. For example, since 1982 the number of charitable organizations and religious organizations in the United States alone has grown from 793,000 to 1.23 million (Independent Sector, 2001). Similar growth patterns are seen in many countries (Salamon et al., 2004; Srivastava et al., 2004). These statistics imply that there are many individuals who are willing to undertake the effort and risk to start such organizations, as well as to assume leadership positions to maintain and uphold existing organizations.

Entrepreneurs, and to a certain extent leaders of NGOs, fuel the growth in the non-profit sector and are key in meeting the social needs of a society where governments are continuously cutting back in their direct provision of many goods and services. Given that one of the functions of non-profit organizations is to supply goods and services not provided by the for-profit or the public sector, understanding the growth of non-profit organizations is important to society. Hence, the study of entrepreneurship in this sector is vital.

In this chapter, we examine women's roles as entrepreneurs involved in initiating NGOs. Entrepreneurship, a much debated topic, has been defined in the for-profit literature as, 'The catalytic agent in society which sets into motion new enterprises, new combinations of production and exchange' (Collins and Moore, 1970). Although the concept of 'entrepreneurship' is closely linked to the for-profit sector and may seem strange in the NGO world, this is not the case. Entrepreneurial spirit is key in initiating projects and mobilizing resources, whether for promoting social causes in the non-profit sector, or promoting a profit-making enterprise. Both kinds of enterprises are the result of the entrepreneur's innovation, leadership, imagination, efforts, and ability. In using the definition from the for-profit literature, we define a non-profit entrepreneur as a self-directed, innovative leader who founds a non-profit enterprise.

In an interview with Young (1999), John C. Whitehead[2] noted that leadership and management in the non-profit sector is far more challenging than in the for-profit sector. This is because the goals of the non-profit organizations are not as clear-cut as those of the for-profit sector. Whitehead says:

> It is more difficult, in my opinion, to manage successfully a not-for-profit organization than it is to manage a for-profit organization. It's harder to manage the American Red Cross than it is to manage General Motors. One of the principal reasons is that in managing a for-profit organization, the objective, the mission, is rather simple—it's to increase profits for the stockholders. Of course in modern management there are other constituencies that a manager needs to be conscious of, but principally if he does a good job in increasing profits for the stockholders, he will serve a long tenure and end up a distinguished manager. But in a not-for-profit, where growth and sales and earnings are not so important, determining the mission of the organization, just what the organization is there to do; developing plans to achieve that mission; and monitoring the performance of the management against those plans are much more complicated things both for the management and for the board.
>
> Another difference is raising the money that an organization needs. A for-profit organization goes to an investment banker, who sells a $100 million bond issue, and they've got it made for the next few years. But in

---

[2] John C. Whitehead helped build Goldman Sachs into one of the world's pre-eminent investment banking and brokerage firms, serving as senior partner and co-chairman. He later worked in the government sector as deputy secretary of state and on retirement served on the boards of many important organizations.

the not-for-profit sector, raising the money from voluntary contributions is a lot more difficult. Trying to find ways to capitalize on some of the products and services that the organization offers, trying to persuade foundations and corporations and individual donors that this is an organization that deserves support, is much more difficult.... The use of volunteers is another example. When the chairman of General Motors tells his employees he wants something to get done, it gets done, because these people owe their jobs to the chairman. But in an organization that deals with volunteers, such as the American Red Cross, managing those volunteers and finding a way to satisfy them to work for nothing is a challenge that for-profit management doesn't have. So there are many factors that make managing a non-profit organization more difficult (Whitehead quoted in Young, 1999: 315–16).

Whitehead's words capture the essence of the differences in the two sectors and point out the key challenges facing non-profit entrepreneurs who must mobilize resources, manage, and govern effectively. Entrepreneurs in the for-profit and non-profit sectors, however, do face similar challenges: identifying opportunities, promoting innovative ideas, implementing ideas into viable enterprises, mobilizing resources, and undertaking risks inherent in starting a new project. A priori, this suggests that entrepreneurship in both the for-profit and non-profit sectors are related phenomena, although the primary motivation in the two sectors differ—making profits versus promoting a social cause or public good. Furthermore, entrepreneurs in both sectors are equally vulnerable to the personal, structural, and cultural environments in which they live.

Scholars such as Bilodeau and Slivinski (1996) have raised questions about non-profit entrepreneurship, for example:

Why would anyone invest time and money to found a non-profit enterprise? More specifically, how could it be rational for the individual who founds an enterprise and might still control it to deny herself the opportunity to appropriate the fruits of her skills and efforts?... If those who control non-profit enterprises cannot appropriate any profits, it is unlikely that profit-maximization is a useful behavioral assumption to employ in studying them (Bilodeau and Slivinski, 1996: 67).

There are, however, seldom responses to such questions in the existing non-profit literature. We already know that there is little known about women non-profit entrepreneurs, and even less when we look for literature on female entrepreneurs in India. For these reasons, in the next section we present a limited literature review and we turn to the insights from for-profit entrepreneurship studies done in less industrialized countries.

We consider a series of questions regarding women entrepreneurs of NGOs: What are the characteristics of women entrepreneurs in this sector? What motivates them? In addition, we examine if there are any structural and cultural factors relevant to understanding women's entrepreneurship of NGOs?

Literature Review:
Women Entrepreneurs

The study of entrepreneurship and leadership in the for-profit sector engages social scientists from various disciplines, notably economics, psychology, and business management. There exist several journals devoted almost exclusively to the study of entrepreneurship and leadership in the for-profit sector. It is outside the scope of this chapter to provide a comprehensive review of the for-profit entrepreneurship literature; however, we will look at a limited number of studies of for-profit entrepreneurship that seem be applicable to non-profit entrepreneurs.[3] Non-profit entrepreneurship studies in academic journals are limited. In particular, there is little material on female non-profit entrepreneurs or entrepreneurship in non-Western cultures. For such insights, we will rely on literature from the for-profit sector.[4]

We divide our literature review into four parts: First, we review the literature on non-profit entrepreneurship. Second, we review the literature on women entrepreneurs in the for-profit sector in industrialized countries, which is the setting for the majority of available studies. Third, we look at literature in less industrialized countries, focusing again on women entrepreneurs. Finally, we focus on women's style of leadership as entrepreneurs.

---

[3] For example, Brandstatter, 1997; Brush and Hisrich, 1991; Brockhaus and Horowitz, 1986; Caputo and Dolinsky, 1998; Carter and Cannon, 1992; Hisrich and Brush, 1984; McCelland, 1987; Sexton and Bowman-Upton, 1990; Watkins and Watkins, 1984.

[4] Baron, 1998; Brush 1992; Fischer et al., 1993; Moore and Buttner, 1997; Naffziger et al., 1994 to name a few.

Entrepreneurs in the Non-Profit Sector

Several authors have suggested that individuals who are driven by motives other than profit self-select themselves into the non-profit sector, either as entrepreneurs or as managers (Frank, 1996; Weisbrod, 1988; Young, 1983). Young (1983) provides an interesting approach to various stereotypes of entrepreneurs. He classifies entrepreneurs by their 'primary source of satisfaction' and suggests that the entrepreneur likely to be attracted to the type of NGO that occurs in our study will be the '*believer*' whose principal source of satisfaction comes from the pursuit of a social cause or mission rather than from the pursuit of profit.

Building on this, Pilz (1995) finds that non-profit entrepreneurs are further driven by personal experiences, perceptions of community needs, and the desire to provide services to others. Non-profit entrepreneurs are as likely as for-profit entrepreneurs to have characteristics such as risk taking, self-directing, innovating, and taking leadership; however, their focus is on what they can do for others. We have no reason to believe that the women entrepreneurs of NGOs in India will be any different, and we expect them to have many similar attributes.

In a theoretical paper on non-profit entrepreneurs, Bilodeau and Slivinski (1996) show that individuals who start non-profit enterprises are likely to incur relatively small capital costs and receive modest private contributions to aid in their enterprise. They are likely to be in the middle-income range and receive a high psychic payoff from the mission of the enterprise. As the kind of NGOs in our study fit their description of the non-profit enterprise, it is likely that the entrepreneurs in our study also receive great satisfaction from successfully advocating for women's rights, ameliorating the conditions of poverty and abuse among women and children, and helping to empower women. They are also likely to come from the middle-income range, which helps to cushion the non-lucrative nature of their enterprise.

We focus on NGOs pursuing women's issues and rights, and consequently expect that our women entrepreneurs have values that are aligned with feminist goals. Also, given that our study is located in India, we expect caste, which plays a significant role in the cultural context of India, will be an important determinant of NGO entrepreneurship. As we noted earlier, a woman's class, an outcome of caste to a large degree, strongly affects her opportunities for an education and marriage which often translates into privilege and status but not necessarily emancipation.

The urban India of the educated and privileged, is replete with examples of gender discrimination and inequalities. Very often even when women in the upper echelons of society fight to end oppression forced by caste and religion, they continue to hold patriarchal values in their personal lives due to the strong influence of their extended families. The opposite is not always true either. Women in rural India are not always submissive to the patriarchal forces. Increasingly, the poorest of rural women are joining women's groups or 'mahila mandals' where they collectively identify their own needs and priorities, and choose ways to determine their own futures. Moreover, they have come to recognize their rights and use the power of mahila mandals to resist male domination and abuse. We present a more detailed description of mahila mandals later on in this chapter.

Women Entrepreneurs in the For-Profit Sector in Industrialized Countries

Many previous studies have attempted to identify the characteristics that determine which women in the for-profit sector in industrialized countries take on entrepreneurial roles. Many have tended to focus on the demographic and psychological characteristics of women entrepreneurs—the challenges they face, and their motivations.[5] Some studies look at socio-cognitive and behavioral theories, while some take an integrated perspective or use a feminist approach.[6]

Given that the primary motivation of entrepreneurship in both sectors is significantly different, we use this literature with caution. In the for-profit literature, certain socio-demographic characteristics and motivations emerge among women entrepreneurs (Brush, 1992;

[5] For example, Brandstatter, 1997; Brush and Hisrich, 1991; Brockhaus and Horowitz, 1986; Caputo and Dolinsky, 1998; Carter and Cannon, 1992; Hisrich and Brush, 1984; McCelland, 1987; Sexton and Bowman-Upton, 1990; Watkins and Watkins, 1983.

[6] Baron, 1998; Brush 1992, Fischer et al., 1993; Moore and Buttner, 1997; Naffziger et al., 1994 to name a few.

Naffziger et al., 1994).[7] A study by Hisrich (1986) found that the majority of women entrepreneurs in the for-profit sector in the United States were married, from middle and upper-class families, had college degrees, and operated mostly service-related businesses.[8]

In our study, we expect that the women entrepreneurs who began NGOs and who are successful in providing services or advocating for change will have either training or prior experience in social services, as well as educational qualifications to enhance their credibility. We expect, a priori, that non-profit women entrepreneurs will also be married, and come from middle or upper middle-class families.

Start-up financial capital is frequently mentioned in the literature as a barrier to founding an enterprise. Inheritances and other familial financial assets that can contribute towards securing capital are found to positively affect a woman's decision to undertake entrepreneurship (Blanchflower and Oswald, 1998). Starting an NGO, however, does not require substantial capital because NGOs tend to be service-oriented and do not require the capital resources necessary in launching most for-profit businesses. But NGOs do need capital of a different kind, that is, social capital. Social capital includes the network of social, political, familial, and community networks that provide public credibility and legitimacy as well as donations of time and money.

Volunteer labor used by many NGOs is a form of social capital which can be considered a special kind of asset to NGOs. Volunteer labor not only provides the initial organizational capacity to launch the NGO but it also represents an invisible contribution to the economy as it represents a form of economic return to the economy (Quarter et al., 2003). Thus, an initial lack of financial capital is unlikely to be a constraint for NGOs, but the lack of other resources, namely volunteers and charitable donations will be constraints. This means that an NGO entrepreneur needs access to resources that are initially dependent on personal, family, and social connections (Pilz, 1995). That said, NGOs and their entrepreneurial leaders understand that

---

[7] Although there is some controversy about socio-demographic and individual characteristics having explanatory or predictive powers (Krueger, 2000), there are sufficient numbers of scholars who believe that these characteristics do have certain explanatory powers.

[8] In recent years there has been an increasing variety in the types of women entrepreneurs and in the types of businesses they own (Allen and Truman, 1993; Fischer et al., 1993; Gundry and Welsch, 2001). However, these studies do not invalidate the typical profile offered by Hisrich (1986).

start-up capital is linked with access to potential donors with time and money.

Household assets and income were found to be important factors affecting decisions for entrepreneurship in the for-profit sector (Blanchflower and Oswald, 1998). Household assets and income can also provide the necessary financial security for women entrepreneurs in the non-profit sector, thus they are likely to come from middle-class or upper middle-class households with relatively high assets and stable incomes.

Having entrepreneurial family members is also found to influence and support the women's decision in becoming an entrepreneur. The role that family members play in providing human capital— through mentoring, role modeling, and making available experience and knowledge—has been found to positively affect a woman's decision to become an entrepreneur (Caputo and Dolinsky, 1998; Cooper et al., 1994). We suggest that family influence is an important factor in non-profit entrepreneurship, but with an interesting twist, as we will explain later.

Early on, Goffee and Scase (1985) took an integrative approach (a combination of personal and environmental characteristics), and classified women entrepreneurs with varying commitments to entrepreneurial ideals and conventional female roles. One of the four types of entrepreneurs they defined includes 'radical' entrepreneurs—those who have a low commitment to both for-profit entrepreneurial ideals and conventional female roles.[9] This type of entrepreneur will closely resemble our NGO entrepreneurs.

For example, it is not uncommon in India for an educated and well-to-do woman to shrug off the limitations of domestic roles as a wife or mother and take part in the broader society. In addition, if she is a self-proclaimed feminist this ideology pushes her to fight for women who are subject to the abuses of deep-rooted patriarchy in India. In doing so, she often finds herself using her leadership and entrepreneurial skills outside of the accepted mold of pursing monetary profits through the aegis of an NGO. According to Goffee and Scase (1985), this type of entrepreneur sees the enterprise as a means

---

[9] The other three types are: 'conventional': women who show high commitment to for-profit (FP) entrepreneurial ideals and conventional gender roles; 'innovative': women with high commitment to FP entrepreneurial ideals and those who reject conventional gender roles; 'domestic': women with low commitment to FP entrepreneurial ideals and high commitment to conventional gender roles.

through which she can live by her feminist ideology, and considers this a means to promote social and feminist causes as well as being an economic unit. Profits are used to further feminist causes.

Carter and Cannon (1992) suggest that behavioral and motivational factors could differentiate women entrepreneurs. They classified women into five types: (i) young achievers: These individuals are likely to be well-educated and move directly into entrepreneurship after completing their education; (ii) drifters: women who seek entrepreneurship as a last resort in order to make a living and become entrepreneurs as an alternative to unemployment; (iii) achievers: women with related work experience who intentionally choose entrepreneurship over employment in order to gain the flexibility of combining family and career; (iv) returners: women who have taken time away from work in order to have families and upon returning to the labor market find entrepreneurship as a better opportunity and investment; and (v) traditionalists: women who came from entrepreneurial families and see entrepreneurism as a way of life. In this study we expect, a priori, to find all types, even traditionalists, if we allow that families who promote social causes and are engaged in social movements have children who see this as a normal way of life.

There is an interdisciplinary literature on the cultural aspects of entrepreneurship in the for-profit sector (Berger, 1991). Scholars argue that entrepreneurship is influenced by forces such as morals, norms, and values. This forms the context within which individuals pursue entrepreneurial opportunities, where cultural values and norms are critical in explaining entrepreneurship. For example, in India, entrepreneurial culture is prevalent at all socio-economic levels, from the pavement vendor, to the one-person enterprise, to the larger corporation. Entrepreneurship is also regarded as an honorable way of life, often more respectable than wage labor employment. For example, matrimonial advertisements may exhort a prospective groom as a 'business man' despite his business being limited to goods sold from a cart.

In our study of NGOs advocating and pursuing women's issues and rights, we expect women entrepreneurs to have values and beliefs that are aligned with such goals. In other words, to advocate women's rights in a patriarchal society will require our entrepreneurs to be strong and committed believers in the rights of women. The motivation to undertake such work must come from personal values and commitment to women's issues as there is no profit motive involved.

Finally, we expect that the cultural context of caste in India will come into play as we explore other characteristics of women entrepreneurs. When we explain the caste system in more detail in the Section on Findings, we will see how careers, marriages, education, class, and other socio-economic determinants are influenced by caste. Then it will not be surprising that our women entrepreneurs come from certain castes that may also reflect their socio-economic status.

Entrepreneurs in the For-Profit Sector in Less Industrialized Countries

In the two studies relevant to India, determinants of entrepreneurship include caste, family support, and previous experience, as well as individual characteristics (Gupta, 1991; Naffziger and Terrell, 1996). Although both these studies deal with male entrepreneurs of for-profit enterprises, we believe that factors dealing with caste, family support, and previous experience, with relevant variations which influence male entrepreneurs, will also influence female NGOs entrepreneurs.

In a study of women entrepreneurs in Pakistan (Shabbir and Di Gregorio, 1996), the authors investigated factors influencing the decision of women to start a business in an urban area. They argue that qualifications and a women's experience, location of the enterprise, availability of finances, and support of family members, suppliers, clients, and employees, constitute most of the factors that have an impact on women entrepreneurs. The extent to which women are influenced by these factors depends largely on their individual personal goals. In other words, all of these factors influenced women, but the relative influence of each factor differed among women entrepreneurs. The impact of these factors resulted in different expressions of entrepreneurship.

These personal attributes were classified as follows: *'freedom seekers'* were dissatisfied women who started enterprises as a way to get independence from their current employment; *'security seekers'* were women facing personal mishaps who wanted to maintain or improve family income and status while keeping flexibility in the hours worked and location; and lastly the *'satisfaction seekers'* were women with no formal experience, generally housewives, who wanted to demonstrate their ability to be productive.

In the case of women entrepreneurs of NGOs, we expect that the women are more likely to be either *freedom seekers* or *satisfaction seekers*, as running an NGO is not likely to be financially lucrative. In this case, according to Shabbir and Di Gregorio (1996), the factors most likely to impact the women's decision to become an entrepreneur would be education and family support. We expect that education and family support are crucial determining factors for women NGO entrepreneurs. Women, the majority of whom are married with children, will find it difficult to take on the struggles and challenges of starting and running NGOs that are largely self-financed and motivated by a commitment to women's causes. The family support factor occurs in different ways: being available for childcare, providing financial support to the NGO, volunteering to help, and providing psychological support. Such support cushions the entrepreneur's risk-taking venture.

Leadership by Women Entrepreneurs

Our literature review of women entrepreneurs would be woefully inadequate if we did not include a section on 'women's style of leadership'. Thus far we have been examining qualities such as 'innovative' and 'risk-taking' and classifications such as 'freedom-seeker'. These are useful but do not provide the specific characteristics and details about women entrepreneurs. There is a tendency among feminist scholars to adopt conventional male-defined standards so that the world gets framed ideologically from a male standpoint devoid of women's lived experiences. It also ignores the domestic realities central to most women's lives, such as their roles as mothers, spouses, and daughters[10] (Campbell, 2003). Women do indeed have

> ...a different way of doing things, a different way of working, of building capacities. Therefore, women will create alternative ways of doing things.... Women's ways of building capacities allow women to try things and make mistakes. In fact, you are encouraged to take risks. You are allowed to learn from each other so a caring space for learning is created rather than intimidating settings. This also stems from what mothers learn to do

[10] For example despite the influx of capable women entrepreneurs, Powell et al. (2002) found that most men and women still described good managers as having male characteristics.

with their children. For mothers, the question is how they can help bring out the talents of each and every child (Jaeckel and Purushothaman, 2000: 169).

This insightful observation indicates the emergence of a new work culture that is inclusive and participative as women find ways to do things that resonate with their perspectives and values as well as the many hidden demands that often remain invisible to others.

Moreover, women's leadership does differ from traditional forms of leadership. It is often intrinsically non-hierarchical, a far cry from the pyramid model of leadership. As a matter of fact, Aburdene and Naisbitt (1992) coined the term 'women's leadership' to describe the style that women assume while leading, a style that reflects their feminine values and behavioral characteristics. This style of leadership is more natural to women than to men. For example, Pierce and Newstrom (2003: 112) found in a meta-analysis of gender and leadership styles that 'men were more autocratic or directive than women, and women were more democratic or participative than men'. Women achieve organizational goals by encouraging people to transform their self-interest to feed into the goals of the organization through sharing of power and information and enhancing their feelings of self-worth. Men, on the other hand, were found to lead through 'transactions' rewarding good employee performance and punishing employees for inadequate job performance (Rosener, 1990).

By leading in a way that best suits their life experiences and traditional socialization patterns, women succeeded by encouraging employee participation, sharing power and information, and energizing their employees in the same way they interactively infuse moral strength and give structure to their families (Rosener, 1990). An unexpected finding in a study of women leaders, by the 2000 Winds of Change Foundation, was the identification of leadership skills and leadership metaphors with those arising from 'mothering' (Erkut, 2001).

Women leaders often form personal and social networks, a traditional socialization pattern, that becomes a prized source of information enhancing the leader's social capital. The fact that women spend much time maintaining personal networks is, therefore, not seen as an obstacle but an apt conduit to garnering information that is crucial to the success of the organization (Neilson, 1987). Male leadership, on the other hand, leaves out an important element which women's leadership does not, which is one of shared ownership. Male leaders often focus on rewards and punishment in a way that does not allow for shared ownership, which could possibly impact long-term sustainability.

Recent studies show that women are especially suited to the forms of leadership called for in the current work force; 'one that is right for the times' according to Moldt (in Nelton, 1991).The current approach in business literature that the business leader best functions as a team leader creating dynamic teams is especially well suited to the way women naturally lead (Acebo, 1994). The empowering style of leading and developing the capacities of others is evident in literature on women's entrepreneurship in the NGO sector in India. For example, many women-led NGOs encourage rotating leadership roles among other women—giving women opportunities to acquire multiple leadership skills.

This style of leading by empowering other organizational members can help overcome leadership transition and succession challenges that often occur when a founder or powerful leader leaves. Second line leaders can step into the leader's shoes and thereby preserve the organizational culture and assure leadership transition.

As many NGOs encourage and support the formation of women's groups, called *mahila mandals*, a short digression on *mahila mandals* at this point would be useful. *Mahila mandals*, depending on their location, attract women from all walks of life for the purposes of getting together and achieving collective goals. Although *mahila mandals* have been in existence for decades and are found throughout India, they were initially formed during the 1950s and were given a boost during Indira Gandhi's administration to facilitate an increasing involvement of women in the economic and political life of rural India. The aim of the *mahila mandals* in rural areas was to draw women, essentially poor women, into the mainstream of village life and to give them a voice in local development. Women were encouraged to come together and realize their power as a group and function as instruments of social change.

The formation of *mahila mandals* is often the first step in bringing women into the economic and political life of villages in rural India. The *mahila mandals* provide women members with a venue to discuss issues of women's rights, education, community needs, individual problems, and to come up with ideas and plans of action to address these issues. In some cases, the *mahila mandals* become fairly well-organized and register as NGOs, holding elections for the positions of president, secretary, and treasurer, etc. In other cases, they remain informal and unregistered.

Ideally, women hold regular meetings and take an active role in the design and implementation of the new development projects in their villages introduced by NGOs or by the government. In *mahila mandals*, rural women learn about and practice leadership and decision making. *Mahila mandals* also play an important role in creating collective public ownership of assets by women and empowering women through collectivities. Collective ownership can stop these assets from being taken away from the woman by men or families. Collectivizing them also gives women a face and legitimacy to access loans and government funds. Women with assets also gain self-confidence and are willing to take on new leadership roles in their communities.

There are numerous stories about women who, under the aegis of *mahila mandals*, gain access to assets, work to lobby for basic services from government authorities, protest injustices by landowners, and together fight against wife and child assault as well as alcoholism. Over time, through their *mahila mandals*, women have risen to protest successfully and overthrow salient anti-women customs in their communities, have gained assets, and have taken on leadership roles as the narratives in the book will show.

Findings

In this section, we present our findings on the women entrepreneurs of the twenty NGOs we studied in Pune. We organize our findings as follows: we first describe some characteristics of our sample of women entrepreneurs who founded the NGOs and are still leading them; next, we report on the findings related to their motivations, followed by the self-evaluation of personal characteristics. We then turn to the social and cultural factors that may influence entrepreneurship.

The NGOs in our sample range from five to thirty-five years old, with the average age being 13.7 years. They are all involved in providing basic services for mainly rural women and children. These include counseling, primary health services, family planning, literacy training, and a variety of legal and administrative services. Many are also involved in advocacy of women's rights with local politicians and the judicial system.

The women who started these NGOs came to this role at different ages and via different routes. As we shall see, there are underlying commonalities in their backgrounds and personalities that help explain their roles as entrepreneurs of NGOs. We first look at their family backgrounds, then turn to education and experience, beliefs and values, and the influence of culture. We then offer a typical profile of a woman NGO entrepreneur before presenting some concluding remarks.

Family Background

The ages at which women founded the NGOs varied, and ranged from twenty-four to sixty-five years old with the average being thirty-eight. The average age of founding NGOs was past the childbearing age for most women and few had the burden of meeting immediate needs of very young children. At this relatively mature age women who had careeers had gained some professional experience.

Twelve women in our sample were currently married, five were previously married but currently single and three had always been single. In our discussions with them, the married women reported encouraging partners who supported them in taking on new initiatives. Those single or separated found that they had sufficient energy to channel into the founding of their NGOs despite being single parents. Many of those single or separated also received support from their extended families.

Our findings show that although the overwhelming majority of women had children at the time of starting the NGO, the issue of childcare was not pivotal in their decision making. All ten women with young or school-age children lived in extended families which allowed them to work outside the home. Of the ten others, five women had adult children when they founded the NGO, four had no children, and one had put her child into foster care (more on this last case in the narrative that follows Chapter One).

Thus, in our study, marital status and childcare responsibilities did not affect the women's decisions to start NGOs, as suggested by scholars of women entrepreneurs in western countries (Caputo and Dolinsky, 1998). One explanation for this could be that living and family arrangements in India differ from those in highly industrialized countries. In India, the cultural norm dictates that young couples live with the husband's family as an 'extended family', or what is sometimes referred to as 'joint families'. This means that the 'extended' families will generally consist of the parents, their unmarried daughters, and sons with their own families. The daughters-in-law who marry into the family benefit from the additional help available for sharing domestic and childcare duties. Furthermore, upper and middle-income households have access to inexpensive labor to help with household and childcare chores.

All but three of the founders in our sample came from upper to middle-income groups, which reflect the findings by other scholars in India and elsewhere. Sufficient family income allowed these seventeen women to pursue their goals in starting NGOs. In doing so, they often had to give up other careers with attendant higher incomes. In the three cases where family income was insufficient, human and social capital allowed a couple of the women to continue earning an income in work-related activities while founding their NGO. In these two cases, the women continued with the income-bearing activities until the NGOs were stable and could afford to generate sufficient revenue to pay them a modest salary.

This finding underscores the importance of women's financial security in undertaking entrepreneurial activity (in both the for-profit and non-profit sectors). The need to have some kind of income security is not surprising, given that most entrepreneurs are involved in fairly risky activities (Bilodeau and Slivinski, 1996; Blanchflower and Oswald, 1998; Hisrich, 1986; Pilz, 1995).

In the case of non-profit organizations they are not financially at risk, especially in terms of capital investments, and there is no expectation of financial rewards. In this event, the entrepreneur does not require much up-front capital to facilitate a start-up. She does require some financial support for day-to-day living expenses. This support usually comes from her savings, family, friends, or her own income generating activities. One of our interviewees reinforced this recurring theme: 'I received financial support from my family at the time of starting. I was not expected to contribute to the family income.'

Nearly all of the NGOs started with little financial capital because their needs were minimal. Start-up financing from other NGOs was common in many cases. In most cases, volunteer labor was the most important resource; this usually included recruiting friends and family members. Personal networks gave over half of the women access to friends and acquaintances for volunteer labor and donations. This is consistent with the findings concerning non-profit entrepreneurs in the West (Pilz, 1995). This suggests that access, or the lack thereof, to financial capital is not a crucial factor affecting decision making for NGO entrepreneurs. This finding is contrary to findings among for-profit entrepreneurs (Blanchflower and Oswald, 1998).

In the for-profit world, it is common for women entrepreneurs to have entrepreneurial husbands and/or family members. The entrepreneurial culture of family members often positively affects women's decisions to become entrepreneurs. This is also true, with some variation, in the non-profit sector. Despite the diverse family backgrounds, seventeen founders came from families where the parents were highly involved in either the provision of, or advocating for, social services.

Parents, as role models, are highly influential in inculcating the values of social justice among the women entrepreneurs. Parental influence, they claim, 'made me decide to do social work and volunteer'. We found that parental influence is pivotal to shaping the values needed to motivate their children to establish and operate an NGO. Parents as role models and active supporters of the missions of the NGO also provide important emotional assistance and help meet the exigencies along the way by volunteering at the NGOs, and donating money.

This kind of parental support provided to non-profit entrepreneurs is in sharp contrast with entrepreneurs in the for-profit sector. In the for-profit sector, parental influence is important due to their experience and skills in the for-profit arena. Parents of for-profit entrepreneurs, who often are also entrepreneurs, are able to share their experience and skills in helping an entrepreneurial daughter found and run her own enterprise (Cooper et al., 1994).

Education and Experience

The general educational levels of women entrepreneurs in our sample are very similar to those of women who establish for-profit enterprises—most are university graduates (Hisrich, 1986). It is not surprising that NGO founders are well-educated because in a bureaucratic country like India, being educated facilitates successful navigation and negotiation of administrative and legal requirements necessary in founding an NGO. Of the twenty entrepreneurs, eighteen had university degrees, thirteen of whom had post-graduate degrees. Although a majority of them chose social work as a career, not all had social work degrees.

For example, one of the entrepreneurs with a post-graduate degree in science chose a career in social work because she was always interested in social change. Influenced by her father, a trade unionist and activist, she grew up embedded in discussions of social justice and questioning the status quo. As an adult she had a supportive husband and family who encouraged her to pursue her passion for social justice and to found an NGO. She credits her parents for her insights into the need for social change and is grateful for their continuing support of her NGO work.

One of the women, whose story appears in a narrative discussed in this chapter, is an example of a self-taught woman who has become a highly articulate, charismatic, and powerful speaker. As we talked to her, she delighted us by reciting quotes from well-known Indian poets in order to elucidate points that she was trying to make. She was well-known for her oratory skills as well as for her singing. Both of these skills played a major role in her success with her NGO.

All the women who founded NGOs had been involved either professionally or as volunteers in social movements and had been activists for change. Moreover, more than half of them had previously worked as social workers, either as professionals or as volunteers. This was often the starting point for many of them, for not only did it give them insights into current social issues and pathways for social change, but it made them aware of their own potential to bring about change. All of them reported that these early experiences gave them such enormous satisfaction that they realized that bringing about change is what they wanted to do in the future. One woman reported, 'Having succeeded in preventing the police from beating up on the poor, I realized I had the power within me to change the system. This is what made me happy and I wanted to continue this work.'

We asked the women founders to describe the skills and experiences that they found most useful in setting up their NGOs. 'Interpersonal skills' was chosen as the first and foremost skill. This is hardly surprising given their leadership roles for social change, which required that the women be able to communicate effectively as well as motivate people to believe in their vision of social justice. One entrepreneur suggested that over and above interpersonal skills, it was also important to be able to 'evolve strategies' necessary for survival and achieve one's personal and organizational goals. Founders also discussed the need for deep empathy for the underprivileged and oppressed women and the desire for change. One woman put it succinctly, that prior to establishing an NGO one had to first and foremost 'be uncomfortable with the status quo'.

In founding and running an NGO, half or more of the entrepreneurs declared the importance of having specific kinds of practical skills. These included administrative skills, prior NGO experience, and business-related skills. These were extremely helpful in the day-to-day management of the organization and also allowed them to interact effectively with government and other NGOs. Their administrative know-how contributed to the smooth functioning of their organizations, especially as they grew more complex. They used their skills and experience in hiring professional staff and obtaining funding from donors who wanted greater accountability.

Finally these women founders talked about the importance of recognizing that despite their best intentions they needed to limit their reach in what they could achieve. This, they said, helped them limit their activities in order to maintain a focus on their goals and not be drawn into crises management. As one woman put it, 'to accept that all problems cannot be solved and learn to draw a line'.

Beliefs and Values

Although the twenty women founders came to entrepreneurship via a variety of paths, they shared the feminist conviction that attention to women's issues is paramount for social justice. They all identified themselves as feminists. They were strongly committed to helping women, especially poor, rural, and tribal women who are illiterate, have no access to healthcare, and are often victims of domestic abuse. Most (seventeen of the twenty) came from family backgrounds that shaped their worldview regarding social justice. For example, a majority of the parents of the entrepreneurs were social activists. The venue for their social activism was mostly in the context of the national independence movement, although in two cases the women's fathers were leaders in trade unions.

A few entrepreneurs followed the examples of their parents who had started NGOs, while most had parents who were involved to some degree in issues of social justice. In these instances it was clear that the women's awareness of social problems started with their parents, and this acted as a catalyst for their own beliefs and values. This awareness, compounded by the current pressing societal problems, spurred many of the women into action. Initially they chose careers in social work and then went on to founding their own NGOs.

The question that intrigued us most was: What motivated these women to choose to leave their professions and launch their own NGOs? For example, why was it not sufficient for them to pursue their commitment to social justice issues regarding women through employment or volunteering in social service agencies? The four most frequent responses were the desire to serve others, the awareness of unfulfilled needs in the community, the opportunity for self-actualization, and the desire to affect social change. When asked to elaborate on their motivations, an underlying issue for many founders was that mainstream organizations, even in social work, did not have the capacities to deliver what the founders thought was needed. Furthermore, most of the founders did not necessarily identify with or feel comfortable with the organizational culture.

All twenty women indicated that they were motivated by the need to serve others, particularly women. They believed they could best address the concerns closest to their hearts by founding their own NGOs. Some of them reported frustrations with jobs held previously because they could not serve the women in the ways that they best understood. Although twelve of them previously held jobs in the field of social work, they felt that their work did not address problems in ways that affect long-term change.

Most of them also perceived a failure on the part of mainstream institutions that often reinforce traditional attitudes, which adds to problems in the long term. According to them the solution lies in making attitudinal changes and raising awareness among women about their human and constitutional rights. Hence, starting their enterprises was a remedy to address this shortcoming.

For four women, the founding of an NGO simply allowed them to continue doing what they were already doing informally; the NGO helped them increase the scope and legitimacy of their work. The motivations reported by all of our founders, regarding the need to serve others and the unfulfilled needs in the community, replicates the findings by other scholars (Pilz, 1995; Young, 1983).

Fifteen of the twenty women were motivated by the needs of women in the rural communities that have been ignored. These needs require specific political or judicial action. Our respondents claimed that there is a 'great need to bring about self-awareness among rural women', and to 'make them understand that there were alternatives to [their] situations through legal and other means'. Ten of our founders articulated that the lack of action to stop observed injustices against women in the community was the singular driving force behind their initiatives to start NGOs.

One example of a woman who worked in a social service agency may illustrate why the step to founding her own NGO was taken. She was working with an agency in an area related to her feminist beliefs, and found that the agency was effective in helping women who were abused and marginalized. However, she did not find it satisfying to deal with problems after they occurred, a typical response of many of the existing organizations. She wanted to prevent wife abuse and the oppression of women and children. Hence, her motivation to start her own NGO was with this goal in mind: to create and disseminate awareness programs in order to deal with problems of discrimination against women and abuse of women before they occurred.

Given that all twenty of our respondents see themselves as feminists, social justice issues concerning women are significant to them. Thus, it is not surprising that three-quarters of the women reported that starting an NGO dealing with women's issues was also a process of 'self-actualization' for them.

One respondent believed that, 'Only women can create a platform and empathize with other [women] at a grass-roots level', and another said, 'Women require women to create space for themselves'. This suggests that founding an NGO with a mission congruent to their feminist beliefs gave the entrepreneurs a high personal pay-off, a finding repeatedly found in the non-profit literature (Bilodeau and Slivinski, 1995; Pilz, 1995; Young, 1983).

Since all of the respondents had some previous experience in social movements, and many came from families that were involved in issues of social justice, sixteen of the twenty founders stated that they were motivated to found the NGO in order 'to achieve change'. All the women saw themselves as agents of change, and they believed they could bring about progressive change through their experiences using their NGO as the principal vehicle of change.

Social injustice and the lack of awareness were often repeated themes in the need to achieve change. For example, one respondent said she was motivated to, 'change people's outlook towards unwanted children'. Another believed that it was necessary to 'Make changes in the structural and legal facilities to fight injustices towards women'. There was a consensus among the respondents that the lack of education and resources, combined with an unsympathetic police force and judicial system, make lower-caste rural women vulnerable to social abuse, and that change was paramount in achieving social justice. The founders understood that the short- and long-term solutions required both awareness raising and attitudinal changes in the community. Moreover, many of the mainstream institutions often reinforced the traditional attitudes rather than changing the attitudes that would lead to long-term solutions.

Over half the respondents also said that creating the NGO allowed them to enhance their social connections. Half the women said that their peers expected them to do social service. Fewer than half indicated that the desire for independence was a motivating factor. Unlike the for-profit sector (Hisrich and Brush, 1984), independence does not seem to be an important motivating factor in founding an NGO in India.

Typical Profiles

We asked the respondents to elaborate on the characteristics that best describe themselves. They all saw themselves as hardworking and persistent in achieving their goals. Almost all saw themselves as self-confident and extroverted, enabling them to marshal resources and confront many levels of bureaucracy, especially in rural areas where women rarely participate in public or political action.

The following story illustrates how such characteristics make these women successful in achieving the goals they set out for their NGOs. There was a case of women in a village being harassed by men on an on-going basis as they went to the fields early in the mornings. This village was typical of many villages of rural India where men control and dictate the norms that subjugate women. Thus the women in this village had little opportunity to complain or put a stop to this verbal assault. The torment continued for several months and began to take on many forms including being followed and threatened sexually. The women could not count on the local police for help as the police were on friendly terms with the perpetrators. Their complaints were summarily dismissed and the police refused to come to their aid. The village women brought their problems to Maya (a pseudonym), the founder of an NGO, who was visiting their village.

Maya has always been concerned with the plight of rural women. She had founded an NGO that specifically deals with the empowerment of rural women and took this opportunity to teach women how to help themselves. To do this in a way that would empower the village women over the long term and increase their self-confidence, Maya organized a meeting where she invited all the women in the village to come and speak about these problems of harassment and any other problem. Her organizational and leadership skills helped her quickly mobilize the women into a *mahila mandal*. Maya believed that the *mahila mandal* would be the locus of future problem solving in the village.

Maya then turned to the problem at hand. Since she was highly educated and outspoken, Maya was able to go to the local police and confront them about their inaction. She also threatened to take this case to their superiors at the district level. She produced the necessary documentation and was able to navigate through the bureaucracy sufficiently to make her threat credible. At this point, with the help of the local women, the police arrested the accused men and brought them to a meeting at the *mahila mandal* where the women voted on their punishment. The men were to wear their sandals around their necks and go barefoot for a period of time, as a mark of shame. The harassment ended! More importantly, the *mahila mandal* now liaises with the police and the local village council so that women have a collective voice. Maya continues to drop in and give them advice when needed, but the *mahila mandal* now functions as an autonomous group that is recognized and respected in the village.

Thus organizations like *mahila mandals* can creatively use mainstream institutions to gain attention and support for their concerns. The *mahila mandal* provides for a collective voice of women that cannot be easily ignored and thereby ensures that institutions like the police stand by gender justice.

Other characteristics that founders use to describe themselves include being ambitious and willing to take risks. As forming an NGO is a risky and innovative venture these characteristics are important. This risk is not necessarily financial but can result in social repercussions when women fight against historically-ingrained social norms. This may adversely impact the founder's social standing, putting her reputation on the line. The founder is often in the public eye, and as such is continuously judged on her actions, which may be both controversial and unwanted. The goal of social change embraced by the entrepreneurs is risky and ambitious. It is not surprising then that many of the entrepreneurs see themselves as risk-takers.

These findings of risk-taking and ambitious behaviour replicate the findings by Pilz (1995) and McCelland (1987). It is interesting to note that fewer than half of the women see themselves as altruistic. They do not see themselves as do-gooders, but rather as people who act from a place of strong convictions and beliefs in eradicating social injustices.

The Influence of Culture

In the introduction, we briefly described the caste system and the plurality of religions in India. Here, we touch on the likely relevance of caste and religious systems to non-profit entrepreneurship. Our findings on caste and religion among our entrepreneurs show a striking convergence. We first note that only one woman of the sample is not a Hindu, she is a Christian. The predominance of Hindus among our entrepreneurs certainly reflects the distribution of religions in India. However, there are a few areas in India where this predominance does not hold, and a sampling of NGO entrepreneurs from these areas may not be consistent with our findings.

Although the overwhelming majority of our sample is Hindu, religion is not reported as a motivator or even a factor for actions undertaken by our respondents. This is in contrast to Gupta (1991) who suggests that religion is an important factor in explaining for-profit entrepreneurship in India.

For Hindus, where caste is a relevant issue, we find that fifteen are Brahmins, the highest caste. Three are from lower-castes, and one of them belongs to a 'scheduled' caste (this category includes tribal people and groups of the very lowest caste, including the 'untouch-ables'). This finding that nearly 80 per cent of the founders are Brahmins, suggests that there may exist certain factors that make it likely that women of higher-castes are attracted to, and are successful at, NGO entrepreneurship in India.

Often social status makes higher-caste women more likely to have the power to combat traditional forces and legitimize socially controversial issues related to women. In the case of one of the lower-caste women founders, we found that her significant educational background (she is a lawyer), likely compensated for her lower-caste status when dealing with local authorities and obtaining resources.

A common characteristic among our sample of entrepreneurs is their overall deep and long-term commitment to feminist ideology. Unlike religion, feminist ideology is overwhelmingly offered as the motivating and rationalizing factor to begin an NGO. Many of these women have been involved in social movements, and came to their feminist beliefs during this time; others developed their ideology through workplace experience and at home. Entrepreneurial women in the for-profit sector in the West also often see themselves as feminists who undertake unconventional roles (Allen and Truman, 1993; Brush, 1992; Fischer et al., 1993; Moore and Buttner, 1997).

Although feminism invites a universal understanding of patriarchy as an oppressive force, the cultural and historical context in India gives rise to certain divergences in the meaning of oppression and social justice (Gedalof, 1999; John, 1998; Niranjana, 1998). Feminist ideology, as understood by our respondents, recognizes this difference resulting from the values and norms held in society, as is evident in their concern for the oppression of lower-caste women.

For example, the women entrepreneurs were cognizant of the problems faced by poor, lower-caste rural women due to the traditional social and political institutions that recognize and often promote the subordination of women by male family members. Although not legal, caste often also dictates the subtle, and sometimes not so subtle, discrimination faced by lower-caste women. This awareness, combined with their experience and ideology, spurred the women founders to do something to alleviate the problems of other women. They did so by founding NGOs whose missions and goals actualized their feminist beliefs.

The expression of feminist beliefs, as well as a deep commitment to dealing with social injustices, suggests that non-profit entrepreneurs derive great satisfaction in pursuing a cause that is so strongly connected to their beliefs. This finding closely aligns with the findings in the typology suggested by Young (1983) in his study of non-profit entrepreneurs. He categorizes them as 'believers', those who believe in a particular cause and pursue it single-mindedly. It also replicates the findings in the literature of non-profit entrepreneurs (Bilodeau and Slivinski, 1996; Frank, 1996; Pilz, 1995; Weisbrod, 1988).

Women's Style of Leadership

Many of the more mature women in our study have a strong under-standing of the systemic nature of women's oppression that affect them at both a personal and a societal level. Hence, the 'personal is political' resonates for many of the women entrepreneurs. The expe-riences of oppression in many of its forms contribute to their work. They strive to challenge and remove barriers that keep women locked into their state of continuous subjugation. In several cases women see their role as a special kind of 'mothering' which extends to the community. This is especially true for those whose work deals with children. Their maternal instincts energized and informed their work on several levels; offering protection to the children and helping women become better mothers through health education.

The women founders in our study also used this special kind of mothering with their clients as well as their own staff members and volunteers. They cultivated growth of their staff and clients much as they would for their own children with an emphasis on the growth of the individual: learning to become independent decision makers and becoming aware of problems facing other women and children.

Women in leadership positions in the NGO felt comfortable with brainstorming, which was inclusive and personal. In several cases, staff members and clients were encouraged to bring up issues that affected their own family lives as a springboard for discussion of problems facing other women. This encouraged a dialogue among staff and clients, which was egalitarian and not hierarchical.

Bringing the personal into their work is a natural aspect of the use of social capital for women. The women founders find that their personal lives and networks are an important form of social capital,[11]

---

[11] In 'Forms of Capital', Bourdieu (1986) expands the notion of capital beyond its economic conception that emphasizes material exchanges, to include 'immaterial' and 'non-economic' forms of capital. Bourdieu suggests that an individual's social capital is determined by the size of their relationship network, the sum of its accumulated resources (both cultural and economic), and how successfully (quickly) the individual can mobilize them. According to Bourdieu, social networks must be continuously maintained and fostered over time in order for them to be called upon quickly in the future.

which often surpasses other forms of capital available to them. For example, some women used their personal networks to gain land and physical resources to house their projects and serve their client populations. Others used their personal and professional connections to secure funding and favorable terms on loans for the women they are helping. Almost all used their personal connections to secure donations of time and volunteers who are so necessary to help fledgling NGOs take hold and continue to thrive and be successful. Founders also rely on volunteer boards of trustees for governance, advice, and social capital. Our interviews and narratives suggest that our women entrepreneurs prefer to lead their NGOs in 'their own way'. Drawing on the commonalities of the two narratives that conclude this chapter, we learn some new and interesting facts about 'women's leadership'.

Conclusion

Can we say anything about entrepreneurs in the non-profit sector based on the findings on women entrepreneurs of NGOs in India? Given the limitation of our data to one geographical region, it is difficult to generalize; nevertheless, we suggest that the data points in a certain direction and we can draw some conclusions from our findings.

The salient factor in our study is that all of our women entrepreneurs share a feminist ideology and a desire to help others. By founding an NGO whose mission is closely related to these ideologies, the women are able to actualize their beliefs, and this provides them with the professional and personal satisfaction that continuously fuels their actions. Clearly, this does not imply that all feminist women who desire to help others should (or do) start their own NGOs. We simply suggest that risk-taking and ambitious entrepreneurial women, who are social activists and dedicated to changing the status quo, are likely to found NGOs that are closely aligned to their beliefs and goals.

Earnings and independence, on the other hand, seem to be secondary to pursuing the mission of the NGO. Lack of access to financial capital does not pose a major challenge to entrepreneurs in this sector. Essential in founding a non-profit organization is access to volunteers and donations, initially achieved through personal networks. Neither the number of young children nor the presence of a husband affects women in their decisions to start an NGO in India. It is not that the women are exempt from childcare and domestic responsibilities, but that they typically receive help from either their husbands or family members. This is facilitated by the custom of living in extended family structures so common in India. This gives them the flexibility to pursue their goals of founding, directing, and running their NGOs. Thus, their choice is not contingent on childcare costs or household responsibilities. These resources, of course, would also have been available for other kinds of employment. Thus, this factor does not completely explain why women choose entrepreneurship in the non-profit over the for-profit sector.

Parental role models and early professional and volunteer experience also served to raise the women's awareness and motivated them to become pioneers in their pursuit of social justice. It is not surprising that as self-professed feminists they chose to start NGOs addressing women's issues to remedy social injustices and work for change. Our NGO entrepreneurs describe themselves as ambitious, persistent, hardworking, and willing to take risks. They are self-confident, extro-verted, and energetic. All of them feel that their inter-personal skills were paramount in starting NGOs, especially as resources such as volunteer labor and donations often had to be mobilized through the help of family, friends, and members of the community.

We find that the most important factors affecting non-profit entre-preneurship are women's human and social capital: education and experience as well as relational, family, and social connections. Tradi-tional external resources that are crucial for for-profit entrepreneurs, such as loans, have little impact on non-profit entrepreneurs. However, we found that financial stability in the household was essential for many (but not all) women establishing a new NGO.

Given a small and geographically limited sample, we cannot say whether our findings on caste and religion indicate a preponderance of one religious group or caste among women entrepreneurs of NGOs, or if the findings are representative of the larger population. However, our findings do indicate that caste—and maybe religion—should be further investigated as possible determinants of NGO entrepreneur-ship in India. In Maharashtra, where there exists a greater proportion of Hindus than many other states in India, we did not get the plurality of religions among NGO founders.

A significant proportion of our entrepreneurs are Brahmins, which is not surprising given the cultural context. In India, despite the many attempts to rid society of the ramifications of the caste system, the system continues to operate subtly—and not so subtly—at many levels. The élite in India are often the educated Brahmins; they enjoy certain privileges of social connections amongst other Brahmins, and are respected as leaders and intellectuals. Since starting an NGO requires an unusual reliance on friends and the local community to mobilize resources, being educated and belonging to a high caste provides the required connections to facilitate this resource mobilization.

Many of the issues that NGOs take on are deeply embedded in the traditional, cultural, and religious fabric of society and it is often extremely difficult to rally support of local communities, especially in rural areas. Women who take a strong stand against the local practices are often victims of harassment within their own communities. Much of the time they receive little or no support from the local police when they file complaints or seek help from other local public agencies. It is no surprise that feminist, educated, self-confident, and affluent Brahmin women from respected echelons of society are much more likely to succeed in dealing with local bureaucracies and police when they raise socially controversial issues. It is, therefore, likely that the woman entrepreneur of an NGO dealing with socially-sensitive and controversial issues is usually an educated individual who comes from middle to an upper-income household. Being from a high caste as well as being highly educated, she is usually respected and can exercise power and influence as well as mobilize resources.

Most of the women manifested a holistic style of leadership, which may account for their success as entrepreneurs. It is evident that their personal networks gave them access to important resources and continuing family support that allowed them to flourish. Holistic and inclusive processes that include teamwork, concern for others, effective interpersonal skills, intuitive management, and creative problem-solving are the important descriptors of the way these founders led their NGOs.

These women founded NGOs that foster teamwork and participatory decision making. They created a crucial democratic and administrative model for potential use in the transformation of mainstream organizations. The type of leadership we see typically practiced among these twenty women entrepreneurs is the same kind of leadership now recommended to for-profit businesses in the twenty-first century (Loden, 1985).

This coincidental meeting of women's form of leadership with the paradigm shift of leadership styles seems to fit with Weber's notion of 'elective affinity'. If a particular practice coincides with the requirements of a particular status in such a way that each is particularly favorable to the other, when this favorable coincidence of socio-cultural sphere occurs, there can be a quantum leap forward on the part of the socio-cultural system (Weber, 1930).

Narratives

The Lesson of the Cow: Sindhutai—Saptasindhu

Find a purpose, the means will follow... (*Gandhi*).

It all began with cow dung, a flap over dung. Sindhutai was only twenty years of age, already with three young boys, and now pregnant with her fourth. Everyday while the men tended the cows, Sindhutai gathered dung with the other women from her jungle village. The men received a rupee for each cow they cared for, but the women received nothing in exchange for their efforts in collecting dung. They were also not allowed to keep the dung for their own fuel needs. All of it had to be given over to government agents and their friends for their private use. Sindhutai, a feisty woman with an inherent urge for advocating for fairness, led the women in a protest and secured a change in the law so that the women received remuneration for their work. This was her first social awakening and consequently the women of the village started to regard as her as a leader.

Sindhutai's effort, however, so angered those who had profited from the village women's labor that they sought to get rid of her by spreading rumors and telling her husband that someone else was the father of her soon-to-be-born child. In anger Sindhutai's husband kicked her out of the house, kicked her in the belly, and banished her to the elements. That first night she sought refuge in a cowshed where without food and water she fell unconscious. Later, when she awoke she gave birth to her daughter and cut the umbilical cord with a stone. In the morning she saw that a cow stood over her, protecting her from a stampede of other cows that would have otherwise surely trampled her. 'If the cow can protect me as a mother, she thought, why can't I protect others as a mother?' She tried to return to the village and sought help from the women of the village she had once helped. However, being afraid of the consequences of supporting Sindhutai, the women chased her away by throwing stones. Even her mother, who had sent her off to be married at nine to a 35 year old man, had nothing but contempt for her and turned her away without any food. She feared her daughter would keep returning to her family for help. So Sindhutai had nothing, neither strength nor capacity to look after herself and her child. Now, at the age of twenty, her life was dismantled, the institutions and family traditions she had grown to trust had let her down. She had to find a new way of life. She was determined to be a good mother and in that way show her own mother what it meant to be a good mother.

The Tree

Sindhutai had no purpose, no hope, and at one point felt that suicide was her only option. To her it seemed that she was unfairly fated to endure this extreme sorrow and pain, having done nothing to warrant it. The memory of the cow that had stood over her and protected her, however, gave her the courage to go on.

To make a living for her daughter and herself, she resorted to begging and living at bus and train stations. As groups of beggars competed for the meager offerings from the public, Sindhutai sang songs that touched the hearts—and pocketbooks—of people. Sindhutai thus received more coins than the rest. Being vulnerable as a young single mother, she wanted to become part of the community of beggars and get their protection. She, therefore, began sharing her bounty with them and in her act of compassion discovered the satisfaction that sharing brought. She also discovered that this sharing made her a valuable member of the beggar community. This became her new life. As she hopped trains all over India to protect her child from the harshness of the seasons, this charismatic beggar-singer began to draw around her other beggars and orphans of the street. Sharing her plenty with them and receiving in return protection for her child, Sindhutai's social commitment was enhanced. She continued this compassionate and nomadic way of life for five years. However, often tired and depressed of this nomadic way of life she contemplated suicide many times. One day, tired and resting against a tree, she observed that the tree was 'wounded'—slashed in many places—and yet it lived. She saw that the tree provided shade from the sun for her, yet it itself had no shade. She wondered if she could be like the tree for others, not protected from the sun and also wounded. Could she provide for others what the injured tree provided for her?

It was then that she made her bargain with God. 'You allowed me to live, my daughter to live, now talk to me. Give me direction and help me out. I did not ask to be born. You must have a purpose for me. There must be a reason that I am here. Now you must show me the way and provide for me. I will do what you ask of me.'

From then on Sindhutai became aware of her own gifts, her leadership, and her gift of song and oration. She discovered that she had the power to change peoples' lives. She decided that her mission would be to take care of the beggar orphan children who gathered about her. For another five years she continued to live her itinerant life, taking care of the orphan children and having them sleep in a circle around her at night. This is now my life, she thought. I must take care of all of these children. But how was she to take care of these orphans and her own daughter? Was this possible? Would others think she was always favoring her own child, saving the food morsels mostly for her? She decided if she were to take care of the orphans she must give up her daughter. She had to make the break and made the decision to give her daughter over to a trust for destitute children.[12]

---

[12] Sindhutai's daughter thrived at this trust, and over the years prospered and grew. She was to receive an education through the trust and eventually earn a Masters degree in social work. She later joined Sindhutai to work alongside her until she married. In taking care of the children with her mother, she found both purpose and direction in her own life.

The Hut

In her wanderings among the villages and jungles, Sindhutai began taking care of the tribal children while their parents worked. As a result, the tribal people built her a hut to live in with the children under her care. It was this hut that inspired her to build an orphanage. From then on the orphanage became her life's mission and work.

Aie, as she was now known to all of the children, a name meaning 'mother of all', had little access to resources. She came from a low caste, she had no education, she could not read, yet her pleas from the heart brought in the resources that she needed to build the orphanage and accept abandoned and orphaned children. In 1986, Aie registered her orphanage as an NGO. To this date, Aie still seeks resources from private donations to support the several orphanages she has opened. Aie does not apply for grants. She continues to speak at schools, meetings, and conferences to tell the story of her life and of the orphanage where she is the 'mother of all'. And she never worries whether there will be enough money because she made a bargain with God. In this way she is spiritual in her commitment to help others and is, therefore, confident that resources will follow.

Sindhutai told of one incident of getting money from an unexpected source. The first child of her orphanage, Gaikwad, now forty-one years old, came into an inheritance of property and donated it to Aie to help build another orphanage. Many former residents of her orphanage volunteer and support the institution and act as mentors to new generations of orphans.

As a leader and entrepreneur, Aie believes that fate—and God—brought her to this work and that the necessary resources will materialize. 'This is why I was born' she believes.

Sindhutai/Aie Returns to Her Village

Seven years ago, Aie was invited back to her village to be honored for her work with orphans. Those who had thrown stones now presented her with flowers. She met her estranged husband again after twenty years, and as she was not sure to recognize him it was arranged that she be introduced to him. While she was invited to her old matrimonial 'home', she felt only like a guest. She saw that her husband was in tears amidst this ceremony honoring her. She struggled with mixed emotions: uppermost was the urge to take revenge for his behaviour and for abandoning her to the elements. Then she thought, 'if he had not kicked me out, I would not be the mother of so many'. She pressed her husband's hand and said: 'The same people who threw stones at me are now giving me flowers. Nobody belongs to anyone. Don't wait for flowers. Come as a child not as a husband. I am ready to be a mother not a wife. I forgive you as the biggest child of all'.

Commentary

The story of Sindhutai (Aie) is an extraordinary one of an extraordinary woman from a backward rural community and of the lowest caste, who defies the common profile of women founders of NGOs in India. The study of the twenty NGOs revealed that there are four principal factors influencing successful entrepreneurship: higher education, prior experience in business or non-profit work, a supportive family system, which provides both role models of parents working in social moments or volunteering, and resources such as funds and freedom of time, and lastly, the social connections and networks of influential and/or people of means.

None of these factors is evident in the case of Sindhutai. As a backward rural villager, she had no rights and little access to education. She was under the control of her husband to whom she was married at the age of nine; her husband was twenty-six years her senior. Her only experience, which was the beginning of her social awakening, began when she protested on behalf of the women of the village who collected dung with her. She successfully drew attention to the injustice meted out to the women of the village and ended the practice of having to give up cow dung to the local agents and their friends. While the ire of the men in the village who lost their fuel resulted in her being abandoned to the elements, she had discovered her own courage and her skills as a leader to others.

Her family, if anything, was a negative influence. Her family was most likely poor and desperate not to have to feed and care for one more child. They married Sindhutai off at a young age of nine, to a man of thirty-five. This made her the responsibility of her in-laws. When Sindhutai returned to her parents' home for help after her daughter was born and she had been thrown out of the house, she was rejected rather than protected and supported. She was entirely on her own, and her parents suggested that it would be better for her and her daughter to die.

As for social connections, there were none, unless one counts the beggar community that had protected her in exchange for her financial support. So what was responsible for the rise of this woman to a status of a highly visible and successful entrepreneur? The research indicates that while these previously mentioned factors represent the most typical profile of successful NGO entrepreneurs in India, the internal resources likely play the most important role. In Sindhutai's case, she exemplifies all of the characteristics of NGO entrepreneurs found in the study, including: a strong spirit and commitment, an ability to mobilize resources, demonstrate innovation and leadership, have imagination, ability, and is willing to take risks and show innovative approaches to problem solving and program development. Sindhutai had all of these characteristics even though she had none of the advantages of most of the entrepreneurs in the study.

Cultural influences in her case were negative rather than positive. She had everything against her coming from a backward jungle community; she lacked family support, education, organizational qualifications as well as the typical socio-economic profile. She clearly had a strong will, personality and a spirit that would overcome all of these negative factors. It is likely, however, that these negative factors pushed her to break away from her background and better understand the oppressive plight of other women and children.

What we do understand about Sindhutai is that she very much fits the profile of other entrepreneurs when it comes to motivation. She was influenced by her faith in God to guide her to live her life for a meaningful purpose. Her strong belief that abandoned and orphaned children had a right to live and grow up in a caring environment, coupled with her first-hand personal experience of oppression, gave her a keen understanding of the needs of the marginalized. This included beggar groups, poor children, and many poor women in her village. She ultimately was driven by an insatiable desire to serve them and better their circumstances. She was willing to take risks—had she not lived a wanderer's life for nearly seven years, taking care of her own daughter and many of the other beggars and village children even at the risk of jail and starvation? She survived and became more committed to her cause. Did she not discover her own personal power to sing and earn money and to motivate others by her gift of oratory? And had she not shown how innovative she could be in her wanderings by using her gifts in positive ways rather than engaging an enemy—the system—that did not want to grant her any rights? Was she not willing to give up her own daughter in order to become Aie, 'the mother of all'?

In many ways, Sindhutai is the antithesis of the common profile of successful entrepreneurial women founding NGOs in India. At the same time, she absolutely typifies the values, characteristics, persistence, and commitments that describe most of the women in this study. It is an important lesson for researchers, practitioners, and policy makers to understand that it is possible to find and develop entrepreneurs from every class and caste and from every kind of lifestyle—without education or means—and become entrepreneurs of the future. Sindhutai is the exception that opens the window of hope and possibility for different futures in India. Moreover, her story reminds us that typical profiles are just that—typical. We find in cases like Sindhutai that the more important factors influencing entrepreneurship are the inner resources, the commitment to serve others, her faith in God, and an unflagging perseverance in the face of insurmountable odds to succeed. She sang the following in concluding her interview:

> God gave me a voice to sing
> He gave me oratory skills
> This has been my life
> Now I live for others
> I am their Mother
> You can become their relatives.

A Woman for All Women: Medha Samant—Annapurna

> *A woman's identity is considered her family and home...*
> *as if she does not have any other identity!!!...* (Prematai Purao).

In many ways Medha Samant's life has been highly influenced by that of her mother's. But she also has her own story. Medha Samant is an extraordinary woman, competent and self-assured, who left a lucrative career in a public-sector bank to found Annapurna Mahila Mandal of Pune—hereinafter referred to as Annapurna—in 1993.

Medha's story begins with her parents, who were revolutionaries and social activists. Her mother, Prematai Purao,[13] was an underground freedom fighter in the revolution against the Portuguese in Goa in the 1940s. Prematai not only carried messages back and forth across lines but participated in the fighting, and still bears visible scars from the bullet and knife wounds she suffered in the revolution. After the war she married a Marxist trade union leader, Narendra Shantaram Purao, and together they continued to fight for social justice. Prematai's revolutionary spirit continued in her chosen life work, the emancipation of women. In a 2003 interview, she was blunt about women's subjugation: 'A woman's identity is considered her family and home, as if she does not have any other identity.... She is supposed to play a supportive role. I hate it when people don't consider a woman being equal to a man, or when they say women are the weaker sex!'[14]

Medha, one of two children, grew up hearing stories of revolution and social action focused on relieving the oppression of others and improving the human condition. In our interviews with Medha, she frequently talked about how her family's beliefs influenced her life and shaped her desire to relieve the miseries of others. Under her parent's guidance she became a confident, self-reliant, independent person committed to helping others. As a daughter in a well-to-do Brahmin family she had many advantages that others did not have. She went to college and then became a professional banker at the Bank of India. She was well-trained, well-respected, and well-remunerated. She hoped her banking position could also help her serve the people she most cared about—abused and disenfranchised women.

Medha's Story

We met Medha on an unseasonably hot winter's day in Pune. We drove out of the city to the slums, winding our way through narrow alleys of slum structures, arriving at the office of Annapurna in the

---

[13] Prematai Purao is the founder of one of the NGOs studied. As she was not available for the case study, we interviewed her daughter, Medha, who was instrumental in recently founding a related NGO.

[14] Interview with Medha about her mother, 2003.

late afternoon. We were ushered in to meet her in a very small office—
under a very hot tin roof! She was working at her desk with two
members of her staff crammed into an office hardly bigger than a large
closet. At first it seemed rather odd that 'Medha the Director' held
a visitors' interview for two hours in the presence of the staff, who
continued to work at their assignments. Later we began to understand.
It was her feminist philosophy about egalitarianism that explained in
part their continued presence and the fact that she sometimes drew
them into the conversation as well.

Medha is an energetic woman in her early forties with a husband
and one child. One of her first remarks was to note the support of
her family in her work: 'My husband and my family have stood by
me and helped me in every possible way. It is because my family
nurtured and supported me that I am here today. My growing up years
were important in choosing this kind of work, but I believe that it was
in 1975 that I had a real awakening. I didn't realize it at the time.'

'Let me explain', she continued, 'it was 1975, and it was the first
International Year of the Woman. It was the year that a comprehensive
international report came out on the status of women. At long last the
issue of women's emancipation was not just a village, state, or country
issue in India; it was an issue that caught the attention of women—
and men—everywhere, all over the world! It was an important time.
It was also the year that my mother, Prematai Purao, started Annapurna
Mahila Mandal in Mumbai. Then it was still called Bombay. I
watched my mother fight for displaced women mill workers who had
become entangled with ruthless moneylenders. She saw that they had
no way to support themselves; they had lost their jobs. My mother
knew about a new source of funding, an alternative to moneylenders;
newly nationalized banks were required to give 1 per cent of their
loans to the poor. She approached the banks and launched a lending
program for slum women. She hoped these women could start new
small businesses—running household inns—so they could support
their families and work without fear of harassment and exploitation.
This is how my mother, Prematai, started Annapurna Mahila Mandal
in 1975. I believe this was my inspiration—and my own awakening.

In the early 1990s, while I was still working for the bank, I noticed
that the slum conditions in Pune were not much different from those
in Mumbai. Women in the marketplace were having big problems
with unscrupulous moneylenders who charged exorbitant interest
rates and harassed them daily on the job. I knew this from personal

experience because I walked through the marketplace everyday going to and from work. I went to the same stands to buy my vegetables and after awhile developed a personal rapport with a few of them. They began to tell me about their problems, especially about those with the moneylenders. Since they had to buy fresh produce everyday and they needed cash on a daily basis, moneylenders were their only source of funds. The moneylenders, however, were ruthless exploiters and charged exorbitant interest rates.

They badgered the women on a daily basis to repay their loans. For each day that they missed a payment, the moneylenders compounded the interest. Their debts became so high they despaired of ever being able to repay them. I wanted to do something about it. I wanted to help them so I went to my bank and requested loan funds, under the 1 per cent requirement, to make loans available to the poor. The bank refused. Their excuse was that making small loans to slum women was not only too risky but the service costs would be very high. It was not worth the trouble. Discouraged by their lack of support, I quit my job. That was in 1993. I wanted to find some way to help these and other women like them'.

The Rest of the Story

With the help of her mother, friends, and other family members, Medha opened the Pune branch of the Annapurna Mahila Mandal in 1993. She worked out of her home along with friends whom she gathered around to help. Initially she used her own money for the first project—to make loans to the market women.

Medha believed that the women themselves would be able to discover solutions by coming together in a group and discussing strategies. She was a little worried that the moneylenders would resent the fact that Annapurna was providing loans, and either come after Annapurna or further victimize the women. She need not have worried because the 'group of nine' market women developed their own strategy to take care of the moneylenders. They decided to meet the moneylenders each day with a promise to pay the next day. On the following day they would do the same.

They kept up with this strategy long enough to frustrate the moneylenders who no longer found it profitable to harass the women or attempt to make them new loans. While there were many moneylenders in the marketplace, the moneylenders were not organized and so the women's strategy worked and they left the marketplace. Because it was the group of nine who created the strategy and took the initiative to confront the moneylenders, there was no backlash against Annapurna.

There were special aspects to this first lending program that have become basic principles for all eight of Annapurna's programs. Medha believes that women's emancipation occurs when they have the opportunity to develop self-confidence and believe in themselves. She believes that all individuals have the solutions to personal and societal problems within themselves. It is just a matter of creating a safe and supportive environment to bring those out. She laid the groundwork for Annapurna's approach to empowerment by gathering the women from the marketplace together to solve their problems. Their success in getting rid of the moneylenders gave them confidence.

Now all of Annapurna's programs are established on similar group models. Bringing groups together for problem solving and decision making is one of Medha's strategies for women's empowerment. She encourages ingenuity and self-reliance by involving members of Annapurna to participate in the process of problem-solving, decision-making, and creating ideas concerning new and continuing programs of Annapurna. She takes their suggestions for new programs and helps them organize projects that best suit the needs of their own slum communities.

Today, Annapurna has reached out to more than eighty slum areas in Pune. In 2003, more than 3,000 women from these slums participated in credit, savings, and insurance programs as well as the many other programs offered by Annapurna, including childcare, job training, and job placement.

Eighty plus Eight

Annapurna's first program, providing loans to nine market women, has grown to eight programs offered in eighty slums in Pune. Today Annapurna has more than 4,000 members.[15] Annapurna's first program has grown to include more than 12,000 loans to the poor over the past ten years. There have been no defaults. That 100 per cent

[15] Members include all of those who participate in Annapurna in any way, including staff, volunteers, slum dwellers, Medha, and the management committee.

repayment record has been the envy of every bank in Pune. In fact, bank officers come to Medha and ask, 'How do you do it? Can you show us?'

Annapurna's members always have ideas for new programs and projects. New projects are on the drawing board or in early stages of implementation as members design ways to improve life in their slums. Since 1993 Annapurna has added seven more programs with plans for continued expansion. As Medha puts it—and her wall program posters illustrate—Annapurna is building a whole galaxy of programs, 'stars that contribute to the emancipation of women and build stronger and healthier families. We have also been covering poor women with insurance since 1993. And we have offered credit savings program since that time as well'. In 2001, they launched Shantipurna—'peace at home'—which provides family counseling, procurement of ration cards, birth certificates, legal counseling, and legal literacy training. This is a program that includes individuals, groups, and whole communities.

Annapurna started another new program in 2001—a vocational training program 'Tantrapurna' for youth who were dropping out of school. They are trained in trades such as small appliances repair, electrical wiring, working in beauty parlors, and the like. In 2002, Annapurna reached out to men in the slums to help them develop their own enterprises to support their families. This program, 'Udayampurna' (enterprise) helps them with savings, loans, and insurance. It also provides training to help them become rickshaw drivers and owners, cobblers, and the like. Medha believes that women cannot be truly empowered and emancipated if men do not play a constructive and contributing role to their emancipation and so Annapurna continues to reach out to men and boys as well as women and girls. One additional program, 'Swasthyapurna', is a 'health mutual fund', which takes care of the health problems of 5,000 slum dwellers.

The programs that Annapurna has planned, launched, and continues to develop come from ideas from the community, or 'members' as Medha calls them. 'We are all members of Annapurna; none of us is a client. We work together, we share responsibilities, and we create ideas and programs that respond to the needs of all members. While founded on a base of credit, insurance, and savings programs, Annapurna also has a placement service, "Sandhipurna", a low cost childcare program, "Vatsalyapurna", and soon a program for house financing, "Gruhapurna"'.

Medha is clearly pleased and proud that 4,000 members have already made significant changes in their lives. She is pleased that their loan program has been so successful. She also sees that by building new programs in a holistic way, members can take advantage of a number of them at the same time. Most members, she says, participate in at least three different services. The favorites are micro-finance, family development, placement services, health planning, and vocational training.

It is more than services that makes Annapurna successful; it is really about the way in which Annapurna gets its work done. It is a bottom–up approach according to Medha: 'We discuss everything we do and offer in group meetings. Then we have cluster meetings where decisions get made. The staff also meet and represent their needs and the needs of other members. Finally, there are management committee meetings. They participate in decision making as well.' Medha, however, is the principal decision maker and she is the one who is the catalyst for new ideas. She has an ongoing commitment to all of the people who live and work in the slum areas of Pune. She stays busy building new programs with the ideas provided by members, so that Annapurna remains responsive to the changing needs of the communities. They have been successful so far. And, all the new programs are self-supporting. Everyone is proud of that.

The Dreamer and the Doer

Medha is a woman of vision, but she has the energy and the know how to make the vision happen. She has a big picture in mind for Annapurna that is comprehensive and holistic. Because she believes that women can be strong only if the entire family is empowered, Medha encourages members to design programs for men and children. Their next project will be building houses in slum areas and connecting them to municipalities and municipal services. After that they have plans to work on a new program focused on caring for the environment.

Medha Samant lives and models her philosophy of empowerment everyday. Her tiny little—and hot—offices are in the middle of the slum they work in. Most of the staff live in this slum. They are also members of Annapurna. Medha has hired them to train them in office work, hoping to prepare them for other paying jobs in the future. She is their mentor, and sometimes their mother.

· Medha Samant is a dreamer and a doer. Her incredibly rich educational and professional background in the banking industry—with all of its networks—has made it possible for her to apply knowledge, experience, and understanding to complex projects. Her business acumen and leadership is evident everywhere. As is her heart.

Medha Samant never sits still. She is always looking to the future. She is always imagining a better world for the miserable and marginalized of society. From the very beginning she has dreamed about what might be and has turned those dreams into reality. When we asked her what was next for Annapurna, Medha replied: 'In the future we will be a big galaxy, providing all of the different services in all of the fields of social development. All of our programs and projects will be independent yet linked, just like the stars that make up the galaxy'.

Commentary

In our research we found that women founders of NGOs were largely driven by beliefs, personal experiences, their perception of community needs, and the strong desire to serve others. They are innovative, self-directed, and willing to take risks. And most of them are extroverts who are hardworking, persistent, and undaunted by most obstacles. Medha Samant is one of those entrepreneurial women who seems to be the perfect composite of all of the factors we found significant among women founders of NGOs in our study.

Medha comes from a Brahmin family. She had an excellent education. She had considerable professional experience in the private sector as a banker and she had a strong and supportive family. She did not have financial worries and she had good connections throughout the community should she need them. All of these resources played a significant part in the founding of Annapurna.

Growing up in a family of social activists, Medha's family fostered a desire to help others and modeled a zeal for taking personal responsibility for social justice. Her family had an almost missionary attitude about helping women escape the subjugation and exploitation of men. Medha's mother was a role model; she had a strong personality, deep convictions, and assertiveness to effect change. She enthusiastically accepted any and all risks that might intimidate others.

As a daughter, Medha could have been intimidated by her mother's accomplishments. That was not the case. Medha has exercised the same strong commitment to women's emancipation. She has used her status and expertise in the banking world to connect her to the knowledge and financial resources she needed to establish Annapurna. Her banking background has also helped her create Annapurna's financial self-sufficiency.

Medha is an entrepreneur and catalytic agent who seems almost gleeful in initiating creative ways to help others. Her energy seems to grow exponentially as more schemes come off her drawing board. Each of them builds on the needs revealed by earlier programs or new ideas offered by Annapurna members. She does not grow programs in a horizontal and additive way—they are not just a collection of 'would it not be nice to have' new programs. She attends to their vertical interconnections in order to build permanent pathways to independence and self-sufficiency.

It is clear that Medha delights in creating new 'stars' in her galaxy. Some might say that if Medha with her energy and drive were to disappear, the spirit and effectiveness of Annapurna might disappear with her. Medha, however, has put into place a sustainable organization not likely to disappear because every new program is self-supporting. Perhaps most important, however, is that she has fostered confidence and self-reliance among Annapurna's members. She knows that they will provide solutions to problems that might threaten Annapurna's longevity when she is no longer around.

What is different about Medha Samant as a founder and entrepreneur is that she is a thoroughly modern woman who has brought professional knowledge developed in a traditionally male institution—the Bank of India—to support Annapurna's social justice mission. In many ways her story is not the same as other feminist entrepreneurs who have resisted—even eschewed—bureaucratic structures in favor of collectives. Medha has intentionally designed an organization that uses some pragmatic bureaucratic principles and practices as effective strategies for accomplishing Annapurna's social mission.

Contrasting our Stories

The stories of Sindhutai and Medha seem in sharp contrast to one another. Sindhutai and Medha seem to be as opposite as they could be. As we wrote in our commentary to Sindhutai's story, she displays none of the factors that are so common across our study of women founders of NGOs. Medha, on the other hand, seems to be the perfect composite of all of those factors. To come to this conclusion would be to dismiss too quickly some intriguing subtleties about what characteristics and factors these two women founders share.

In the case of these two women, the external factors affecting their founder profiles are sharply different. Sindhutai's family drove her away, leaving her unable to count on family support. She had no education beyond the third grade. She comes from the lowest caste of Indian society as a tribal woman. She had no financial resources or social connections that would help her become successful in her own life much less contribute to the success of others. Medha, on the other hand, had it all: a supportive family with resources; role models for social activism; an advanced education that prepared her for success and so on. But we have learned in our study that many of the advantages that Medha had are 'external resources'.

What Sindhutai and Medha share in common are what we have described in our study as 'internal resources'.

(*a*) Both have strong spirits;
(*b*) both can mobilize resources;
(*c*) both are strong innovators;
(*d*) both take risks in the face of significant obstacles;
(*e*) both have strong self-confidence;
(*f*) both demonstrate zealous persistence;
(*g*) both believe that they can have a significant impact on improving the lives of others;
(*h*) both have compassion for the oppressed; and
(*i*) both recognize and use their personal power.

As we and others continue to study the factors that influence and motivate women to found and lead NGOs, perhaps we should investigate the relative importance of external versus internal factors. These two stories, as different in circumstances as they are, make a strong case for the primacy of internal resources. Perhaps internal factors are better predictors of entrepreneurial leadership in NGOs than external ones and should be more closely studied.

Chapter Two

Organizational Structures: Does a Feminist Ideology Matter?[1]

Introduction

Organizational structures are not carved in stone. They depend on many factors: the environment in which the organization functions, why it was founded, what it does, what the organizational goals are, and who are the people who make the organization function. Our study was based in a specific geographical region in India, and the NGOs were chosen because they were founded and led by women, and serve clientele who are largely poor and marginalized women. Given the similarities in the characteristics of our sample organizations, we expect that the NGOs under study to have developed similar organizational structures that allow them to work optimally.

As we noted in Chapter One, all of the founders rejected conventional employment and chose to strike out on their own to start organizations that would allow them to pursue their own goals of helping other less privileged women. More importantly, almost all the founders of the NGOs in our study were self-declared feminists.[2] We believe that the underlying ideology of a founder has a profound impact on the structure of the organization and the services they

---

[1] This chapter is based on the results that first appeared as 'Feminist Social Service Delivery in India' published in the *Pakistan Journal of Women's Studies* in 2002.

[2] We do not mean to imply that there is one blanket feminist ideology. We acknowledge that there are significant variations between Marxist, liberal, and radical feminism, as well as home-grown versions of feminism among ethnic groups.

provide. We discovered that all the founders have a core set of values and beliefs that shape the organizational culture. This culture is 'tacit, deep-seated, and often remains constant in an ever-changing external environment' (Rondstadt, 1984).

We noted that all of our founders proclaim themselves to be feminists, even though a couple did not like the 'label'. They all strongly espouse a feminist ideology and are passionate in promoting social justice for all women. Hence, we expect that the NGOs under study will reflect this philosophy, although often mediated by the particular social and cultural environments in which they function.

We first look at what the literature has to say about organizational structure and social service delivery of NGOs. We were curious whether or not the non-profit organizations would simply adopt the organizational structures of existing organizations and in particular the ubiquitous for-profit organizations, or would the difference in the non-profit and for-profit ethos influence the organizational form? As most of the founders of NGOs in our data are guided by feminist visions and values, we are particularly interested in how feminist ideology might influence the organizational structure of the NGOs. If a feminist ideology promotes inclusion and consensus building, what is the impact on the organizational structures? And through what channels do these influences affect decision making in the NGOs?

We also examine the management styles of the NGO leaders to see if they adopt styles congruent with their feminist philosophy or whether they adopt traditional management practices that are more typical of bureaucratic organizational structures (Segal, 1996). We wondered whether feminist ideology was potent enough to prompt feminists to adopt organizational structures and management styles that reflect their values and vision.

Literature Review

The literature suggests that non-profit organizations created to provide care and human services are rarely started as hierarchical and bureaucratic organizations. In an attempt to increase their efficiency, scope, and attend to the complex needs of their clientele, would organizations over time become formal and adopt features of a bureaucracy? Specifically would they mimic the business practices of the for-profit domain in order to increase their efficiencies or develop new revenue streams that would be more predictable than the whims of donors (Gonyea, 1999)?

The suggestion that non-profit organizations should be 'run like businesses' is a frequent recommendation but it is not without controversy. Those who insist that non-profit organizations are different from for-profit enterprises concede that non-profit organizations should be 'run like a business' only to the degree that they should obey the law, balance their budgets, use revenues efficiently, and be accountable as stewards of their resources. The similarities should end right there (Smith, 2000).

The ethos of generating care and well-being is the goal of most non-profit organizations. This is clearly different from the ethos of organizations in the for-profit sector that focus on generating profits and the government sector striving to fulfill political agendas. This caring ethos in non-profit organizations is a radical and fundamental challenge to the mainstream institutional culture and its ethos of 'hire or fire', 'publish or perish', or the waste of resources in the form of expense accounts and entertainment expenses allowed under the aegis of corporate culture.

Scholars have suggested that if non-profit organizations model themselves on organizations whose missions are the antitheses of their own ethos, it would likely affect their ability to set and meet their own goals. This prompts us to ask, will the organizational structure borrowed from other sectors negatively impact a non-profit sector organization from meeting its mission? Does organizational structure matter?

Non-profit organizations are not a homogeneous set of organizations. They range from the informal grass-roots organizations to the more formalized and large multinationals. Whether they are explicitly modeled after for-profit businesses in organizational structure or not, non-profit organizations must organize themselves in appropriate ways to effectively meet their missions and ensure a stream of revenues to do so. The idea of organizational efficiency suggests that there must be an overall structure that encourages the provision of care at reasonable costs, accountability, knowledge of the donors and clients, continuity, and reduction of overhead costs.

According to Weber (1968), the guru of organizational structure theory, optimum efficiency can be reached in those bureaucratic forms of organization which have a known chain of command and fixed hierarchical structures. This general process of bureaucratization inevitably follows the growth of an organization. In other words, as an organization grows it also becomes more complex: there are more staff, volunteers, donors, and clients. All of this demands certain bureaucratic features to allow for the organization to function efficiently. For example, decisions must be made in a timely fashion, costs must be allocated, revenue streams must be predictable, employees must have some specificity in their roles within the organization, etc. Weber also pointed out the negative consequences that bureaucratization could bring but he strongly believed that the shortcomings were outweighed by the benefits: the survival and success of the organization.

Feminists have taken on the challenge of rejecting Weber's claims by repudiating the inevitability of the 'iron cage of bureaucracy'. They point out that the efficiencies that Weber regards highly are social constructs. They suggest that the nature of efficiencies that require bureaucratization are indeed driven by gender, and that bureaucratization ignores efficiencies that are inherent in more consensual organizations where members feel included and empowered regardless of their role in the organization (Ferguson, 1984; Mills, 1988). Democratic participation and flat hierarchies indeed have their own efficiencies that mainstream literature disregards.

Another issue of contention is the optimal size of an organization. Size of an organization is a matter of choice. Hence, the deliberate attempts to grow may result in large organizations which in turn may become impersonal and bureaucratic. This choice of size may then undermine the advantages of small organizations that use small consensual groups and where skills and resources can be easily shared (Goffee and Scase, 1985).

Early feminist literature stated that hierarchical structures found in bureaucratic models were repugnant to feminists, because they were seen as synonymous with oppression, dominance, and authority (Rotschild, 1976: 28). The feminist case against bureaucratization insists that the manner in which an organization is structured is as important as the goals of the organization. There must exist a congruency between the two. For example, an NGO involved in promoting social justice cannot discriminate against minorities in its own hiring policies, nor can it set up an organizational structure that is oppressive towards any of its employees. Organizations based on collectivist principles, where all employees have a voice in the operation of the organization, meet the requirements of consensus and the culture of care. This, feminists have claimed, is the ideal organizational form (Matthews, 1994).

There are examples of early feminist NGOs initially organized with flattened hierarchies. As they grew larger over time and became more elaborate they were faced with traditional issues of management efficiencies, timeliness, and fiduciary responsibilities. Both clients and funders demanded that accountability standards be met, which often required the hiring of professional bookkeepers and administrators to manage the complexities of growth (Ferree and Hess, 1994: 125). Over time, the demarcation between the collectivist and bureaucratic forms of organization melded as the collectivist structures gave way to an increasing diversity of structural forms that included certain bureaucratic features (ibid.).

The obsession with ideology-driven organizations based on collectivist principles lessened over time to meet the realities faced by feminists running organizations, and attempts to integrate ideology with the practical task of running organizations led to new hybrid organizational forms (Mansbridge, 1984; Martin, 1990). For example, timeliness and efficiency demanded that only those closest to the routine and local issues were involved in decision making, while decisions that affected the whole organization, or were critical to its future, were made collectively (Ianello, 1992).

Collective decision making may be costly and time consuming, as all participants (or at least their representatives) must be made aware of all the issues and consulted prior to making of decisions, as all actions require some form of agreed upon consensus. A mixed 'pragmatic' form of organization has persisted through time as a compromise between attempts to realize feminist ideals of collective decision making and the need of a larger, more complex organization. However, such compromise, we argue, does not signal that the feminist model has failed and that the male model has been unabashedly adopted as the optimal form of management. It only suggests that certain pragmatic changes are adapted to enhance and complement an inherently feminist model of organizational structure.

The National Foundation for Women Business Owners (2003) reported that women and men business owners do, in fact, have different management styles that influence the culture as well as the structure of the organization. These gender differences are related to differences in experiences, environment, socialization and biology, thereby giving rise to a different value system, attitudes, and psychological characteristics (Billing and Alvesson, 1994). The management styles will impact and influence organizational structure.

Women typically have caring and participatory management styles (Rondstadt, 1984). Women are less hierarchical, may take more time when making decisions, seek more information, and are more likely to draw upon input from others, including fellow business owners, employees, and subject-matter experts. Hughes et al. (2002) reported that female managers show greater concern for others, consider how others feel about managerial decisions, and were more likely than men to act with the organization's broad interest in mind. Women tend to use more socially-facilitative behaviors to lead (that is, an interactive, cooperative, people-centered approach), while men use a more task-focused style (that is, a transactional approach based on dominance) (Eagly and Karau, 1991). Interdependence, cooperation, receptivity, merging, and acceptance characterize women's management values.

Several scholars report on the gender differences among male and female founders of for-profit enterprises; women tend to have smaller businesses more geared to lifestyle (Rondstadt, 1984). Among equally qualified male and female entrepreneurs, female entrepreneurs establish a more relaxed creative entrepreneurial setting favoring a more egalitarian management style. For example, women provide more progressive employee benefits, and have greater sensitivity to the challenges of balancing a family and a career. Accordingly, the goals and intentions of the entrepreneur during the start-up phase determine many of the characteristics of the business. This suggests that women are more involved in lifestyle ventures that give greater importance to independence, autonomy, and control of the enterprise than to generating profit margins (ibid.).

Given the historical dominance of men in the field of management and organization there is a gender bias in organizations: 'Males have structured the game, the rules, and manufactured the arena in accordance with their specialties, skills and interests' (Billing and Alvesson, 1994: 222). Hence, organizational structures and processes are largely dominated by culturally-defined masculine values. Masculine values are culturally mediated and stress features such as 'hard, dry, objective, independent, rationalist, and materialist' (Hines, 1992: 328). These features then become the yardstick against which organizational behaviors are measured in order to determine if they are successful and efficient. Some of these measures can be argued to be antithetical to efficiency or ownership or even sustainability of small NGOs.

As organizations are evaluated by funders and clients, vis-à-vis accepted masculine defined parameters, women struggle to maintain organizations that reflect their own values. In order to survive in a male-dominated arena in a country like India, women with feminist visions must find ways to navigate between appeasing their donors (often from organizations modeled on the male model) and following their own values. They often need to be pragmatic and respond to their environment without adopting the male meanings of efficiency and success.

This 'pragmatic' form of compromise was evident in the investigation of women-led NGOs in New York carried out by Rebecca Bordt in 1997. A hybrid form of organization appeared most frequently (45 per cent) in the ninety-five organizations that she studied. She called this form 'collectivist pragmatic', as it draws on both bureaucratic and collectivist characteristics. The classical forms—the bureaucracies and collectivists—were found least frequently: 19 per cent and 8 per cent respectively. Bordt concluded that age and size rather than ideology are the only useful predictors of organizational structure in non-profit organizations.

Changes in organizational structures are also explained in the literature on organizational life cycles. It suggests that the organization exhibits characteristics similar to collectivists in the early stages of the life cycle, and takes on characteristics of the bureaucracy as it evolves (Perkins et al., 1983). However, this explanation is problematic as it implies the inevitability of the bureaucratic structure over time, and negates the collectivist structure as an end it itself (Bordt, 1997: 54).

Size, as measured by the number of paid employees of an organization, may also affect the structural form. As organizations employ more people they are subject to greater regulation by the public sector. It is often inevitable that the logistics involved in managing and running an organization will necessitate developing formal structures with hierarchical reporting procedures. Hence, we expect that the larger organizations will be more bureaucratic in nature than the smaller organizations. Thus, if the predictions of organizational life cycle hold true, then one would expect that all older organizations that have grown over time are bureaucratic, and the younger and smaller organizations are collectivist.

However, this type of argument implies that the growth of an organization is inevitable for success (or efficiency). The size of the organization itself is a choice that is endogenous to the management/founder. Organizations that deliberately choose to stay small and eschew the 'success' of growth may be intentionally measuring 'success' using a different yardstick.

This yardstick includes process and output, and not output alone.[3] In other words, the decision by an NGO to maintain a collectivist structure by foregoing the opportunities for bigger grants and their ensuing obligations may be the result of how they evaluate their own success. Furthermore, in contrast to the bottom line, a for-profit measure of success, the provision of a nurturing environment that requires a flat hierarchy may be the key output—and, therefore, a key success factor—for women-founded NGOs. This output is in addition to the services they provide.

Although the literature does not offer any explanations for what choices an organization makes in the objectives it wishes to pursue and the types of services it offers, in Chapter One we saw that this is largely driven by the beliefs and values of the founder. Feminist founders of NGOs, as we saw, were primarily offering services congruent with their ideals. Then, when the opportunity to grow confronts the founder with attendant changes of the nature of the output and organizational structure, the founder's response determines what happens to the organizational structure.

It is also important to investigate the drivers of change: demand for services, wishes of the funders, etc. The response to each driver may differ; this raises questions we explore further in this and later chapters: How does a feminist ideology influence the type, number, and the nature of services offered by feminist organizations? What we cannot know is whether the nature of services an organization chooses (to meet client demand, donor preferences, or other reasons) influences organizational structure, or vice versa. This question, as interesting as it is, remains outside the scope of our study. However, we return to the nature of services NGOs offer when we consider their impact in Chapter Three.

---

[3] Even if output were a measure of success, if output is measured in proportion to funds received or spent, perhaps the output to cost ratio of small organizations may on average be higher than that of large organizations whose overhead costs are usually high.

Organizational structures often reflect not only the nature of services provided, but the kinds of people who provide it. By this we mean whether the services are provided by paid professionals, by volunteers, or a mixture of both kinds of personnel. This is evident when we look at organizations that rely on volunteers. Since no one is forced to donate their time, NGOs must make efforts to recruit volunteers. Volunteers, in numerous studies on motivation, say that they volunteer for a particular organization because, 'I believed in what the organization was doing' (Clary and Snyder, 1999). Thus, we would expect that organizations that are inclusive and collectivist in structure are more likely to recruit volunteers who may also espouse the feminist vision, as they would be easier to attract and retain.

Some feminists eschew volunteer labor, arguing that such labor, especially when provided by women in social services, is another form of female exploitation (Christiansen- Ruffman, 1990; Ellis and Noyes, 1990). In other words, feminists suggest that when women are encouraged to donate their work as an unpaid labor of love through acts of volunteering, the savings accrue to the organization. However, such theoretical predictions are not borne out in the real world where feminist organizations are shown to use volunteers (Metzendorf and Cnaan, 1992).

Moreover the very term 'volunteer' implies 'choice'. If the basic needs of a 'poor' volunteer are not met, she, in all likelihood, would leave her volunteer position to seek a paid position. To choose to continue work as a volunteer is then a personal decision and cannot be seen as exploitive. Moreover, there are many who volunteer their time because they both believe in the cause and can usually afford to do so due to some family support.

In India, we also find increasing use of '*sewa bhavis*' (volunteers) by NGOs, and the notion of exploitation of women does not surface, as women often regard volunteerism in the aid of the poor as fulfilling their religious '*dharma*' (duty) (Kassam and Handy, 2003). Furthermore, accepting donations of time is not considered a form of exploitation by feminist women founders as they themselves are often forgoing market value for their labor to pursue their vision. We recognize that much of the volunteering in the NGOs in India is done by women who come from the middle and upper classes, thus negating the kind of exploitation claimed by some feminist theorists.

As we have explained the cultural context of our study in Chapter One, we will not repeat this discussion here, but only mention briefly those concepts that may impact organizational structure. Many of the founders belong to the Brahmin caste (the highest caste in the caste system) and come from relatively well-to-do families. Women from the higher-castes tend to be educated and financially secure. Living in 'joint families', they are likely to have fewer time commitments towards domestic duties and childcare. This may make them more willing to devote energies to running collectivist organizations that are congruent with their beliefs and are also less constrained by the demands of bureaucratic organizations that are hierarchical and less consensual.

The nature of donor support also influences the nature of organizational structures and the manner in which they evolve. If a large number of people give donations in small amounts, this mitigates any donor control. Governments often act as agents for the donors inasmuch as they monitor and regulate the NGO for fraudulent behavior. In the case of larger donors, where the donation is of significant size relative to the budget of the NGO, a donor may require additional guarantees of fiduciary accountability by asking to sit on the board of trustees or actively engaging in the organization as a volunteer.

For example, international donor support in India is often an inescapable reality for women-led NGOs. Non-governmental organizations accepting international donations are subject to additional bureaucratic stipulations from the Indian government, under the Foreign Contribution Regulation Act (FCRA). Under this law all foreign donations are supposed to be credited into one single bank account. All NGOs receiving such aid are required to register with the Union Home Ministry and file an annual statement of the utilization of these grants. In the period between 1990 and 1995, it was estimated that over 10,000 NGOs received nearly twenty billion dollars over this period from fifteen different donor countries (Nanavatty and Kulkarni, 1998). In addition, the donors themselves had rather stringent accountability requirements which no doubt added to the paperwork burden of the NGOs.

While donors and the government require strict accounting mechanisms, this does not necessarily imply that NGOs must become bureaucratic in order to comply. It simply requires that NGOs have the right accounting structure, services which professional chartered accountants well versed in non-profit accounting can provide. In addition, accountants can advise the NGO on efficient record keeping in compliance with donor norms. Often small organizations are more flexible compared to larger organizations in terms of accommodating a variety of accounting norms and do not respond with a change in their structures in response to donor's accountability requirements.

When an NGO receives large funds and this changes the size and scale of operations sufficiently, it may be necessary for the NGO to change its decision-making mechanisms. This can result in changes in governance and reporting practices and affect organizational structure. Moreover, it is possible under certain circumstances that even if the scale does change but other parameters remain the same, such as the number of permanent staff or clients; there may not be any need for NGOs to alter their organizational structures.

While the common assumption is that accepting foreign funds inevitably brings bureaucracy is not always valid. It might be true for large foreign government funders like the European Union or USAID, but it is not always true of other smaller foreign funders. Nonetheless, we expect that donor and government requirements, whether necessary or not, often do influence the organizational structures of many NGOs pushing them to adopt more bureaucratic characteristics. In addition to donor and government accountability requirements there are other factors mentioned earlier that may mitigate this influence or exacerbate it. It is difficult to say which kinds of influences may dominate.

Will NGOs retain the collectivist forms as reflected by the vision of their organization? Or will they be pushed towards the practical features of a bureaucracy? To answer these questions, we turn to the literature, which suggests a continuum of organizational forms that NGOs can take that lie between the two organizational extremes: those organized on collectivist principles (referred to as collectivists, from now on) and bureaucracies.

In her study, Bordt (1997) offers a typology of organizational forms based on a variety of dimensions. As we explain next, we use Bordt's classification with some modifications. Closely following Bordt, we use two hybrid organizational structures 'professionals' and 'collectivist pragmatics'. We retain the former from Bordt, but intentionally invert the latter from Bordt's 'pragmatic collectivist' to our 'collectivist pragmatics' to stress the differences along the collectivist dimensions of the organization. In other words, our collectivist pragmatics are closer to the pure collectivist organization than bureaucracies on the continuum, as seen in Figure 2.1, which illustrates the continuum of the NGOs from collectivists to bureaucracies.

FIGURE 2.1
A Continuum of Organizational Structures

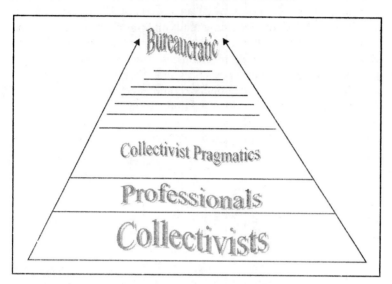

In Table 2.1, we list all the dimensions of organizational structure and use them to categorize organizations as collectivists, professionals, collectivist pragmatics, and bureaucracies. For each type of organization the dimensions are marked as 'high', 'medium', or 'low' to reflect how different types of organizations are structured on these dimensions. For example, *material incentives* would be 'high' in bureaucracies and 'low' in collectivists. Conversely, *shared norms and beliefs* would rank 'high' in collectivists and 'low' in bureaucracies. The two hybrid forms would reflect 'high' to 'medium' for shared norms and beliefs and 'low' or 'medium' for material incentives.

The first dimension, *formal structure*, corresponds to the degree of formality existing in an organization's policies. It examines whether rules and policies are formalized in writing or simply exist as unwritten contracts between the members; whether written job descriptions exist or whether employees just do what needs to be done. It also includes formal accountability controls such as audits.

The second dimension focuses on *material incentives*, which is measured by the existence of detailed payroll information and description of scales for employee salaries, benefits, vacations, and opportunities for promotion. At the low end of the spectrum, salaries

TABLE 2.1

Dimensions of Organizational Structure

	Dimensions of organizational structure						
Type of organization	Formal structure	Material incentives	Normative incentives	Decision-making authority	Formal decision making	Shared beliefs and time	Informal decision making	Differentiation
Bureaucratic organizations	High	High	Medium	High	Medium	Low	Low	High
Pragmatic collectives	Medium	Medium	High	Medium	Medium	Medium	Medium	Medium
Professional organizations	Low	Low	High	Medium	Medium	High	Medium	Medium
Collectivist organizations	Medium	Low	High	Medium	Low	High	High	Low

are also described but there is less divergence between the values of the salaries across the organization. The *material incentives* across the organization in collectivist organizations are ranked 'low' and tend to be more equitably distributed and they do not reflect premium salaries to those who may command more in other labor market.

Normative incentives emphasize personal satisfaction by making values and norms explicit without being connected to monetary incentives. Recognition and appreciation are general normative incentives. *Decision-making authority* is the fourth dimension and measures whether authority is vested in a few individuals or in many. Concentration of authority in a few suggests a bureaucracy; it has a 'high' ranking in decision making. Conversely, if the decision making is based on consensus, it suggests a shared decision-making process with 'low' authority invested in each individual. Accordingly, the latter is ranked 'low' and is prevalent in collectivist organizations.

The next dimension is a measure of *formality in decision making* and corresponds to the existence of explicit and written criteria for evaluation. For example, the control for termination or disciplinary actions for employees may be informal or formal according to written procedures. The higher the degree of formality, the closer the organization is to a bureaucracy. Conversely, the more informal the decision-making criteria, the more it resembles a collectivist structure.

In bureaucratic organizations, it is not necessary for members to share norms and values or socialize outside the workplace, as hierarchies are characterized by high depersonalization. The opposite holds true in flattened hierarchies, where members relate to each other in a more personal manner. They, therefore, generally have shared values and norms in order to function efficiently, and tend to socialize outside the workplace. Furthermore, shared political, ideological, or ethnic beliefs lead members to share time outside of the workplace. This is particularly true in organizations that have informal structures and few formal controls or material incentives. Thus, bureaucracies rank 'low' on *shared norms and beliefs*, while collectivists will rank 'high'.

Informal decision-making criteria measures ad hoc decision-making actions, such as using individual judgment in issues of fairness. It often involves taking into account the opinions of other members of the group and not following rigid or formalized rules. Collectivists generally rank 'high' on this criterion and bureaucracies rank 'low'. The final dimension is *differentiation*. This dimension measures the number of job titles, as well as the economic and educational diversity of the members of the organization. Higher differentiation on this dimension corresponds to a greater diversity in the status of the employees and is, therefore, a characteristic of bureaucracies. Conversely, collectivists rank lower in differentiation.

We invert Bordt's organizational structure to collectivist pragmatics (rather than pragmatic collectivists as in Bordt's 1997 study, as previously mentioned) because of the cultural context within which our feminist-mandated NGOs function. We find that some of the dimensions used by Bordt to explain hybrids do not resonate with the NGO environment in India. For example, pragmatic collectivist organizations in Bordt's classification exhibit 'low' levels for the dimensions of shared time and beliefs, 'high' for normative incentives, and 'medium' to 'low' for material incentives.

Many of the women founders (over 90 per cent) in our sample come from middle or upper-middle echelons of society in India (as seen in Chapter One) and they were not generally expected to support their families financially at the time of founding their NGOs. This suggests that women founders are less likely to be concerned with earning high incomes from work in their NGOs. Thus, collectivist pragmatic organizations score 'high' on normative incentives, 'low' on material incentives, and 'high' on shared norms and beliefs (and time) as do collectivists. We note that Bordt's pragmatic collectivists are closer to bureaucracies than collectivists while on several dimensions our collectivist pragmatics are closer to the collectivist model. This is also true for our NGOs structured as professionals. These modifications to Bordt's findings reflect the reality of the NGO organizational structures found in our sample.

Table 2.2 shows the rankings for each of the dimensions for the four organizational structures: Bureaucracies (B), Professionals (P), Collectivist Pragmatics (CP), and Collectivists (C). Using these categories and their specifications along the eight dimensions (described earlier), we organize our findings and discuss them in the next section.

Findings

In this section, we present our findings for the organizational structures of the twenty NGOs in our study. The interviews were done over

TABLE 2.2

Variation in Dimensions of Organizational Structure

	Formal structure	Material incentives	Normative incentives	Decision-making authority	Formal decision criteria	Shared beliefs and time	Informal decision criteria	Differentiation	Organization type
1	H	H	H	H	M	L	H	H	B
2	M	H	L	H	M	M	L	H	B
3	M	H	L	H	M	L	M	H	B
4	H	H	L	M	H	L	M	H	B
5	H	H	M	M	M	M	M	H	B
6	M	L	H	M	M	H	M	L	CP
7	M	L	H	M	M	H	M	M	CP
8	M	M	M	M	M	M	M	H	CP
9	M	M	H	M	M	H	M	L	CP
10	M	L	H	M	M	H	M	H	CP
11	M	L	H	M	L	H	M	L	CP
12	M	L	H	M	M	L	M	M	CP
13	L	L	H	M	M	H	M	L	P
14	L	L	H	M	L	M	M	L	P
15	M	L	H	M	M	H	M	L	P
16	L	L	H	M	M	H	M	L	P
17	L	L	H	H	L	H	L	L	C
18	M	L	H	H	L	H	M	L	C
19	M	L	H	M	L	H	M	L	C
20	L	L	H	M	L	H	H	L	C

Notes: B = Bureaucratic; CP = Collectivist Pragmatic; P = Professional; C = Collectivist; H = high; M = medium; L = low a period of six years to track the changes in scope and depth of services, size and funding, and organizational structures. To obtain organizational characteristics we chose to interview the managerial staff as well as the founder. We hoped we would get better insights concerning the day-to-day management of the organization from which some of the founders were often far removed.

In Table 2.2, we list our NGOs and then rank them as 'high', 'medium', or 'low' according to the eight dimensions. Although in some cases we have ranked the dimension as medium, this is not to be construed as a true midpoint between high and low. We use 'medium' for ease of tabulating and to suggest an interpretive place that is neither high nor low. These rankings are based on the information elicited by the interviews. The ranking enables us to infer the NGOs organizational classification as bureaucratic, professional, collectivist pragmatic, or collectivist organizations.

Ranking them as 'high' or 'low' was relatively simple when the organization's mode of operation coincided fully with a bureaucracy or collectivist organizational type. In the cases where an organization did not strictly follow a prescribed dimensional pattern, or it followed a variation in the pattern suggested in Table 2.1, we ranked it as 'medium'. For example, if organizations reported that they sometimes used individual judgment and sometimes based their decision on written policies, we ranked them as 'medium' on the informal decision criteria dimension. It was sometimes difficult for our respondents to say how often one kind of practice was used over the other requiring us to make an estimate based on their responses. Hence, the caveat that 'medium' did not reflect the midpoint on the scale. Table 2.2 provides rankings of all our NGOs on the eight dimensions.

Since there are so many variations in how organizations score along the eight dimensions, it is not surprising that many NGOs in our sample are not pure bureaucracies or purely collectivist. Just over half the NGOs in our sample (11/20) are hybrids having features of both collectivists and bureaucracies. There are only five NGOs that can be classified as pure bureaucracies and four as pure collectivists.

Structure and Ideology

When we asked the NGO founders about their organizational philosophy, 75 per cent (15/20) identified that their organizations had a feminist ideology. Despite this finding, there are only four pure collectivist organizations in our sample. This may suggest that feminist ideology and organizational structure as traditionally described do not go hand-in-hand. However, given that many of the NGOs turned out to be hybrids that have important collectivist features and also continue to be managed as collectivist organizations, we need to conduct a more detailed analysis before dismissing the connection between ideology and organizational structure.

During the interview with the founders we asked them to identify their organizations as collectivist or bureaucratic by providing them a list of factors to consider. These factors included whether decisions were made by committees or by individuals, by virtue of their office or expertise, or whether it was voted on by the members or delegated officers. We also asked them to consider whether formal rules existed, or if there were any minimal stipulated rules with ad hoc decisions made by the group or elected officers. Other questions concerned whether social relations were role-based and impersonal, or less segmented and more personal. We also wanted to know whether there was social stratification based on a hierarchy, or if there was a more egalitarian distribution. Finally, we asked questions about their policies of recruitment and whether or not there were incentives for advancement and the nature of the incentives.

With one exception, every organization that identified with having an organizational philosophy of feminism, also self-identified as being a collective, based on the criteria mentioned earlier. Overwhelmingly, the respondents chose the items listed under collectivist structure over those listed under bureaucratic structure. However, in examining our triangulated data, which was obtained by asking the staff and the founders at a second interview[4] to carefully describe their day-to-day activities along the eight dimensions, only four organizations qualified to be called 'pure' collectivist (prescribed using the dimensions suggested in the literature).

For example, when asked about decision-making authority regarding personnel matters, founders would often reply that *all* such matters are subject to group decisions. This, however, often appeared to be a normative wish on the part of the founder. When pushed for recent examples, the founder and the staff normally conceded that some decisions were either made by the founder or one of the trustees.

---

[4] We gave them an open-ended structured questionnaire this time.

Making a group decision would have taken 'too much time, and would have been detrimental to the immediate goals' as one respondent commented. This sentiment was echoed frequently and referred to localized decisions that did not impact the core of the organization. However, such decisions were subsequently discussed at group meetings, but only for purposes of information.

Thus, decision making was not always a collectivist endeavor. Some interviewees insisted that there was an important distinction between critical and formal decisions on one hand, and minor, informal decision making for more mundane matters on the other hand.[5] In this case we gave them a medium on the ranking, noting that our hybrid organizations for the most part lie closer to a collectivist structure than to a bureaucracy.

A few of our founders sounded exasperated with the demands of a collectivist form: 'It's just not practical', claimed one. Another admitted, 'We really tried and then decided we could not continue this way'. Several feminist founders blamed the bureaucratization of the original collectivist structure on the hiring of new professional staff: 'We had to get accountants and others once we received funding from an international agency', claimed a growing NGO that had received a substantial donation a few years previously. Another shook her head despondently, 'The new staff just don't have the same values'. It is puzzling why there is a discrepancy between self-identification, beliefs, and actual practice.

We believe that given all twenty founders self-identified as feminists, and that fifteen founders had identified their organizations to have feminist ideologies, their answers in most cases tended to be normative. Of these fifteen founders, all but one believed her organization to be collectivist. In addition, they used management styles that suggest that they inherently remained feminist organizations in the eyes of their founders, despite having adopted some bureaucratic features. Only four founders, who did not claim to have a feminist organizational philosophy, identified their NGOs as having bureaucratic structures.

Ideology and normative tendencies may call for self-identification as collectivist organizations, but the reality differs somewhat in some of their practices. We got the sense from the interviews that some of the responses came from strong ideological beliefs despite the fact

---

[5] Bordt (1997) and Ianello (1992) have also mulled over this distinction.

that many founders had to acquiesce to external demands or the professionalization of their own staff. This explains why organizations that may start out as firmly ensconced in feminist ideology, continue to see themselves as feminist organizations although they may have to adopt a few bureaucratic features to adapt to the changing exigencies of their environment. Without doubt the ethos in all of the NGOs in this study was strongly feminist. We believe that is why the NGOs have been so resourceful in preserving many of the participatory features of collectivist structures.

Organizational Structures

Collectivists

Feminist women providing services for women, advocating for the rights of women, and undertaking projects to promote social justice tend to initiate and manage NGOs that adhere to a feminist ideology. This ideology, as seen in the literature, predicts that these NGOs will be collectivists. However, the data did not bear out this fit between organizational structure and ideology. The founders of these NGOs, like many others describe their organizational philosophy as 'collectivist'; however only four NGOs retained characteristics congruent with their ideals.

As seen in Table 2.2, the characteristics of collectivist NGOs are 'low' in material incentives, 'high' in normative incentives, 'low' in formal decision-making criteria, and 'low' in differentiation. We found that members of collectivists share political and other beliefs, and they tend to socialize with each other. All but one relies on donations from private individual donors and receives no funds from other organizations, government or international funders. This latter point suggests that they may not have to adhere to rigid accountability requirements facing other NGOs who do receive this funding. Thus they are able to preserve their collectivist organizational structure.

When we examine the four collectivist NGOs, we note that only one receives international funding. We have argued earlier that foreign funding has pushed some NGOs to take on bureaucratic features. However, this one NGO had managed, in its eleven years of operation, to retain its collectivist features. That said we note that it has no paid staff and one of the highest numbers of volunteers. It is likely that this NGO is able to attract the kind of volunteers, which makes it possible for them to meet their donor and government requirements without hiring professional staff and moving to a bureaucratic organization.

Although, from the Table 2.2, the low scores of 'professional' and 'collectivist' organizations on dimensions such as formal decision criteria, differentiation, and formal structure, may give rise to the notion that these NGOs are unplanned, unstructured, and naturally chaotic, it is entirely contrary to the picture on the ground. These organizations are highly efficient and have managed very well despite their informal structures.

Bureaucracies

Given our discussion of the feminist ideology of our founders, we may expect that women-run organizations promoting social justice do not tend to develop bureaucratic structures. However, we find that among our NGOs there are more bureaucracies and hybrids than collectivists. Of the twenty organizations we studied, five of them are bureaucracies using the dimensions identified in Table 2.1. Bureaucracies represent one end of an organizational continuum. It is interesting to note that in the case of four out of these five bureaucracies, our finding coincides with the organizational form identified by the founder. Despite their own personal feminist ideologies, these founders were aware that their NGO's organizational structure did not reflect the kind of structure that would be expected of a feminist founder. This warrants some explanation.

It is often the case that a personal feminist ideology does not necessarily match the organizational form. We think there is a reasonable explanation for this. Most founders started small with the help of friends and family. While they remained small they were able to apply their feminist ideology to their organizational arrangements and practices. They remained hierarchically flat, operated with shared beliefs and norms, and practiced participatory and democratic decision making. On all eight dimensions shown on Table 2.1, these organizations likely started out as collectivist organizations because of the founder's feminist ideology.

The growth and the influx of international funding and changes to the number and types of services, however, often resulted in structural compromises. Although these may seem to have compromised the founding feminist principles, this is not necessarily the case. For the sake of managing growth many of the NGOs took on bureaucratic features and in our classification some became hybrids (retaining some collectivist features) while a few became bureaucratic.

Founders who perceived their organizations as collectivists, we believe, may be referring to particular features of their organization that function as a collectivist one. It is unlikely that their vision of feminist collectivist organizations matches our eight dimensions used for analytical purposes. Furthermore, as all hybrids maintained some collectivist features, it is entirely possible and reasonable that these features are paramount in viewing the organizations primarily as collectivist ones.

Adopting bureaucratic features does not necessarily mean that feminist principles were abandoned just because the organizational form changed. (We take this issue up later in this chapter.) Those that did not adopt bureaucratic features may not have handled growth or change in the same manner as those that became wholly bureaucratic. This can be explained by considering the many different kinds of change, for example: growth in revenues, types of services, number of clients, etc., that warrant organizational responses. Each different type of growth can determine changes on different dimensions of structural form. For example, growth in the services requiring specialization and hiring of professionals may push an organization into adopting differentiation in job descriptions and material incentives.

Source of revenue and foreign funding is an important influence on organizational structure. Consider what happens when an NGO diversifies its revenue streams. It is likely that once an NGO receives large funding from a few sources, especially when they are international sources (such as large government agencies or other NGOs), it usually responds by implementing formal structures and takes on bureaucratic characteristics. One of our founders voiced the dilemma faced by feminists as they try to stabilize their NGO's services by attracting external and international funds: 'We are now in a better position to serve others. But we find the collectivist model cannot work anymore. I don't know what to do—should we stay small and collectivist, the way we want to be? Or should we grow and serve more people and abandon our collectivist ideas?'

The size of the organization, measured by the number of paid staff, seems to suggest that bureaucratic organizations use more paid staff than other organizational forms do. As organizations gradually move away from the collectivist end of the continuum, they seem to have a much higher ratio of professional staff to volunteers. When paid

Is coll. better than bur.?

staff outnumber volunteers it is likely that material incentives become more important than normative ones. While volunteers may respond to normative incentives, paid staff may find material incentives more attractive. This may apply particularly to lower-level staff who are dependent on their pay for their livelihoods. Higher-level managers or professionals, who may be better off financially, may not depend on salaries for their whole livelihood. In those cases, material incentives may not constitute a significant incentive because they can more easily postpone their paychecks or accept reduced salaries in times of fund scarcity.

Many of the features described as bureaucratic also characterize many large and/or well-funded organizations. The question is, does becoming larger or well-funded imply that the organization stops using democratic values of grass-roots collective decision making? Some founders think that it does, but others disagree. In some organizations internal staff decisions related to daily decision making are not made collectively. At the same time, however, consensus decision making is the norm for decisions that are considered major and related to the overall operations and goals of the NGO. In other organizations, grass-roots decision making is encouraged at the smaller group level which the NGO as a whole facilitates. Non-governmental organizations working closely with *mahila mandals* encourage this approach to collective decision making.

It is interesting to note that bureaucracies have fewer volunteers than other organizational forms. Here we find an inverse relation in that bureaucracies as measured by the volunteers (as compared to paid staff) rely on volunteers far less than the smaller collectivists that tend to rely more on volunteers than paid staff. Our findings show that the average ratio of paid staff to volunteers in bureaucracies is 4.67 staff to 1 volunteer, whereas in the hybrid forms, the average ratio is 1.4 staff to 1 volunteer. Collectivist organizations have a ratio of 1 paid staff to 4 volunteers.

From our data we cannot determine whether this finding suggests that bureaucratic organizations have sufficient funding to use paid staff in the delivery of services, or whether they offer services for which they cannot use volunteers because of training and liability issues, or whether volunteers are not attracted to working in bureaucratic organizations.

Within the larger NGO organization, paid staff who have specialized roles may make decisions related to their own area of specialization rather than taking decision making to the organizational level.

This raises the question of whether and when organizations move to non-collective decision making. Does it relate to particular aspects of their size, their age, the nature of their services, or to their bureaucratic features in general?

The emergence of bureaucratic organizational structures may also be due to the age and size of the organization, as the life cycle theory predicts. Our findings lend partial support to this theory. We find the largest as well as the three oldest organizations in our study are bureaucratic in nature. The average age for our bureaucracies is 33.4 years. One of the largest and oldest of our NGOs is a bureaucracy, despite its founder's professed commitment to a feminist ideology. In this case, we discovered that external factors, such as funding arrangements exerted sufficient pressure to make the organization adopt bureaucratic characteristics. In another NGO the increase in the sheer number of paid employees pushed the organization away from collective decision making to a more bureaucratic form. In this case it was difficult to maintain timely responsiveness to its clients without delegating decision making to a few staff members.

The organizational pressures of adapting to changing environmental demands result in changes in size, funding, staff specialization and differentiation, adoption of material incentives, timeliness of decision making, fiduciary responsibilities, etc. These change the organization's proclivity towards the use of bureaucratic features rather than collectivist structures.

In our interviews with the founders of the bureaucratic NGOs, three out of four did not espouse any organizational philosophy. Although they all had a personal feminist philosophy, they did not see a contradiction in leading organizations that had bureaucratic features. Adopting financial reporting mechanisms, doing strategic planning exercises, having explicit criteria for evaluation, and offering staff material incentives was a reflection of their successful status and obligations to funders. Although they lamented some of the changes that decreased shared decision making and beliefs, they explicitly made a choice in favor of growth, accepting its attendant changes.

Growth did not imply that the founders were willing to compromise on the quality of their work, their commitment to empowering women and bettering the lives of the poor or other important issues related to their core mission. The tradeoffs they were willing to make were to compromise on the organizational processes to further their reach among the poor, and offer specialized services that were otherwise unavailable to poor women. The leadership in these bureaucratic

NGOs in no way resembled the kind of leadership normally encountered in traditional patriarchal bureaucracies. The women founders' leadership, even when they adopted certain bureaucratic features, had retained leadership characteristics of inclusiveness, egalitarianism, and participatory democracy. At the core, the feminization of leadership also focused on the personal among its staff and its leadership.

Given that the founders had started the NGO and have remained at the helm of their organizations, they are mindful of not letting their organizations become inefficient or wasteful. We found that in all the bureaucratic NGOs the founders were partially involved in all aspects of the organization, including, in most cases, contact with the clientele. In this respect they were unlike the leaders of highly differentiated organizations. Although all of the founders said yes to 'differentiation' in levels of education and job titles in the organization, there was in practice considerable overlap of roles, especially in the case of the founder.

Hybrids: Collectivist Pragmatic and Professional Organizations

As NGOs grow in size and complexity, taking on bureaucratic features moves them along the continuum between collectivist and bureaucratic organization. In this context, two additional structures arise—professional organizations and collectivist pragmatic organizations. Our data reveals there to be eleven hybrid organizations, four professional organizations and seven collectivist pragmatic organization (See Table 2.2). They have an average age of ten years and are relatively younger than the average bureaucracy (33.4 years). This suggests that if they started out as collectivist organizations they have responded to demands that face organizations over time and adapted to their particular organizational structures, or that they have adopted their organizational structure at the outset.

One seven-year-old NGO is an example of an organization that transitioned from a collectivist to a hybrid form, what we have called a collectivist pragmatic form. This NGO started intentionally as a collectivist organization, in keeping with the feminist ideology of the founders. It managed to stay collectivist as evidenced by its members who met informally with the trustees and worked out strategies to execute and develop their programs. They were all heavily involved in the day-to-day activities. In this case, change happened gradually because the trustees found that they could no longer be personally responsible for the needs of a growing organization. They distanced themselves from decision making and assumed traditional roles of governance. This was followed by a degree of differentiation in the roles of members and staff. This is a classic example of the process of a growing NGO as it changes from a pure collectivist form to adding practical bureaucratic features.

Of our twenty NGOs, seven (35 per cent) fall primarily into the collectivist pragmatic hybrid organizational form. We find that a majority of the collectivist pragmatic organizations have adopted bureaucratic features in response to the demands of international funding. Hence they exhibit moderate amounts of formal structure, decision-making authority, and formal decision criteria, but they also have features of the collectivist organization. All but one exhibit 'high' normative incentives, 'high' shared norms and beliefs, and the majority of them measure 'low' on material incentives. Although they do not retain all the characteristics of collectivists they function more like collectivists than bureaucracies in their leadership styles. Thus it is not surprising that all their feminist founders continue to see their organizations as collectivist organizations.

Similarly, professional NGOs are hybrids that have structures from collectivists and bureaucracies. As shown in Figure 2.1, they are closer to collectivist organizations than to collectivist pragmatic ones, and function even more like collectivists than bureaucracies. We call them 'professionals' because many of the members are professional women, such as social workers and teachers; they also take management and leadership roles in the NGO.

We find four (20 per cent) of our NGOs to be classified as professional organizations (P). This hybrid organizational form possesses fewer of the characteristics of a bureaucracy than the collectivist pragmatic organization. For example, all the professionals score 'low' on material incentives, 'high' on normative incentives, and 'low' on differentiation—like collectivists; however, unlike collectivists, they do not all score 'high' on shared norms and beliefs.

This last finding may be surprising given that the members share high levels of education, income, and are all from the upper class. Most of them volunteer their 'professional' time to helping other women; this suggests a sharing of altruistic norms and beliefs. However, they do not spend time together after work, which is also a component of 'shared norms and beliefs'. Thus scoring low on this dimension does not suggest that they do not share norms and beliefs;

rather they do not engage in socializing outside the workplace. We speculate that many of these professional women have other commitments that do not leave them time to socialize. For example, many professional women, who volunteer a set amount of their time to the NGOs, must return to their professional workplace leaving them little time to participate socially despite their shared norms and beliefs. On the other hand, the finding that normative incentives are frequently found in the professional organizations is not surprising. It is commonplace for professional women, who volunteer to spend money from their own pockets to finance the activities of an NGO, not to be subject to material incentives. They are more likely to respond to normative incentives.

One of the NGOs in our sample that did score 'high' on shared norms and beliefs, and 'low' on material incentives, is more typical of professional organizations. It was founded by two professional social workers. With the help of a group of professional women, mainly social workers, they provide counseling services for women and youth to prevent marital and family problems. They have also undertaken advocacy to prevent problems dealing with wife abuse and family conflict. They firmly believe that intervention done early can alleviate tremendous suffering and reduce further abuse. More than 75 per cent of the members of this NGO are trained professionals who volunteer their expertise to do the intervention and advocacy work.

Noting the move towards bureaucratic features in all but four of our NGOs, it is worth pausing a moment to understand this move, and to understand what it means to NGOs, especially in India. India is a highly bureaucratic country in which the 'red-tape' involved in negotiating anything that has a legal structure is horrendous. Many see bureaucracies as inept, inefficient, wasteful, and corrupt. Thus it is not at all surprising that many organizations do not want to admit to being bureaucratic. This does not imply that all the features of a bureaucracy are ineffective. It may suggest that mediating bureaucratic functions with a feminist ideology and its inherent collectivist features allow our NGOs to be resourceful, efficient, and successful in achieving their mission. Indeed, democratic participation in feminist organizations reduces the negative impacts of bureaucracy (Paavo, 2002).

In summary, our findings concerning organizational structures of the NGOs imply that despite the fact that only four of the organizations were run entirely as collectivist organizations, the other organizations were still highly influenced by feminist ideology. Neither the feminist principles nor the goals of the organization are displaced due to the choice of any particular organizational structure. The organizations, for example, do not turn to motives that we know drive for-profit or government bureaucracies the moment they grow big. However, some elements do change with the adoption of bureaucratic characteristics. For example, methods of decision making which are no longer collective, job differentiation due to specialization, lines of authority to meet additional accountability standards, and the appearance of material incentives with an increase in paid and professional staff. These changes, however, do not change the feminist essence of the organization. Vision, goals, and motives remain constant. We find that feminist leaders with strong ideological commitments can meet the practical exigencies of changing environments in creative ways and not function like traditional bureaucracies.

Discussion of Differences: East and West

In this section, we briefly note the differences found in our NGOs, as compared to those found in Bordt's (1997) study of NGOs in New York, USA. Given that our NGOs are based in Maharashtra, India, and are women-led NGOs dealing with issues related to women and children, we can contrast our findings with those of Bordt to see what similarities and differences there are between NGOs that are grounded in two different cultures.

Although all of the women who founded and led the NGOs we studied claimed to be feminists, only fifteen out of twenty of our founders declared that their organizations were structured on collectivist principles. However, when they were carefully documented, only four of the feminist-mandated NGOs were truly run as collectivists, but the remaining eleven organizations were hybrids that did maintain many of the collectivist structures. Recalling that we made changes in the dimensions that characterize organizational structure, for reasons explained earlier, we classify our sample of twenty organizations as five (25 per cent) bureaucratic, seven (35 per cent) collectivist pragmatic, four (20 per cent) professional, and four (20 per cent) collectivist. Bordt's sample, which comprised ninety-five organizations, were classified as nineteen per cent bureaucratic, forty-five per cent pragmatic collectivist, twenty-seven per cent professional, and eight per cent collectivist.

Notwithstanding that our sample sizes are different, and so comparisons of numbers may not be valid, at first glance there appears to be an overall similarity between the two studies. Over half the organizations in both countries are hybrids, suggesting that neither classical bureaucracy nor collectivist forms dominates the four organizational structural types. We found that there are interesting cultural differences within these types that are worth exploring and we elaborate on these next.

Ideology and Organizational Structure

Although the Hindu religion emphasizes the need to serve others and sixteen out of twenty women founders are Hindus, religion is not suggested as the motivating factor by any of our respondents. Feminist ideology, on the other hand, professed by all founders, was offered as the motivating and rationalizing factor in fifteen out of twenty of the organizations. There is a deep and long-term commitment to feminist ideology on the part of all of our founders, and they see the need for social justice among poor, low-caste women as the pivotal factor for their undertakings. Founding NGOs to help their less fortunate sisters is their way of actualizing their feminist beliefs. We find, contrary to the findings of Bordt, that feminist ideology is a good predictor of the type of organizational structures espoused.

Our findings illustrate that although there are some changes due to environmental pressures for NGOs to adopt certain bureaucratic features, they continue at the core to espouse a feminist ideology that we see reflected in leadership and management styles, choices of services, and retaining collective and participatory decision making at certain levels in the organizations.

Material Incentives versus Normative Incentives

In Table 2.2 as we move from the bureaucratic to the collectivist organizational forms, a pattern emerges. For example, with the exception of bureaucracies, we find that material incentives get less important and normative incentives become more important. In the case of Bordt's organizations, the material incentives remain largely at a 'medium' level and only get less important in the case of professional organizations. This finding may be explained in part by the different cultures studied in Bordt's study in the USA versus our study in India.

A large majority of women founders in the Indian sample are Brahmins who represent the highest caste; they have a high level of educational attainment and are members of the middle to upper-income class. Higher class and castes are culturally and religiously faced with the moral imperative to 'do good' (Karunanithi, 1991). Thus, it is not surprising that these women are more likely to pursue normative incentives in the hope of actualizing their values. The organizations they founded also reflect this ethic.

The majority of the women founders in our sample live in 'joint families' in which they share fiscal and family responsibilities. In well-to-do 'joint families', women do not have the same responsibilities for family finances as they may have in nuclear families like those in Bordt's study. Although the levels of education do not differ between the two, the practical considerations for women being fiscally responsible for family members in the American sample may suggest why material incentives are so much more important in American NGOs than normative incentives.

The Indian data also displays higher amounts of social time spent together amongst staff. In our sample, many of the women have considerable help with the running of the household and childcare responsibilities by virtue of living in 'joint families', or hiring inexpensive help. This leaves them with more discretionary time. In the American sample, however, the practical necessity of rushing home at the end of the workday to attend to children in daycare and school precludes the possibility of women coworkers from spending time together after work.[6] Once again the practical considerations of American women leaders being more responsible for childcare and household duties than Indian women founders, explains differences in the two studies.

---

[6] Many studies have been done on women in the West who still bear the brunt of caring for the home and family after a full day of work (Coltrane, 1996; Hochschild and Machung, 1990; Shelton and John, 1996).

Age and Size

Bordt finds that organizational age is the strongest predictor for the primacy of the bureaucratic form in her study. In our sample, the three oldest organizations are bureaucracies, which supports Bordt's findings. The newest and youngest NGOs in our sample, however, are not necessarily collectivist, suggesting that some of our NGOs may not have started as collectivists before ending up as hybrids or bureaucracies. It is also likely that they were intentionally started as collectivist pragmatic organizations or professional organizations.

Furthermore, Bordt finds that size is a critical factor. The largest organizations in her study are bureaucracies. Our findings replicate this, in that we find that our largest organization, made up of eighty-seven paid staff and eleven volunteers, is also a bureaucracy. However, unlike Bordt, we find that pattern does not always correspond with size. What we find, in general, is that collectivist organizations tend to have a lower ratio of paid staff to volunteers than do bureaucracies. The number of volunteers in relation to paid staff actually decreases as the organizational structure moves away from a collectivist one towards a bureaucracy. This could suggest that collectivist organizations are better at recruiting volunteer labor or simply may need more volunteer labor than bureaucracies.

Funding and Organizational Structure

We find the kind of funding an NGO receives is a strong predictor of the bureaucratic form. For example, organizations funded by large external or international sources are either bureaucracies or hybrids that have put into place some bureaucratic features in response to accountability standards. In our sample, sixteen (80 per cent) of the organizations do receive external or international funding of which fifteen are either bureaucracies or hybrids that have adopted one or two features of bureaucracies.

Similar findings in Bordt's study may underscore how funding can make organizations adopt bureaucratic features. In Bordt's study 77 per cent of the organizations are funded by more than one source, including external sources. She finds that 73 per cent of them are either bureaucracies or hybrids, which have retained features of a bureaucracy in order to meet the accountability requirements of funders.

Many feminist organizations in our study have accepted elements of bureaucracy in order to respond to external funder demands. However, as Paavo (2002) reminds us, no particular structural characteristics make an organization feminist. We see that feminist organizations in our sample have all self-consciously searched for ways to minimize the negative impacts of bureaucracy on democratic participation. Fifteen out of the twenty NGOs under study have thereby managed to sustain their collectivist features.

Conclusion

Our study of women-led NGOs involved in social service provision to women and children finds that those women who take on this important task overwhelmingly describe themselves as feminist. There is a marked tendency of social service provision for poor women and children to be undertaken by feminist entrepreneurs (Gopalan, 2001). Their ideological commitments influence not only the mission and mandate of the organization but also organizational structure. Over 75 per cent of them describe their organizations as having feminist mandates and as being structured as collectivists that encourage democratic participation.

While one can have strong feminist values that deal with social injustices towards women, it is not necessary that these values only be actualized within collectivist organizational structures. In fact, our findings suggest that feminists can and do operate organizations with bureaucratic structures without compromising their feminist beliefs. These findings are consistent with those found by Metzendorf (2005) in a study of feminist organizations. In her study, managers continue to practice feminist principles within their organizations which over time had adopted many bureaucratic features.

We believe that strong feminist founders of organizations have a proclivity to adopt organizational structures that reflect collectivist principles and this is what we set out to examine in our data. We found that feminist founders certainly do have this proclivity as many saw their organizations as collectivists even though they had adopted bureaucratic features to meet practical exigencies of their environments. In India, a highly bureaucratic country, many founders (80 per cent) had creatively adopted some bureaucratic characteristics in their organizations to respond to the environmental challenges and still retained their feminist approach to leading their organizations.

In particular our data show that our feminist founders have managed to retain many of the collectivist characteristics in their organizations, either in the purely collectivist forms (20 per cent), or by adapting minimally to bureaucratic features, thereby prompting us to name them hybrids (55 per cent).

Indeed, our 'professional' organizations are so similar to the 'collectivist' form that we were tempted to include them with the 'collectivists'. However, for purposes of analysis, we have used the classification from the available literature of 'professionals' to distinguish NGOs that have been run by professionals. As explained earlier, these 'professional' organizations sometimes deviate from their original 'collectivist' model in that they do not exhibit high levels of 'shared norms and beliefs'. As socializing outside of work is a dimension along which we measure 'shared beliefs', it is not surprising that as professional women they scored low in this dimension as they have little discretionary time. However, the fact that they volunteer their 'professional' services suggests a high level of commitment to shared norms of the feminist organization.

We can find two areas in which the feminist entrepreneurs do concede to bureaucratic features. With growth of size and complexity of services offered, we find that a formal decision-making criterion moves from 'low' to 'medium'. On this dimension the more explicit the criteria for making decisions, that is, written rules for evaluation, the higher the score. If we keep in mind the earlier distinction between decision making for routine and local issues as well as critical and core decisions, then the move to 'medium' may largely reflect the fact that there may be a few individuals in the organization who specialize in these tasks and are relegated to attending to local issues that require their specialization.

Accountability is the second area that can often warrant bureaucratic structures. As NGOs accept donations they become accountable to donors and some must employ professional staff to meet accountability demands. We must clarify that we do not imply that feminists or collectivists are not able to plan or provide proper accounts. They are well able to plan and do their accounts. However, the conditions under which the Indian government allows NGOs to accept foreign funding are highly bureaucratic and cumbersome. This includes the requirement that the accounting be done by professionals and that the certification of fiduciary documents be done by a certified accountant. Non-governmental organizations have responded accordingly by hiring professional bookkeepers and accountants. When they are unable to secure the voluntary service of an accountant, the founder has no choice but to recruit a professional accountant and often employ support staff to keep accounts. This sets in motion greater 'formal structures', higher material incentives, lower normative incentives, more formal decision-making criteria, and more differentiation. However, these levels of bureaucratization are low enough to still warrant these NGOs to be labeled hybrids rather than bureaucracies.

When women attempt to structure the organization as collectivists to suit their feminist orientation, they struggle with meeting the realities of the demands put in place by funders and the government. Using features from bureaucratic organizational structures should be seen as an 'empowerment' approach. They are empowering their NGOs based on collectivist principles to survive without sacrificing the core collective values that ensure the success of their organization. The numbers prove this. Of the twenty successful NGOs, only five adopted sufficient bureaucratic features to warrant them to be classified as bureaucratic organizations. On closer examination, not one of them scored as a bureaucratic organization on all eight dimensions. Of the other fifteen organizations, which had adopted bureaucratic features, not a single organization had manifested the bureaucratic characteristics on more than two out of the eight dimensions. This suggests a judicious use of bureaucratic characteristics to meet certain environmental constraints such as fiduciary requirements by funders and the government, or decision making that is localized in place and time.

Even as they grow in size and complexity they do not become bureaucratic to be efficient as suggested in the literature. Most of them continue to deviate from the bureaucratic model and continue to be highly efficient in different ways as we show in Chapter Three. Furthermore, they provide role models of feminist visions for their clientele by making their organizations responsive to the feminist principles of democratic, participative, and egalitarian workplaces. Thus, they are doubly successful: as feminist organizations promoting the feminist vision in practice, and in efficiently meeting their visions and goals to help and empower women.

Can we say anything about NGOs, their structure, and their founders based on the findings of these twenty women-led NGOs in India? Given the size limitation of our data and its restriction to one geographical region, we again emphasize that it is difficult to generalize; nevertheless, we suggest that the data points in certain directions and some tentative but positive conclusions can be drawn on the practice of a feminist vision within an organization. Organizations that are structured on feminist principles as collectivists continue to retain their structure as they grow and evolve, and are successful in promoting the empowerment of women. Leaders with feminist visions can successfully adopt a bureaucratic feature here and there to meet some pragmatic needs of the organization, but on the whole remain highly efficient as small and large organizations without embracing the patriarchal models of bureaucracy.

The feminist collectivist structures embraced by the overwhelming majority of NGOs are evidence of what the founders believe. They believed that their NGOs were organized on feminist principles because they believe strongly that the structure of the NGO was as important as the goals of the organization, and that a congruency should exist between the two for efficiency.

In summary, the NGOs in our study have in the main been organized around feminist principles. The women founders have, as expected, been innovative and resourceful in holding on to their own feminist values, while adopting those changes that are not antithetical to their goals but aid them to meet their objectives. This suggests that NGOs organized by women of strong feminist beliefs are able to hold on to their feminist principles even though they need to be pragmatic.

Narratives

From Protests to Empowerment: The Nari Samata Manch

The early 1980s were alive with feminist activism in India. A number of new NGOs emerged to fight for the rights and equality of women. The Nari Samata Manch was one such organization. Sadhana Dadhich and Vidya Bal had been active in the women's movement for sometime but were especially motivated to take action after 1975, the First International Year of Women. The release of the Convention on the Elimination of all forms of Discrimination Against Women (CEDAW) by the Commission on the Status of Women in 1979, brought worldwide attention to the abuses and the plight of women (Neft and Levine, 1997).

In India, the situation was particularly troublesome because traditional Hindu culture seemed to permit or sustain women's oppression through the custom of dowry. Although outlawed, dowry has continued to be a social problem. New brides whose families could not provide expected dowries to their husbands' families were often abused, maimed by fire and sometimes killed. These became widely known as 'dowry deaths', and were on the rise in the 1980s.

While this group of social activists had been advocating successfully for new laws to ban such old customs through demonstrations, protests, and public forums, Vidya Bal and Sadhana Dadhich knew that such advocacy alone was not enough. With the help of eight other like-minded people, both women and men, they established the Nari Samata Manch—the Women's Equality Forum. They wanted to help women who suffered from abuse, but their bigger vision was to create systemic change; that is, they wanted to change the thinking and behavior of a society that mistreated women.

The publicized murders of two women by their husbands—who were from the middle and upper class—opened their eyes to the fact that the victimization of women was not just an issue for the poor and the illiterate. It was an issue for all women. They formally organized the Nari Samata Manch in 1983 and registered it as a public charitable trust in 1987 under the Societies Registration Act.

Awareness, Support, and Shelter

In the beginning we wanted to do something about women's rights and domestic violence. We had no particular vision and we did not have particular projects or funding in mind. We just knew we had to do something (Vidya Bal, personal communication 2003).

Vidya and Sadhana began initiating programs where they saw needs and felt they could make a difference. As social activists they continued pressing for new laws concerning dowry, rape, domestic violence, sati, female infanticide, and amniocentesis for sex detection. They also started programs to serve oppressed women directly. The first program they organized, which is still a core program of the Nari Samata Manch, was called 'Speak Out'. This program provided a space for women to share their experiences, provide each other mutual support, and help each other regain confidence and self-respect.

The needs expressed through Speak Out led to other programs, including the development of a counseling center staffed by Nari Samata Manch volunteers who provided emotional support and legal assistance. Professionally untrained but highly motivated and experienced volunteers like Pushpa Rode, Shanta Bhat, Nirmala Gokhale, and Kusum Bedekar consistently ran the counseling center for years together. Finally in 1997, when Vidya and Sadhana applied for a grant, they were able to employ trained counselors for the first time.

The growth of the Nari Samata Manch over time is embedded in the history of Speak Out. As women expressed their needs, the Nari Samata Manch responded by launching new programs and projects—often without formal planning. The Nari Samata Manch grew organically—a bit like mycelium, the underground mass of interwoven thread-like filaments that create vast living networks that eventually fruit as mushrooms. Its growth of programs has been like that.

For example, as Speak Out grew into a counseling center, it became evident that there was a real need to create a safe shelter for the victims of domestic violence so that they could have a place to stay. At that point, women had nowhere safe to go and had no opportunity to break the cycle of violence. The Nari Samata Manch sought funding to establish the first short-stay shelter in Pune—'Aaple Ghar' (Our Home). This was largely due to the initiative, unrelenting energy, and consistent follow up of a strong advocate, Latika Salgoankar. HIVOS (Humanistisch Instituut voor Ontwikkenlingssamenwerking) was the funding agency for 'Aaple Ghar' which provided space for twenty-five women and children who could stay there for up to six months. In typical Nari Samata Manch fashion, the shelter became more than an interim residence. Aaple Ghar became the venue for additional counseling and education, including job training. This helped the women coming from abusive environments, who were in a state of total dependence, leave with confidence and with the necessary skills to rebuild their lives. By 2003, Aaple Ghar had helped 400 women and 125 children. Volunteers staff both the counseling center Speak Out and Aaple Ghar.

Vidya, Sadhana, and the other trustees felt that serving Pune alone was not enough. Before long they expanded programs to serve tribal areas and rural villages surrounding Pune and branched out even further. They started a rural village training center, a dairy, an organic farm, and a women's bank. They also initiated a variety of programs for youth, women's health, and women's leadership. In the latter case, Nandini Datar, gifted in developing a good rapport with rural volunteers, was in charge of a leadership program to build these qualities among rural women in Maval.

Oils, Ointments, and Kitchen Gardens

In 1998, the Nari Samata Manch realized that it had successfully been educating and training women and youth about rights, laws, the need for education, how to stand for election, how to start small businesses, but they had not addressed something very basic, women's health. They discovered that women understood very little about their bodies. With all of the new drugs and advanced medical technology, the Nari Samata Manch felt women needed to know more about their health and how to take responsibility for themselves. They felt that if women were to truly take control of their lives they needed to learn about personal health and make informed decisions. They wanted to remove the mystery and mystique surrounding doctors and medical care.

Initially, the Nari Samata Manch simply wanted to provide women with awareness about their bodies and their own health, especially reproductive health. Women had the right and responsibility to know what was happening to them as it pertained to their health. After receiving money from the MacArthur Foundation in 1998, they initiated three levels of health projects: tribal, rural, and urban. In the MacArthur Foundation project, the Nari Samata Manch had young, enthusiastic, academically-equipped volunteers like Preeti Karmarkar and Manohar V.P. who were deeply engaged as they focused on creating general awareness about the human body and issues related to health. The Nari Samata Manch wanted to help women understand the diseases that affected their bodies and understand what doctors could and may do for them. The Nari Samata Manch knew that most women who went to the health clinics asked no questions and passively accepted the medical treatment meted out to them. They would return home and ask their husbands, who usually knew as little as their wives.

In their customary organic approach to awareness education, the Nari Samata Manch moved from body awareness to teaching women about their tribal medicines and traditional herbal treatments. Then they moved on to providing education in food and nutrition. What foods were good for the body and what foods were not? They helped them create 'kitchen gardens' for growing healthy food. As village and tribal women began to understand more about their bodies, medicines, tribal remedies, and nutrition, the Nari Samata Manch began to teach them about reproductive health. They wanted women to begin making their own decisions about reproductive health and family size. The Nari Samata Manch ran its health program in tribal and rural communities for five years until they ran out of funding.

However, when the health project ended, four of the twelve young women who had learned about herbal medicines and their preparation continued to produce them. With some assistance from the Nari Samata Manch and another NGO, they set up their own small businesses selling oil and herb products in their villages. Not only did they create a living for themselves, but they earned new respect and standing in their families and villages.

The health program is another good example of what this NGO is trying to achieve through its many programs and projects. They start with building awareness about issues and interests; they then create education and training programs to build on that awareness. The Nari Samata Manch then equips women with the tools they need to build skills and self-confidence thereby becoming self-reliant, independent of their husbands, and more in charge of their lives.

How Work Gets Done:
Macro and the Micro Levels

Perhaps one of the best ways to understand the Nari Samata Manch is to understand it as an organization that operates at two levels, the *macro* and the *micro*. The Nari Samata Manch would say that at the macro level they still operate as a collective. At the macro level, the Nari Samata Manch focuses on advocacy and creating broad societal awareness about the widespread violence against women.

They hope that these efforts will increase intolerance against such violence. They associate their macro-level work with their advocacy, education, training, and public awareness programs. The women's leadership program, for example, aims at improving gender relations in society by organizing men and women for collective action directed at solving their own problems. The women's leadership program, an umbrella for many projects—that include women and men—has created self-help groups (SHGs). These take on a variety of group activities, including credit banking, formation of credit groups, counseling, and the development of legal literacy.

The Nari Samata Manch established a library that provides books and materials in the Marathi language. It continues to put on street plays and create other kinds of media and public exposure to influence changes in societal attitudes about women's issues. All of these public activities, as well as its direct service programs, provide substantial data for research, and new publications are made available through its library and many program sites.

It is interesting that these macro-level activities have generated substantial enthusiasm among younger paid staff members of the Nari Samata Manch who see that being involved in writing reports about projects is a material benefit to their continuing professional development and will provide opportunities for advancement in the future.

The Nari Samata Manch considers its micro-level activities as including its work at its various centers that offer counseling and other supportive services to protect and rehabilitate victims of violence. Today it operates five micro-level programs, each requiring a mix of professionals, trained staff, and volunteers with job descriptions and reporting responsibilities. These programs include its short-stay home, its counseling center, its youth-for-change program, its women's leadership program, and the new rural skills training center. These are all programs aimed at delivering direct assistance or training to specific individuals or groups of women, and they require financial support.

The Nari Samata Manch began applying for and receiving external funding in 1992 when it first identified a critical need to provide a shelter for victims of domestic violence. In 1993, it received funds to start the women's leadership program. In 1997, the Nari Samata Manch applied for and received funds from the Ford Foundation to initiate its training programs; and in 1998, the John D. and Catherine T. MacArthur Foundation provided funding for its health education program. Each of these programs, either funded by a different foundation, or by foreign NGOs with government sponsorship, has been mired in rules, regulations, and procedures that require an organizational structure that is more formal than a collective. On the eight elements in the literature which differentiate among bureaucratic, collective pragmatic, professional, and collectivist organizations, the Nari Samata Manch shows a curious mixture of features that move it away from a pure collective or at least give it a mixed personality. The Nari Samata Manch's social advocacy work—its macro-level activities—is perceived as collective.

The macro-level programs are still carried on primarily by the original founders and trustees while the micro-level programs are designated to professionals and volunteers. Since the Nari Samata Manch began receiving foreign funding, they have had to establish policies and procedures and establish accountabilities in order to meet the requirements of foreign and government funders. Along with these external demands, the younger staff come from a different generation, a generation that did not know or participate in feminist or other social movements.

The micro-level programs, as they are run by paid staff, are rife with rules, regulations, job descriptions, differentiation of tasks and responsibilities. As Sadhana and Vidya put it, the younger and professional staff must make a living and they want to grow in their careers. They are motivated by material incentives such as insurance, salary increases, vacation benefits, and opportunities for advancement. The new staff do not come from the communities of family, friends, and associates who founded the Nari Samata Manch. They come through public advertisements for new workers and they submit written applications.

The new workers coming to the Nari Samata Manch are, in fact, strangers to the trustees and to the organization. The Nari Samata Manch trustees educate these new staff members about the values and mission of the organization, as well as about the women's movement and the laws affecting women. It has been a dramatic change in the way the Nari Samata Manch gets its work done and the culture shift is perhaps an inevitable reflection of the growth and the changing times.

Sadhana and Vidya now describe the Nari Samata Manch as an organization that has a mixed structure. Macro-level activities seem to be mostly collective but micro-level activities are increasingly regulated by the demands of funders who require more systems and infrastructure to be put in place. Micro-level programs have become increasingly bureaucratic. They have fewer shared beliefs across the organization. The founders and trustees operate from shared values and are content with the satisfaction provided by doing their work for women's equality, and not material incentives. But new members of the Nari Samata Manch are more motivated by material incentives that will advance their careers and help meet the needs of their families in what is rapidly becoming a dual-income and dual-career environment.

This, say Vidya and Sadhana, has created interesting dynamics in the organization, and is often a source of conflict for the 'old guard' and the new young professionals. New staff prefer clear-cut responsibilities, decision-making rules, job descriptions, and material incentives. The 'old guard' prefers to act in an informal and often ad hoc manner. Vidya and Sadhana attempt to make their weekly meetings a platform for creating a more shared understanding of the differing points of view and bring the two sides together.

A Conversation about the Future

In a recent set of interviews, we asked Vidya and Sadhana to tell us how they get their work done at the Nari Samata Manch. If they do not plan, then how do programs and projects develop? Who makes decisions? Who writes the grants? Who does the work, paid staff or volunteers? Where do they get their staff and volunteers? This is their story.

We have never done much planning but have grown in an unplanned organic way, with programs evolving in response to new needs. Now, in addition to our shelter home, our counseling programs, our youth for change and women's leadership program, we also have *bachat gats* (credit groups), a new dairy, a vermiculture project, a catering center, and a legal literacy program. But we have no continuous funding. We have only two paid permanent staff, the rest of our staff are either volunteers—we have fifteen volunteers who work full-time and rotate among the different projects—or staff paid out of the project funding. When the funding ends they have to find other positions.

We really must plan for the future, but this has never been our way of doing things. We have been too busy creating projects and responding to new needs. Many of our programs have evolved from a pattern of emotion and sharing at a personal level. But the times are changing and we see the needs of people being more complex, requiring that our programs become more sophisticated as well. For example: counseling is a profession that requires special skills acquired in colleges and universities. Being good listeners and informal advisors is not enough. We must have people with the proper skills and training to help. It is a more complex world.

In the past, for example, we did not focus so much on establishing self-help groups but rather worked at the individual level. Now, however, the concept of self-help groups has become very important. Because of the market and a variety of other opportunities, Self-help groups have been organized all over India to help women develop savings and create their own small businesses. Organizing, educating, maintaining self-help groups, and helping them develop new schemes for self-sufficiency is complex. If we are going to continue to help with this we have to acquire the expertise to do an effective job.

Even the shelter requires something more than we provided in the past. The people who use the shelter are different now. It used to be that people were just grateful for having someplace to go. Now they are more verbal and educated. They have expectations of what the shelter should provide them. In a sense they take the shelter for granted, almost as if it is an entitlement. Meeting the needs of this new population means we have to respond differently.

Another significant change affecting our work is that the government is decentralizing by giving more power to the local communities. The devolution of power to the panchayat raj in villages is an example. The village governing councils now have significantly more power, authority, and responsibility than they ever had in the past. Neither central nor state governments are going to ensure that villages have roads, sanitation systems, garbage collection, employment, or health care. Villagers will have to learn governing skills in order to meet the needs of their own village people.

We have always preferred to act as initiators; that is, to provide the seeds for development and women's empowerment. We have tried to do this through our health programs, training for service on the panchayat raj, assisting in creating self-sufficiency through organic farming practices, providing temporary shelter and safety for victims of abuse, and many other small and large projects. Nari Samata Manch's programs have grown as a result of perceived needs as well as our ability to respond to those needs. We prefer to seed projects, get them underway, provide people with the tools to do them on their own, and then just move out of the way. That is because we have been more interested in empowerment than building a big bureaucratic organization.

Now we are working on a water project with the government. The problem of supplying water in tribal and village areas is always the responsibility of the women. In times of draught, like we have experienced in the past several years, women have to travel great distances, three or four times a day, to supply their family needs. We feel this could become one of our principal projects over the next ten years. We hope to help create better access to water supplies by becoming involved with the critical water shortage issues that place so many burdens on tribal and village women. We still do not have a strategic plan, a strong base of funder support, or sufficient numbers of volunteers to go ahead. We will just have to see what happens.

Commentary

The Nari Samata Manch began as a collective of like-minded people in 1983, and it continued as a collective for many years. Even in 1999, the Nari Samata Manch described itself as a collective. Its feminist ideology, according to its founders, informed its structure from the beginning. Collectives, as we show in our research, exhibit low material incentives and high normative ones. Collectives do not need formal decision-making criteria and they rarely show much differentiation. They are what we call flat organizations. Most of the NGOs in our study share ideological beliefs and have similar value approaches to their work. They tend to rely on membership fees and private donations—often from their own and their family's pocketbooks—rather than external funds. Because they have strong roots in the feminist movements, they particularly have eschewed government support.

Given this kind of profile, collectives have never been interested in developing internal accountability measures, which are now required of organizations receiving external funds from private foundations, foreign funders, and agencies of government. This was the picture of the Nari Samata Manch in its early days. By 1993, ten years after its founding, the Nari Samata Manch also began accepting external funds. Its first lesson was in seeking funding to support its short-stay shelter, Aaple Ghar. This required that they learn how to respond to the myriad of rules and procedures the funders required.

Today, the Nari Samata Manch runs multiple and diverse projects over a broad geographical area that is both urban and rural. The Nari Samata Manch now needs to have rules and procedures for running its programs as they are often run by paid staff. Many of their projects require high specialization of talents, skills, and education. They have to develop ways to coordinate their many activities and create responsive decision-making processes in order to provide effective program delivery. The Nari Samata Manch now has to be concerned about efficiency measures—a hallmark of bureaucracies—but it is doing so because these measures help it increase its effectiveness in delivering on its mission and in getting external funds. The world has changed and the Nari Samata Manch recognizes it will have to change with it. The pure collective, as an organizational structure, does not work anymore.

When we first reviewed our notes from the several years of interviews we had with Vidya Bal and Sadhana Dadhich, we wondered just how much the Nari Samata Manch's story sounded the same as others. It seemed that the progression of this NGO from a feminist collective to a collective pragmatic was a common and perhaps predictable phenomenon. Could the Nari Samata Manch's structural evolution simply be explained by life cycle theory or by its dependence on multiple external funding sources? Given that the Nari Samata Manch is now 22 years old, has its multi-sited and numerous programs made it inevitable that it become more bureaucratic? If so, why does the Nari Samata Manch continue to describe itself as a collective? Is it self-delusion? At first glance, perhaps so.

In 1999, for example, the Nari Samata Manch measured an unremarkable 'medium' on all eight dimensions of structure that would classify it as a collective pragmatic organization. It would be easy—then and now—to conclude that the Nari Samata Manch is simply an example of the inevitable tendency of organizations to move towards bureaucratization because of its age, size, and complexity. The Nari Samata Manch's evolution may look like it makes the case for such organizational theories, but that would miss some important subtleties of the Nari Samata Manch's organizational evolution.

What we experience with the Nari Samata Manch is not an inevitable evolution from the collective to the bureaucratic. The Nari Samata Manch is collectively supported by an organizational structure that assists delivery of values and philosophy that are the hallmark of collective action. Its fundamental organizational behavior still models its collectivist approach to its mission. It is egalitarian, decision making is participative, and it devolves authority and responsibility to the lowest level, including staff, members, and clients. Because of the increasing complexity of its work, the Nari Samata Manch now is hiring paid staff who are professionally educated and trained. But the Nari Samata Manch also continues to recruit village and tribal people to deliver services in those multiple sites. They strongly believe that there must be local provision of local services.

Sadhana, Vidya, and the Nari Samata Manch's other trustees accept that it would be impossible to deliver its many programs without a supportive and efficient structure. The structure that the Nari Samata Manch needs to do its work effectively—specialization, differentiation, materials and normative incentives, decision-making criteria and authority—are now mostly in place. The Nari Samata Manch has created necessary supports for effectively carrying out its mission. That structure works not so much as a bureaucracy but as a structural support imbued with collectivist values and delivery systems.

Is the Nari Samata Manch still a collective or a collective pragmatic organization tending towards bureaucracy? Traditional organizational theorists might say that the Nari Samata Manch is moving rapidly to a bureaucratic form, certainly further and further away from the collective form. Feminist theorists might say that this is undesirable. We do not believe that this is the case with the Nari Samata Manch. The move toward bureaucracy represents for them not a choice between collectivism and bureaucracy. The Nari Samata Manch sees new structures as instrumental, even a strategic choice. Their new bureaucratic elements are providing supports—and efficiencies—that are not inconsistent with its feminist and collective ideology. The Nari Samata Manch would claim that it has not been on a blind and inevitable slide towards bureaucracy but rather it has made a strategic choice.

The Nari Samata Manch's philosophy and attitudes about formal organizations have not really changed since its inception. It still adheres to the belief that their organization can be open, non-hierarchical, and non-judgmental. They believe that working for the Nari Samata Manch provides equal opportunities for staff and volunteers to use their voices in decision-making processes at the project, program, and organizational levels. The founders claim that all feminist organizations must work like this. They must continue to be egalitarian. All people who work with or are served by the Nari Samata Manch, no matter their caste, class, education, or age—have access and voice in its work. This, the Nari Samata Manch claims, is after all what empowerment and women's development is all about.

Transitions: Swadhar Pune

Veni, vidi, vici (Caesar).

They came, they saw, and they responded. It seemed almost that straightforward in 1995. Twelve years earlier, in 1983, Meenakshi Apte co-founded Swadhar Mumbai with Mrinal Gore, an ex-member of Parliament, to help destitute women become self-reliant and gain control of their lives. Swadhar became very successful, well known, and well supported in the bustling cosmopolitan city of Mumbai. It had a large support base of beneficiaries that provided financial and volunteer support for the many programs under its umbrella.

In 1994, Meenakshi Apte retired and moved to Pune with her husband. So did Sulabha Joshi, a retired lecturer at the University of Mumbai and a volunteer social worker, who worked at Swadhar with Meenakshi Apte. Their mutual commitment to the empowerment of destitute women kept them in touch once they moved from Mumbai. Pune was much smaller than Mumbai, however, Meenakshi Apte and Sulabha Joshi realized that the plight of women in Pune's slums was no different from those living in Mumbai. They contacted Mrinal Gore and asked, 'why not open a Pune branch of Swadhar?'

Establishing Programs in Pune

By January of 1995, Meenakshi Apte and Sulabha Joshi opened Swadhar in Pune and began to organize education and service programs similar to those offered in Mumbai. They moved quickly. Their years of experience in building similar programs in Mumbai shortened the start-up time that most new organizations require. They already knew what to do. They recruited a management committee, they organized a membership program of volunteers; and within six months they opened two counseling centers.

The family counseling centers were established to help women become aware of the causes of their problems and to provide them with help and support in finding alternatives and solutions. While they provided emotional help and education, sometimes Swadhar also provided financial support. The family counseling centers helped women address issues of marital discord, alcoholism, aging, domestic violence, legal matters, and the like. The family counseling centers were staffed by five trained social workers as well as volunteer social workers, working along the same lines as the programs of Swadhar Mumbai.

In the same year that it was founded, 1995, Swadhar created an awareness program in three separate locations and a family life education program. These two programs offered seminars and trainings, all designed to contribute to the development of self-confidence and self-reliance among poor and destitute women, children, and their families. The awareness program taught them their legal rights.

In 1997, Meenakshi Apte, Sulabha Joshi joined by Anjali Bapat—a young enthusiastic worker who had joined Swadhar that year—created a school for the children of prostitutes in two locations. This was a program for children of commercial sex workers who were generally unable to go to school. Swadhar worked with the municipal corporation in order to improve the availability of education for these children.

By 1998, Swadhar had also established an alternative school program, 'Akshardeep' for children in the six–twelve years age group who were either school dropouts or who had never been to school. It is not uncommon for children born into poverty never to attend school in India. They often have the responsibility of looking after younger siblings and doing household chores while their parents are working. In some cases they are forced into child labor. In this activity Anjali Bapat, her colleague Shaila Purandare and a team of young teachers were of great help.

Over the past five years, Akshardeep has become an umbrella for a variety of projects affecting the lives of out-of-school children in slum areas. Swadhar successfully advocated for their admission to nearby public schools and then worked assiduously on their retention. They also held rallies to bring attention to the basic rights of all children, especially the poor. With this success they decided to address schooling questions for young girls also under the umbrella of Akshardeep. They established a sponsorship program for young girls to prevent them from dropping out of the educational system at an early age.

Swadhar created a third family counseling center in 1999, housed in a hospital in the Pimpri Chinchwad Corporation area. This center provides counseling and care—as well as a shelter—to HIV-AIDs victims and their families. Swadhar discovered the urgency of providing a shelter as they helped the children of commercial sex workers. Many of the children, as well as their parents, have tested HIV-positive. Through the hospital counseling center, Swadhar expanded its counseling program to include an educational program about HIV and AIDs, health assistance, and in some cases was able to provide shelter for HIV-positive women and their children.

Organizing their Work

It is not surprising that when Meenakshi Apte and Sulabha Joshi established Swadhar Pune they used the model they were most familiar with and had been successful with in Mumbai. First they organized a management committee of peers who shared the role of governing the board and staffing all of the projects. They had shared norms and beliefs, making decision making fairly easy. There was no need for an authority pyramid. They needed no material incentives as they were financially independent and they derived their satisfaction from helping destitute women improve their lives.

Each of the management committee members organized separate projects and took responsibility for fund-raising to support their projects, thus they often operated autonomously. When organizational decisions had to be made, they used a consensus model in which all had an equal voice. They were, after all, family, friends, and social peers. They were all well educated and shared a history as activists in the women's movement. They were ardent community organizers so they knew how to operate as a successful collective. This was the organizational structure they knew, preferred, and perhaps best understood.

Once Swadhar had organized its management committee and all had agreed on their roles as trustees, they next designed a membership program, again using the Swadhar Mumbai model. They expected to grow a large membership base that would provide volunteer staff for their programs as well as financial support through membership dues. In the early years, up to the late 1990s, everything seemed to be working fine.

Pune is Not Mumbai: The Need for Change

After eight years, Swadhar has become self-sufficient, has multiple and diverse revenue streams, and it seems to be a highly sustainable organization by all the usual measures. Swadhar did not have to struggle to gain a strong foothold in the community. It started from a point of strength, by its experience, reputation, and visibility, as well as its financial stability. Swadhar's challenges now are about its organizational structure, its lack of a membership base, its aging trustees, its emerging organizational culture differences, and its need for professionally-trained staff.

These challenges, according to Meenakshi Apte and Sulabha Joshi, have arisen for a variety of reasons: (i) the Mumbai model did not fit the situation in Pune; (ii) the failure to create a viable membership program meant they had to hire staff; (iii) their pursuit of international funding burdened them with stringent accountability requirements; and finally (iv) the founder trustees and original management committee members have aged and are getting ready to retire.

The management challenges for Swadhar have increased because it initiated so many programs so very rapidly. And, they were widely dispersed. They have multiple programs and projects in multiple sites in both urban and rural areas. These projects require significant co-ordination by some central office and administrative support. But there is no permanent office, there is no office equipment, and there are no administrative workers to help them with that coordination. While Meenakshi Apte and Sulabha Joshi have continually urged other management committee members to consider permanent quarters, the cost is quite high requiring considerable funds from outside sources. They currently rent a small office—with no equipment—on the outskirts of the city on the campus of an elder care facility. It is not near any of Swadhar's projects. It takes a good deal of time to reach the office, and it is a very makeshift arrangement.

Due to their failure to establish the kind of volunteer base that worked so successfully in Mumbai, Swadhar has had to hire paid staff. As their many programs must respond to the changing needs and laws of their clientele, they are also finding that their staff must be more technically and professionally trained. While Swadhar has had sufficient funds to run projects in the past, they do not have the resources to replace volunteer staff with paid professional staff.

They have had to file for government eligibility in order to apply for international funds that can provide resources to hire staff. That has been a mixed blessing. In applying for and receiving such funds, Swadhar has had to establish financial and program-tracking systems. Funders, foreign and governmental, also require that they have sophisticated—and usually very specific—accounting procedures for reporting purposes. Swadhar, which up to this time had acted primarily as a collective, has had considerable difficulty putting these systems in place. With no permanent headquarters or office equipment, such as computers, this has seemed an almost insurmountable challenge.

The new skills required to apply for funding, to train and supervise the fieldwork, and coordinate activities over multiple sites means that Swadhar has to change. As a result, both Meenakshi Apte and Sulabha Joshi feel they must recruit new and younger professional staff to work at Swadhar as well as prepare them to take over its leadership as older trustees begin to retire. Meenakshi Apte, Sulabha Joshi, and other trustees have taken some initial steps towards this change by recruiting new members to the management committee. They are not surprised, however, that some new members are already impatient with the old style of a collective approach to decision making. It seems unwieldy, slow, and inefficient to the new members.

There is a growing cultural split in the management committee over management practices that Meenakshi Apte and Sulabha Joshi see as partially generational. New young professionals have been trained in management and they are accustomed to organizational structures that have clear rules, regulations, policies and procedures as well as technologically-developed systems for reporting. Some trustees resist those new practices just as the newer members resist maintaining the old ways.

What the founders and new workers are beginning to realize, according to Meenakshi Apte, is that Swadhar has actually become an organization made up of multiple silos loosely connected by relationships between founding members of the management committee. Meenakshi Apte and Sulabha Joshi say that the arrangement is no longer viable. The size and complexity of Swadhar's programs make coordination important but seemingly impossible without having structured organizational systems in place. We could sense their frustration and discouragement at Swadhar's situation as we sat outside its temporary quarters in an old folks home far outside of Pune—and far removed from where their programs and projects operate.

Commentary

Many of the organizational characteristics of Swadhar raise interesting questions about ideology and structure. In the beginning, Swadhar acted as a collective. It was a purposeful decision to do so. The founders and trustees—collectively the management committee—felt that in order to have a truly democratic organization Swadhar must operate as a collective. As social workers and community organizers who shared a history as community activists, this was not a surprising preference and it worked well enough in the beginning.

Swadhar, an 8 year old organization (in 2003), has now reached the second stage of its organizational life cycle. It is no longer creating itself; it is moving towards stabilization and establishing the means to maintain itself. Life cycle theory describes this as the typical movement from stage one to stage two in organizational development. The stage often signals the establishment of formal procedures, systems, and other elements of infrastructure. Unlike many NGOs at this stage, Swadhar has few financial worries. It has many and diverse funding streams and its financial base continues to grow, hopefully assuring its long-term stability. It has five stable programs and some new young professional staff. It looks like Swadhar Pune maybe good for the long run.

The challenges facing Swadhar are not so much about the usual ones facing new organizations. Swadhar's challenge is about sustaining an organization in which many of the 'hands on' working trustees will be retiring soon. The work they have done as leaders and innovators needs to be taken over by others. It is not likely that those who will take over will necessarily be trustees. It is more likely that professionally trained and paid staff members will run Swadhar and shape its course, unless steps are taken very soon to groom leaders who share the vision and passion of Swadhar's founders. Even the management committee will be made up of young professionals who are less likely to have participated in the social movements—the values of which have shaped this organization and made it what it is today.

Board roles and responsibilities will likely change during this stage of its life cycle. In many ways this has already begun. The board will need to change from a working board to a policy board. Perhaps it might retain elements of a working board in developing and sponsoring projects, but it will also need to take charge of developing policies and procedures as the organization continues to grow, diversify, and accept more foreign funding.

Meenakshi Apte observed that Swadhar can no longer operate as a pure collective. She says that Swadhar must develop more bureaucratic characteristics for efficiency and effectiveness—and to be transparent to its funders.

When we began our research in 1998, Swadhar was already moving from a pure collective to a 'collective pragmatic' organization. It had demonstrated some development of a formal structure as it built new and dispersed projects in both slums and rural villages on the outskirts of Pune. Swadhar found that it needed more professionalized staff and so introduced material incentives. While Swadhar still measured very high on normative incentives, the addition of paid professional staff created increased interest in material incentives.

In the beginning there was little concern for decision-making authority or having any formal decision-making criteria. As a collective, the members fully participated in decision making, guided by their shared beliefs and values rather than by formal decision criteria. Issues surrounding decision making generally emerge as an organization grows in size and differentiation, in which there are different levels of responsibility and training qualifications. This did not occur at Swadhar until they began to hire professional staff.

One very strong element of the collective structure of Swadhar that has remained throughout its growth and development is its strong belief and values structure. Members of the management committee continue to be passionately committed to Swadhar's mission. This is what motivates them to continue working for Swadhar. Moreover, trustees continue to spend time together outside of their work. They are social peers and friends but this too is changing, at least among members of the management committee that now includes younger professionals.

These younger members are paid professionals who must earn a living in dual-career or dual-job families. They are not social peers of the founding trustees, nor do they have free time to socialize outside of the workplace due to family responsibilities. Finally, the newer members of the management committee do not share the older members' experience in the social movements which inspired the founding of Swadhar. The result of these changes is that by 1999 Swadhar was better described as a collective pragmatic organization than a purely collective one.

Since 1999, the profile of Swadhar's organizational structure has continued to change. The trustees acted as the principal program staff and were unpaid volunteers who were driven by the need to help others and received satisfaction when they felt successful. Swadhar continued to measure low on material incentives until they needed to hire professional staff. Paid staff are interested in material incentives because they support families. They are looking for opportunities to work their way up in organizations, earn more money, earn vacation time, and have health benefits. By adding younger staff members who have not been part of the women's movement and have not been deeply affected by women's struggle for equality and empowerment, the material incentives are higher than normative ones.

Applying measures of decision making in assessing Swadhar's structure, we see other changes. Since 1999 there is even less participation in organizational decision making by members of Swadhar, both paid and unpaid. As measured by the criteria describing decision-making authority, Swadhar's scores have changed, moving from a sense of participation of the many to the participation of the few. The members of the management committee are seen as the key decision makers of Swadhar.

At the same time, however, there is a sense that there are not necessarily more formal decision criteria. Some are frustrated with what they perceive as informal and ad hoc decisions, which are both inconsistent and inefficient. Meenaksi Apte indicated in several interviews her frustration with decision making, explaining that trustees often made decisions based on their own belief systems and experience rather than on any explicit or consistent criteria. This has resulted in organizational discord from time to time.

Shared belief and time, measures of organizational structure, as mentioned earlier, continue to be split among older trustees and young members of the management committee and staff. For older trustees there is still a strong collective commitment to the social issues they have undertaken over these past thirteen years. As long time friends and social peers, the older trustees frequently get together outside of Swadhar. This does not happen among younger board and staff members. First, they are not the peers of the founding trustees. Second, they do not have a history of involvement with the movement or the social issues affecting women. Because these young professionals also juggle work and family—supporting a family in India today requires two incomes—they do not have time to socialize outside of work, or do not choose to socialize with their working peers. Swadhar's programs are now scattered across many sites covering a broad geographical area. Many workers may rarely—if ever—come into regular contact with each other.

Would having a formal and permanent office overcome some of these factors and create a more communal organization? Would having a central office create more consistency and diminish the sense that the organization is run on an ad hoc basis as multiple independent silos? Meenakshi Apte and Sulabha Joshi believe so. Unfortunately there are some on the management committee who believe this is unnecessary.

The big question remaining about Swadhar's organizational structure is succession. If a number of the members of the management committee retire soon, will Swadhar become more like a bureaucracy than a collective pragmatic organization? Meenakshi Apte and other original remaining trustees recognize that they need to think hard about succession and the effect that might have on the kind of organization Swadhar will be in the future. Meenakshi Apte and Sulabha Joshi realize that Swadhar needs more structure, systems, planning, and vision. They hope that by bringing on younger members to the management committee the founding members will pass on the strong set of beliefs that have guided the organization since its inception. They hope to inspire Swadhar's next generation of leaders to champion the cause of development and self-reliance among the most marginalized groups of India's poor.

Chapter Three

Social Impact:
What Makes for Success?

Introduction

In this chapter, we examine the natural evolutionary process of successful NGOs to understand the context of their choices of programs and services offered. We ask the following questions: Do successful organizations, that wish to grow, increase the different types of services they offer? Or, do they increase the number of clients they serve in existing services? Do they do both? In other words, does growth lead to focusing on a few activities and increasing the scope of coverage, or choosing newer services? In doing so, do NGOs make choices as a response to available funding? Or, do they make deliberate choices based on long-term strategic plans? Alternatively, do they grow organically, choosing new services that complement existing services? And, how do these choices contribute to their success?

When organizations are led *by women for women* do they evolve in ways that are ideally suited to respond to women's needs? What specifically is the contribution of women-led NGOs in terms of building the capacities of poor women and empowering them? We expect that women-led NGOs better understand the cultural barriers women face, women's ways of multitasking, and how issues related to the productive and reproductive health are equally important in the lives of poor women. Hence, they make a profound and sustainable impact on the developmental needs of women.

In looking at the gamut of services chosen by NGOs, we find that there is a particular focus on two services related to women's issues. These are *microfinancing*, based on variations of the microcredit programs that reflect aspects of those initiated by the successful Grameen Bank; and, *political empowerment*, responding to the legislative changes of affirmative action consequent to the 73rd Amendment to the Constitution of India.[1]

We first turn our attention to the range of services the NGOs in our study provide. We then evaluate the impact of these services, with a special focus on their role in microcredit and political empowerment. In India, due to the lack of resources, the government does not provide many of the basic services that people in more affluent countries take for granted. For example, in Scandinavian countries and in Canada, many different levels of governments provide citizens with a variety of basic services such as education, healthcare, minimum income supplements, and unemployment insurance. The provision of the basic necessities of life is the safety net provided by governments.

What does 'safety net' really mean to the poor in India? Gopalan (2001) answers this as follows:

> In a country like India, economic uncertainties, loss of livelihood, inflation, erosion of access to natural resources, shrinking employment, increasing social/ethnic unrest, 'natural' disasters, drought, floods, earthquakes, etc. make the poor extremely vulnerable. Given their asset base, they barely recover from one shock (natural or human-made) before another overtakes them. What inputs would be necessary to ensure that the poor are empowered to access development resources and use it to their best advantage? People's existential reality and their efforts to overcome poverty depend a great deal on their ability to seize opportunities and turn them to their advantage (p. 5).

The lack of basic services leaves the poor in India without any safety net and at the mercy of charitable impulses of the well-to-do. Therefore, the poor are often literally without any recourse and 'on the streets'. In addition, the poor generally lack education and are unaware

[1] This Amendment, dated 24 April 1993, directed all state legislatures to amend their respective panchayat legislation, which included a quota for women in all the panchayats. It required that one-third of the total number of seats be reserved for women, and that one-third of the offices of chairpersons of panchayats at all levels also be reserved for women (Jain, 1996).

of their few and meager entitlements and rights. This makes them even more vulnerable to exploitation. Many NGOs that help the poor find that although the provision of direct and basic welfare services meets immediate needs, these needs must be complemented by services that are more enabling and ensure long-term, sustainable autonomy for the poor. Over time, many of these organizations have turned from providing simple relief and direct aid, to adopting strategies related to community development, self-help, microcredit, and political empowerment.

As the twentieth century was ushered in with Indian independence and social movements, many changes ensued; however, the gains made were not evenly distributed. Many poor and rural women, as well as middle and upper-class urban women, were left out of the stream of political and social consciousness-raising. Nevertheless, as we showed in Chapter One, the changes of these reform movements were not without affect. Many feminist and entrepreneurial women found it possible, despite the overwhelmingly patriarchal society that still remained, to form NGOs that catered to the social development of less fortunate women, and often took on controversial issues such as, male domination, abuse, and female infanticide. They also focused on areas of female health, reproduction, education, and self-awareness, using political consciousness-raising and microcredit to provide channels for self-help and empowerment.

In this chapter, we set about to measure the impact that our selected NGOs have had on women's development and examine the effects of women's leadership. The popular way to judge the effectiveness of an NGO has been to examine how well an NGO is able to attain its stated goals. However, it has been recognized by scholars that this is a limited way of looking at NGO effectiveness, as the goal of the NGO cannot be taken as an end in itself with the assumption that all goal fulfillment leads to development. In fact, scholars insist that the goals of the NGO must be placed in the larger context of development in order to assess how the organizational goals address developmental objectives (Sinha and Sinha, 2002). This is not to suggest that there is a single model in measuring NGO impact in the development literature, rather this has led to a controversy over how to best measure impact (Brown, 1991; Elliot, 1987; Fowler, 1985; Korten, 1990; Wolch, 1990). Notwithstanding this controversy, we draw on the recent literature to formulate a framework that we use in analyzing the NGOs in our study.

It is our view that measuring NGO impact must include the types and kinds of activities of the NGO in raising women's awareness in a *holistic way*, so that they are not only educated, healthy, or able to run a microfinanced enterprise, but that she can eventually effectively navigate her way in the socio-cultural environment in which she functions. Such empowerment, we believe, depends largely on the development of the capacity to exercise a certain amount of control over the social, economic, and political conditions that determine her life. The viability and sustainability of empowerment depend on women's involvement in the process and praxis. A Woman can be deemed sufficiently empowered when she is able to take control, and even spearhead political change. Using the literature that deals with the types of activities an NGO undertakes in order to measure impact, we look at the writings of Atack (1999), Korten (1987), Uvin et al. (2000), and Vakil (1997). Taken together this literature introduces a classification of NGO activity by orientations and type to understand impact. We also use Aital (2004), Gopalan (2001), and Purushothaman and Jaeckel (2001), as a starting point to explore the impact of *women-led* NGOs in our study.

This chapter proceeds by reviewing the key aspects of measuring and classifying the impact of NGOs, and we present a framework for what makes for a successful NGO, relying on the seminal models in the literature. We then examine the practices of our successful women-led NGOs, and present our analysis based on the criteria we develop. We then focus on literature on women-headed organizations to assess their unique contribution to women's development. We are able to show that many of our successful women-led NGOs do indeed have practices that positively impact women's holistic well-being, according to the criteria offered in the literature. Many of these practices we find are a result of the NGOs being led by women who are easily able to relate to the multidimensional aspects of poor women's lives. Women leaders often turned to other women in grass-roots women's groups to identify their needs and to find solutions that are embedded in the local culture.

In addition, we are able to show that successful NGOs also practice strategies for greater sustainable empowerment, which often include the two criteria (microfinance and political empowerment) suggested at the outset. However, microcredit and political empowerment are only two indicators, albeit important ones, of a more holistic multidimensional approach discussed earlier. In concluding, we discuss the implications of the findings that may be helpful to researchers and policy makers.

Literature Review

Development literature often equates the success of an NGO with its impact on social development, although a controversy exists on how to measure this impact (Brett, 1993; Edwards and Hulme, 1995; Smilie, 1995). For our purposes, we start with the seminal work done by Korten (1987) in assessing the effectiveness and legitimacy of NGOs. Korten suggests that it is necessary to follow the evolution of an NGO in terms of the *types* of activities it undertakes. He advocates a macro-level view of the NGO in the way it functions in its environment. To achieve these ends, he classifies them in accordance with 'generational' levels of the activity undertaken by the NGO (Korten, 1987: 147).

By using a generational typology, Korten (1987) is simply asserting that activities can vary in the way they help; one could either 'give fish to the hungry' or 'teach the hungry to fish'. A first generational activity simply allows the NGO to meet a basic human need such as feeding the hungry or sheltering the homeless. The second level of generational activity enables people to develop their own capacities and learn to fend for themselves. The next three generational activities help bring about structural long-term change that dismantles disabling barriers and often involves macro policies for broadbased sustainable development. In Table 3.1, we elaborate on the different levels of generational strategies and give examples of the different types of development activities undertaken by NGOs.

Korten recognizes the need for a lower generational activity, such as providing safe drinking water, which provides immediate relief; however, his main argument is that aid alone is not sufficient for the long-term goals of development that include control over one's life. In terms of long-term change and sustainability, this is a 'low'-level activity that may eventually promote dependency on the donor. The 'higher' generational level of activity tries to foster independence from the donor. And, as one goes towards even higher generational level activities, more social change and development is promoted. Thus, activities undertaken by an NGO at higher generational levels, which

TABLE 3.1
Korten's Generational Typology

Generational level strategy	Type	Examples
First generation strategies	Welfare activities	Activities based on the charity model— to meet basic needs, usually in response to disaster/crisis.
Second generation strategies	Development activities	Activities focused on developing the capacities of people to better meet their needs.
Third generation strategies	Advocacy activities	Activities with the intention of influencing policy or decision making.
Fourth generation strategies	Networking	Activities aimed at promoting a broader social vision and assisting other NGOs and social groups towards that vision.
Fifth generation strategies	Research and publication	Activities aimed at participatory research and publicity that allows for legitimate claims for intervention.

Source: Korten (1987).

promote social change (such as advocacy for legislative changes that promote women's rights), have a greater long-term impact on the population through institutional and structural changes (Atack, 1999).

Higher generational activity through education for the lower-castes can represent attitudinal and social change. One of the major outcomes of raising awareness among the poor is to promote their coming together as a collective (often referred to as a *sangha*) to tackle social problems. With the power of the *sangha* the poor can use their collective clout to challenge governance and tackle problems within their communities. For example, they can take on a range of challenges including fighting alcoholism in their communities, negotiating with local municipalities for development programs, monitoring government programs, and grooming members for local elections. These actions can change attitudes and raise levels of self-confidence among the poor. This in turn can create an enabling environment that prepares the community for changes that are ushered in as a consequence of NGO advocacy.

To be sure, the lower level strategies are often necessary as it is hard to picture women, who have been unable to achieve some basic threshold of amenities, running for political office. Thus, lower and higher generational level activities must coexist, at least until the time that all women have achieved basic levels of health, education, and independence. The latter conditions are necessary to ensure the success of the higher generational strategies in the long term.

Other scholars in the field of development studies have added the concept of 'scaling up' to measure impact (Uvin et al., 2000). Rejecting popular notions of impact that suggest that NGOs must grow in size in order to increase impact, they recognize that impact may be fully independent of growth. They propose this new paradigm of 'scaling up' to measure impact, in which they include the organization, its goals, and its sustainability.

In brief, the 'scaling up' taxonomy used by Uvin et al. (ibid.) is as follows:

(a) *Expanding coverage and size:* The NGO becomes a larger organization, manages more funds, employs more skilled personnel, and covers more beneficiaries in a larger geographical area. An example of this can be seen in how one of our NGOs chose to expand its coverage by seeking additional funding from an international donor. This required permission from the Indian government and a commitment by the NGO to the government and the donor to provide detailed reports and budgets. This small NGO, which up until this point was run on an informal basis, was now required to change its procedures and start keeping records. It hired a new employee who was professionally equipped to help meet the NGO's new bureaucratic accountability requirements. Additional funds from the donor also helped the NGO to expand the service coverage it provides.

(b) *Increasing activities:* This entails offering a greater range and number of services to the clientele whom the NGO serves. For example, an NGO that formed mahila mandals to institute programs of microcredit used the same venue to raise political awareness regarding the rights of female representation on village councils.

(c) *Broadening indirect impact:* This involves NGOs seeking to affect the behavior of other actors who work with the poor, or influence their lives through advocacy, knowledge creation, or advice. An example of this is the NGO that did research on the relationship between alcoholism and reasons for spousal abuse. They used these findings not only to help women deal with alcoholic partners, but also to start Alcoholics Anonymous groups among men to reduce alcoholism.

(d) *Enhancing organizational sustainability:* This implies that an NGO must generally go through discrete stages in achieving organizational sustainability. In the first stage, the NGO is initiated with passion, but without much clarity regarding activity involvement. At the next stage, specific individuals, or teams are established to undertake the specific tasks. At this point, resources are not stable and funding is often uncertain. The third stage is project implementation, where the NGO takes on particular projects without a long-term view. It is focused on completion of the particular project. The last and fourth stage is institutionalizing the NGO's projects. In other words, at this level the NGO has an ongoing strategic commitment with a stable source of funding and programs for its clients and beneficiaries.

The 'scaling up' measures, provided here, could well be a result of a natural evolutionary process, which may not need the NGO to grow in size. For example, an NGO may start small and remain small, even when successful. Instead of spreading its influence by growing large, an NGO expands its impact by 'scaling up'; in other words, by undertaking different or additional types of activities. The choice of the activities is crucial in achieving a broadening impact and organizational sustainability.

In explaining NGO impact, we choose to merge the 'generational level' and the 'scaling up' models discussed here. Korten's generational model explicitly details the modes of direct and indirect impact of NGOs, whereas the scaling up model proposed by Uvin et al., subsumes the direct/indirect impact of NGOs within their model of 'scaling up', however, they omit much of the detail on activities undertaken. While the model presented by Uvin et al. incorporates an elegant new paradigm of 'scaling up', this study assesses the various modes by which NGOs expand their impact. However, it is not explicit in detailing the NGO's impact. Hence we incorporate Korten's generational activity lists to enrich the 'scaling up' framework.

In addition, we find that the measures provided by Korten and Uvin et al. are still somewhat incomplete. Simply increasing activities, providing different 'generational' types of activities, or concentrating on a few well-chosen activities, is not sufficient in explaining the increased impact that is important for holistic well-being in the lives of women. For example, an NGO may use resources teaching women literacy, which is an admirable end in and of itself. However, by also teaching the same women how to parlay their new found skills of literacy into being able to read and understand issues related to other parts of their lives, like health or property rights, the literacy skills leverage better lives for women. Leveraging activities with higher complementary activities will yield higher synergistic impacts for both activities. Such leveraging activities are an example of vertical linkage, which reinforces the services provided by the NGO by making them complementary. The sum of the impact of complementary activities will be greater than the sum of unrelated activities.

If the services provided by the NGO are leveraged by one another, or, vertically linked, we believe that the impact is greater than if the NGO serves larger numbers of women with one type of service, or, provides fewer women with many more disparate services. To obtain optimal impact levels, we believe that all, or at least the majority, of services provided by an NGO should include vertically-linked services, thereby enabling women to reap even greater benefits of all the NGO's activities. Thus, the nature of the services the NGO provides, insofar as how they interrelate with each other, is crucial in assessing impact.

Vertical integration, it is argued, often happens when organizations add activities to complement their original services so as to better control external uncertainties like the environment, and to secure long-term impact (Uvin et al., 2000). While we do not disagree with this assertion, we go one step further to argue that vertical integration actually has a multiplier effect on the impact of the NGO.[2] It can be argued that an enabling environment results from integrated services since these services promote a more holistic development.

Having observed NGOs in the field over time, we were struck by the careful attention paid by resource-strapped NGOs in making choices about whether to add clientele or to add services. We observed that, very often, grant proposals were made to secure funding for new programs. Although there is some debate in the literature regarding whether NGO programs are driven by available funding or whether they choose their services on other criteria, we did not find that NGOs were choosing to add programs in an ad hoc manner, or that they were primarily grant driven. We believe that new programs and services are often chosen deliberately to complement existing services, and we observed the increased impact of doing so. Given this state of affairs, we chose to add vertical integration as a dimension contributing to the effectiveness of the Korten–Uvin, Jain and Brown framework in our examination of the twenty successful NGOs.

[2] Although it is suggested by Uvin et al. (2000), they found little empirical evidence.

Given the synergy of vertically-linked services, we argue that the total impact of the services will exceed the sum of its parts, thereby increasing impact and the long-term effects. The overall impact of any NGO will depend highly on the sustainable impact of the whole bundle of services provided by the NGO. For example, providing women with day care services combined with literacy training and vocational guidance may have a greater impact in women's social development and empowerment than by simply offering distinct services, such as family planning, credit counseling, and a traveling library. Furthermore, a number of varied, yet vertically-linked, services will also make for more efficient use of resources when dealing with social problems that tend to be rooted in an intertwining fashion.

A framework that incorporates the issues of scaling, generational activity, vertical integration, and some traditional measures of size and scope is one we feel most comfortable using to assess the impact of our successful NGOs. We examined the NGOs over a period of five to six years for details on the following:

(*a*) *Increase in scope and size:* We measured the changes in a six-year period from 1995 to 2001 in terms of the change in per cent of clients served, change in per cent of budget, change in spatial coverage, and the change in paid staff and volunteers. This dimension encompasses internal decisions to increase size and scope, as well as the influence of factors outside the control of the NGO founders that may have accounted for change. For example, if the government changed its policy regarding accounting requirements for those NGOs getting international funds, this may have increased the NGO's need for professional staff to fulfill these additional and relatively complex tasks.

(*b*) *Generational activity:* We examined the types of activities of the NGOs and categorized them according to their 'generational level', as laid out by Korten (1987). For example, distribution of food to the hungry has a direct impact that is restricted to relieving hunger; this is classified as a low generational activity with limited impact. On the other hand, advocacy undertaken by the NGO for access to education for lower-caste women would be classified as a high generational activity with greater impact, as it brings about long-term structural change.

(*c*) *Vertically integrated services:* We measured the change in the number of services offered from 1995 to 2001 and ranked the linkages between the existing and new services as high, medium, and low. We measured vertical integration in the services offered by their levels of linkage complementarities. For example, if women were introduced to micro-credit and these programs were extended to other villages, this would reflect an exchange of information between the villages that we can describe as low vertical integration (Uvin et al., 2000). On the other hand, if microcredit was combined with a program of teaching women to save and invest their newly gained money, or if it also involved professional development, this would be a high vertically-integrated service with the existing microcredit program.

(*d*) *Enhanced organizational sustainability:* We measured the stage at which the organization was located, in terms of stability, as set out earlier by the stages of development suggested by Uvin et al., and we complement this measure by noting the organizational form of the NGO. As organizations evolve into higher generational activities, increase in impact subsequently entails administrative exigencies that necessitate organizational structures that encompass formality, ac-countability, and some semblance of hierarchy in terms of responsi-bility. For example, one of the factors of the organizational sustainability we consider is the existence of paid staff. Paid staff represents a certain accountability and legitimacy, which, in turn, make for a sustainable organization. This is to say that crucial administrative tasks often require professionals to carry them out on a regular basis, and such tasks cannot be left to volunteers—among whom the turnover rate may be unpredictable and high. If tasks, such as audits or grant applications, are not carried out in a timely and professional fashion, the organization may not survive or grow successfully.

In the last several decades, especially since the very successful NGO microfinancing venture spearheaded by the Grameen Bank in Bangladesh in 1976, many NGOs have tried to replicate helping poor women obtain financing using the concepts of lending groups, with varying degrees of success. In India, there have been two main routes to helping groups achieve financial independence: the Grameen sys-tem, and the self-help groups (SHGs) system. Whereas the Grameen system is more structured and relies on top–down management, the SHGs system involves small, autonomous women's groups that are often initiated by NGOs, but managed at the grass-roots level. Though female clients and microlending dominate both systems, there are important differences. The Grameen Bank model is driven from the top, has well laid out structures, and has a select range of services available. Clients exercise little initiative beyond deciding to partici-pate and organizing into groups that meet on a regular schedule. The meetings are supervised and a tight discipline is maintained regarding savings and repayments. The repayments are collected and recorded regularly by supervisors appointed by the bank.

The strength of the Grameen model is that it allows the very poor and marginalized people access to loans, the services of a bank, and protects them from exploitation by maintaining strict accountability and supervision. The Grameen model is very popular in Bangladesh and has been replicated elsewhere in India with some success. At the turn of the century, the Indian NGOs that received strategic help and funds from the Grameen bank had a clientele of 420,000 (Grameen Trust, 2000). When governments or banks organize women's groups, their activities are limited to credit orientation. Women need credit as a first step to economic empowerment; this is often available to them through the micro credit schemes. However, it is only the first step as women's overall empowerment is a much more complex and nuanced issue that cannot be limited to the economic realm alone— women need to build their own capacities within the family and community at the social and cultural levels simultaneously.

Another form of obtaining credit is through the formation of SHGs. This system tends to be more flexible and encourages other kinds of empowerment when women must negotiate many of the rules of conduct and savings behavior amongst themselves without intervention from banks or the government. There is no need for a bank at the early stages as an NGO often acts as a catalyst in facilitating the formation of groups that start a savings group. When the savings group has collected significant capital, its members are able to take out loans from the accumulated savings on interest rates decided upon by the group.

The group is self-monitored and makes decisions as to which member can take a loan, the size of the loan, as well as the repayment schedule. As a group becomes accustomed to methods of savings and loans, and thereby establishes its reliability and creditworthiness, it may move to a higher stage of securing loans from a bank. How the group proceeds and how the group establishes routines at every stage is entirely up to the group, which functions as an autonomous organization within the SHGs system.

As SHGs manage themselves at the grass-roots level, they are more vulnerable to collapse than the Grameen system, which is systematically monitored by professionals. However, this vulnerability is also its strength. By allowing members the flexibility of choosing their own methods of savings and accountability, SHGs are highly empowering, as they nurture group mobilization skills, management, and decision making, as well as capacity building among group members. Perhaps because they are so well suited to what Gopalan (2001) aptly calls 'credit for empowerment', the growth in SHGs is phenomenal. Membership figures of SHGs in India are expected to reach 17 million women by 2008 (Fisher and Sriram, 2002).

Mobilizing women and encouraging their participation in the political arena and local self-governance are other areas of NGO involvement. This has been particularly heightened since the government of India's affirmative action policies, mentioned earlier, where one-third of the local government seats are reserved for females. Nongovernmental organizations have been increasingly involved in raising women's consciousness regarding their political rights and their ability to bring about change. They have also engaged in training women to take on leadership positions and provided assistance for women who chose to run for political positions at the local and village levels. NGOs also seek to strengthen the capacity of local leaders engaged in self-governance councils called panchayats.

It becomes evident that NGOs that promote the long-term well-being of women now give high priority to promoting economic independence through income generation and microfinance activities, as well as encouraging political participation through political awareness programs and leadership development training. However, economic independence and political empowerment, as stated earlier, are only two indicators of a more holistic multidimensional approach that women-led NGOs tend to adopt. It is for this reason, and in the context of the NGOs in our study, that we raise the question: How do women-led NGOs fare in providing a more holistic and hence sustainable development for poor women?

Development literature has more recently emphasized that when women head organizations they seek to provide multidimensional programs for women that are sensitive to the invisible demands and the gender constraints under which women operate (Bushley et al., 2003; Moser, 1991). A strong woman-centered approach involves providing an enabling environment for women on two levels. The first level takes into consideration the more immediate practical aspects that allow women to access programs that are offered, that is, child care support would allow her to attend a literacy class. Also, because of the great demands on her limited time, she should be able to access other essential services/needs simultaneously. As discussed earlier, we call this type of bundling of related services as 'vertically-integrated services'.

As economic value is not assigned to the work women do, it often remains invisible and ignored by mainstream development approaches. Feminist development literature outlines the multiple roles and complex interrelated issues that make up the work and lives of women. Women are often the principal suppliers of water and fuel, cultivators, livestock managers, and the backbone of the subsistence economy in the rural environment. They are also the principal workers within the home—as wives and mothers they are the first suppliers of food, health, and education (Sadik, 1988: 1). Often their contribution to the informal sector by engaging in small trades and services support the family and local economy. Their contribution to daily life provides the essential underpinnings of society. Feminists have argued that development agencies have to relate to their whole lives; by segmenting development approaches they cannot hope to make a lasting impact on the lives of women. (Bushley et al., 2003; Purushothaman and Jaeckel, 2001).

Second, at a more holistic level, when NGOs provide programs that are broadly linked and take into account the social, political, psychological, and economic dimensions in order to empower women, they are said to provide 'an enabling environment'. In many instances, social programs address the barriers that women face in accessing programs offered for their health and well-being. For example, the development experiences of Catalyst, a consortium that specializes in the delivery of reproductive health services in Latin America, suggest that programs have to account for the broader social realities that influence peoples' lives. As a case in point, their dairy cooperative allows women to safely market the milk from the cows they raise at home, thereby giving them access to finance. However, this meeting ground allows women to bond and take advantage of talks offered there on health, family planning, and education. At that same time they are able to access contraceptives that they can now choose to buy from the money they make on the milk (Bushley et al., 2003: 6–17).

A multidimensional empowerment approach is needed to successfully tackle deeply-entrenched societal as well as personal problems confronted by women (Everingham, 2002). However, women's role in childbearing and raising and caring for children involves numerous subsistence activities—processing food, administering health care, cleaning, collecting water and fuel. These are assumed to be 'natural' rather than essential work. Mainstream development ideology downplays this reproductive role of women and simply expects it to continue without recognizing the real resources that must be devoted to women to successfully bear and raise children. Instead, if changes are sought in the productive sphere there is an emphasis on income-generating projects (Everingham, 2002: 47). However, it cannot be assumed that if a development intervention promotes women's empowerment along a particular dimension, for example, the economic dimension, empowerment in other areas, such as childbearing and reproductive health, will necessarily follow (Beegle et al., 1998; Hashemi et al., 1996; Kishor, 1995, 2000b; Malhotra and Mather, 1997).

Moreover, the way poverty affects women is inherently different from how it affects men, given that most households do not share the male income equally among the family members. Due to severe imbalances of power across gender, a women's poverty means that the whole family, especially female members are severely affected. Hence, in order to bring women out of poverty, it is important to initiate policies for their empowerment through development strategies that address the specific needs and grievances of women. For example, providing easy access to reproductive health or clean water is distinct from addressing employment levels in the village, or access to equity by male members in the households (Saadallah, 2002). Women are also more likely than men to experience 'poverty and economic dependence… violence, negative attitudes, racial and other forms of discrimination, limited power [over their sexual and reproductive lives] and lack of influence in decision-making… [that]… adversely impacts their health… (Beijing Platform of Action, para. 92). Hence, though health services may be offered by NGOs, local poor women may not be able to access these services because of their domestic responsibilities, economic demands, or gender constraints. Thus the individual and the levels of her enabling environment, that is, the family, community, services, and policy must be taken into account when programs are offered (CEDPA, 1997).

Shields (1992:171) found that women experience empowerment as a multifaceted expansive process that includes the development of an internal sense of self and the ability to take action based on such a sense of self. Shields argues that empowerment for women should be a transformative strategy for poverty eradication. However, as empowerment does not occur in a vacuum, the provision of an 'enabling environment' helps. The enabling environment results from integrated services, in particular vertically integrated services that advocates for a more holistic development. Consciousness-raising also leads to an enabling environment where changes from above can be more easily absorbed on the ground due to changes in attitudes and higher awareness.

It has been argued that women who lead NGOs are more likely to realize the objective of sustainable development because they often adopt a bottom-up approach. They encourage women to identify their own needs and find solutions to meet these needs by participating in the decision-making process (Vijayanthi, 2002). This is in keeping with a marked trend in recent literature to shift away from top–down paternalistic approaches in development towards what Jaeckel (2001) calls 'advancing governance through peer learning'. Aital's (2004) work with NGO's serving women in south Asia led her to call this learning process 'learning from the subaltern'. She had observed a woman-led NGO in south India that asked rural women to identify their own needs. The women pointed to the broken neighborhood water pump that caused them to go a much greater distance to the next working water pump. The ensuing hardship arose from their inability to coordinate their cooking time with the trip to fetch water, which resulted in less time for the women to attend to their other chores. The NGO staff asked the rural women how they wished to resolve their problem. After much discussion the rural women asked to be taught the mechanics of repairing water pumps so as to break their dependence on the male-governed village panchayat that did not give priority to their needs. Their newly acquired skills allowed them a permanent solution rather than the stopgap measure proposed by the NGO staff.

We note that the solution came from the women at the grass-roots level. They took pains to show up in great numbers to learn and then diligently repair pumps, the knowledge soon spreading to other villages (Aital, 2004). Purushothaman and Jaeckel (2000) explain the success of such a strategy: If all stakeholders are present in the planning stage itself, the participation of all groups is likely to be higher since everyone feels a sense of ownership of the process. In the Houairou Commission Report, Purushothaman and Jaeckel (2001) suggests that many development projects go wrong simply because they fail to listen to the affected people, the people on the ground. Partnering with women at the grass-roots level not only gives a handle on the problem, it is also part of a long-term solution. Women at the grass-roots have access to a body of knowledge that is acquired from everyday life experiences and from the wealth of local culture and spiritual traditions.

Findings

As this part of the study was done at a later stage than that reported in the earlier chapters, one of our twenty original NGOs did not participate in the final round of interviews. Our findings are, therefore, based on nineteen out of twenty NGOs that participated in the earlier phase of the study. We interviewed the founders and key personnel of these nineteen NGOs using an instrument that asked more detailed questions on the nature and scope of their services, changes in the size and scope of their organization (including their budget and personnel), and services offered from 1995 to 2001, as detailed next.

As the reader may recall, the NGOs we examine are a diverse group in terms of size and age, and all are active in addressing women's issues. Their activities range from providing health services, food, shelter, and education to the provision of vocational training. Many are also involved with SHGs so that women will learn to act cooperatively and gain support from each other. These groups are organized around savings and credit, vocational training, and other issues. Some of the NGOs participate in advocacy work, promote networking, and conduct their own research. They are often involved in publishing their research for educational and advocacy purposes, as well as using it for needs assessment.

We organize and report our quantitative and qualitative data according to four dimensions: size and scope, generational strategies, number of integrated services, and organizational sustainability. We later focus on the qualitative data we gathered on the role of the women founders and examine their impact on organizational choices especially from a gendered perspective that results in a culture of inclusiveness.

Size and Scope

In Table 3.2 we provide data on the scope and size of each NGO by listing the age, change in the percentage of clients served between

TABLE 3.2
Increasing Size and Scope

	Age (years)	Change in number of clients (1995–2001)	Change in number of services (1995–2001)	Change in budget (Rs in Lakh, 1 lakh = 100,000)	Source of funding	Change in number of paid staff	Change in number of volunteers, full-time employees
1	12	60 to 120	2 to 3	1 to 16	FF[a]	3.5 to 7.5	Varies
2	8	500 to 3,050	2 to 3	1.5 to 8	LF[b]	2 to 10	0
3	8	40 to 550	1 to 4	N/a	LF	10	N/a
4	6	54 to 501	2 to 3	3 to 9	LF, FF	21 to 61	4 to 40
5	6	10,000 to 15,000	3 to 4	1 to 5	M[c]	2.5 to 8	5 to 10
6	9	7,000 to 2 million	1 to 2	0.97 to 5	FF	1.5 to 6	0 to 3
7	5	500 to 1,000	3 to 5	1 to 5	LF	2 to 12.5	0 to 10
8	5	18 to 80	2 to 3	0 to 2	M	0 to 1.5	4 (no change)
9	6	175 to 250	2 to 4	1 to 10	LF	40.5 to 61	4.5 to 4
10	14	80,000 to 90,000	2 to 4	3 to 5	M, LF, and FF	28 to 51	40 to 50
11	19	650 to 900	2 to 5	1 to 45	FF	2 to 20	2 to 5
12	15	150 to 350	4 (no change)	2 to 6	LF	0 to 7	8 (no change)
13	37	9,000 to 32,000	6 (no change)	1.5 to 3.5	LF and FF	49 to 74	30 to 40
14	11	20 to 170	1 to 3	0.20 to 1.26	M and FF	0	35 to 47.5
15	10	300 to 1,000	6 to 9	12 to 25	FF	10 to 29	0 to 30
16	19	100 to 1,000	2 to 3	2 to 8	FF	7 to 10	1 to 1.5
17	6	30 to 190	1 to 4	0 to 3	LF and FF	0 to 7	0 to 10
18	7	30 to 250	2 to 4	0.07 to 3	LF and FF	1 to 2.5	9 to 16
19	52	225 to 192	4 to 5	3.3 to 8.5	LF and FF	8 to 10.5	15 to 20

Notes: [a]FF = foreign funding
[b]LF = local sources of funding, private and public
[c]M = membership and other income

1995 and 2001, change in the percentage of budget in the same period, change in the spatial coverage, and change in numbers of paid staff and volunteers. All the NGOs have increased in scope and size, often significantly. For example, one NGO's budget increased from Rs 100,000 to Rs 4,500,000 and its clientele increased from 650 to 900. Only one NGO decreased its clientele despite an increase in its budget, the reason being that this NGO devoted part of its increased funding to the construction of buildings to house the increase in its future clientele.

We found that the availability of donor funding was the principal factor in the increase in budget; this finding replicates the findings of Uvin et al. (2000). We also note that a significant amount of funding came from public sources within India, as well as international funders. Sometimes it was both. For example, one NGO received funding from a national foundation as well as from international funders, whereas another NGO received its entire spending increase (which was significant) from international sources.

Of our nineteen NGOs, two raised revenues only from individual membership dues within India, five received funding only from sources within India, five relied solely on international funding, and seven received both Indian and international funding. The two NGOs that relied solely on membership dues from within India were relatively young organizations and had smaller operating budgets. They are still in the process of legitimizing themselves and stabilizing their funding sources. Non-governmental organizations often need a modicum of initial success and healthy bank balances before they can attract long-term international donor funding.

We know from the literature that stable sources of funding allow NGOs to experiment, respond to changing needs, and to reach their goals. Funding uncertainties can delay or side rail what many NGOs set out to achieve. Furthermore, the lack of funds can prompt NGOs to apply and accept grants that may not coincide with their mission.

We find that eleven out of the final nineteen NGOs score high on impact and high on vertical integration. Examining their sources of funding, we find that nine of these eleven received foreign funding as part of their funding sources (four received their complete funding from international sources and the other five received part of their funding from international sources). Of the eight who did not score high on vertical integration and impact, only two received foreign funding as part of its revenue sources.

We cannot say whether successful NGOs were able to attract foreign funding, or whether foreign funding helped them to succeed. However, we can raise certain issues for consideration. In the literature we have come across some evidence of NGOs being ambivalent about foreign funds because funding agencies control the development agenda and there is no real partnership. The process of seeking foreign funding is often frustrating and expensive, especially for smaller NGOs. Funding agencies often cut agreed upon budgets unilaterally, and visits by funders and the reporting procedures can be time consuming and cumbersome (Charlton and Everett, 1998). However, many of our NGO founders suggested that foreign funding, despite the strings attached, is typically available for longer periods of time than national or local funding. This contributes to organizational stability and allows the NGOs to develop a more reliable long-term vision, rather than living from hand-to-mouth.

Our data suggests a positive relation between levels of activity and type of funding received by the organization. Of the six NGOs limited to the first three generational activities, only one received part of its revenues from foreign funders. Conversely, of the thirteen NGOs involved in 'fourth generation' or 'fifth generation' activities, eleven received foreign funds. Is it likely that foreign funding helps to advance the NGO on the evolutionary scale of development?

The sentiment of the founders suggests that this may be the case. For example, the founder of one of our NGOs claims that in 1996 'there were no funds'. This NGO, like many others, had started with little or no money and with volunteer help from family and friends. This allowed them only to cater to immediate needs. It was with some difficulty that they were able to expand and offer more services at the second generational level of activities. It was only after receiving a stable source of funding, in this case from an international donor, that this NGO was able to grow without relying on volunteer labor and private gifts. It currently receives foreign aid and is able to offer research and publication services. These are advanced generational activities that have wider impact and help spearhead change through developing increased awareness. Similarly, another NGO started out by counseling poor and lower-caste women in a makeshift garage. Professionals donated their time to help these women. With international donations, however, it has been able to provide a shelter for its clients and also offer services in the education of women. It now is involved in publicizing their plight in society to raise awareness and garner public support.

The study by Uvin et al. (2000) suggests that NGOs typically start small and stay small, even when successful. They increase their impact through 'scaling up', or offering services that expand NGO impact beyond the local level. In applying the scaling up paradigm to the NGOs in our study, we find that almost all of the organizations have grown larger, though one does sense a deliberate attempt to limit growth. We note that despite the fact that some budgets grew tenfold, the staff size only doubled, and volunteer staff grew even less (see Table 3.2). The growth in staff size does not reflect the phenomenal growth in the size of the operating budgets for many of the NGOs. Furthermore, there was a dramatic increase in the number of people served (as shown in Table 3.2), although the spatial coverage of their services increased only moderately for almost all of the NGOs. This, combined with a small increase in staff, may suggest increased efficiency of our NGOs.

Generational Strategies

We find that eleven of our nineteen NGOs are involved in 'first generation' welfare type of activities. Some of our NGOs provide very basic relief to women and children (see Table 3.3). For example, one NGO's mission is to provide immediate relief for the victims affected by a gas leak in Pune; another helps distressed women and very poor children; yet another provides shelter for women; a fourth provides a home for abandoned girls. Seventeen of the nineteen NGOs are involved in 'second generation' development activities. These activities increase the capacities of the local populace to provide for their own needs. For example, one teaches forestry management methods to tribal women (Adivasis) in the region; another provides vocational counseling and training for the underprivileged such as skills for office work and the food industry; yet another counsels women who lead enterprises and also acts as a liaison between clients and the banks, which provide them loans—their client population now consists of 2000 members.

Fifteen of the nineteen NGOs were also involved in the 'third generation' type of activity involving advocacy work such as influencing the process of policy formation by governments and organizations. Besides direct advocacy on behalf of clients, these NGOs were also engaged in participating on the national policy committee for

TABLE 3.3

Generational Strategies

	Age (years)	Number of first generation welfare activities	Number of second generation development activities	Number of third generation advocacy activities	Number of fourth generation networking activities	Number of fifth generation research activities	Impact of services*
1	12	1	1	1		1	High
2	8		2			1	High
3	8	1	1	1			Medium
4	6	1	2	2	2	2	High
5	6	1	1	1			Medium
6	9		2	1	1	1	High
7	5		2		2	2	High
8	5	2	1				Low
9	6	1	1	1			Medium
10	14		1	1	1	1	High
11	19	1	1	2		1	High
12	15	2	2	1			Medium
13	37	1	1	2	1	1	High
14	11	1	1	1			Medium
15	10			3	2	2	High
16	19		1		1	1	High
17	6		1	1	1	1	High
18	7	1	1	1		1	High
19	52		1	2	1		High

Note: * Impact of Services: high: >third level activity
medium: third level activity
low: <third level activity

women's health. They represented the voice of poor women on a variety of national and local committees such as the 'Safe Motherhood Committee' and the 'Expert Committee on the Ban of Sex Determination'. Another NGO has played an influential role in the writing of legislation regarding wife abuse, making policy recommendations regarding global child adoption, and working to change government regulations on child marriages.

Nine of the nineteen NGOs were involved at the 'fourth generation' level which is networking. For example, NGOs network with other NGOs, to share information and work cooperatively and collaboratively to lobby for change. Some of the NGOs also network to help identify poor working women and provide accommodation for them. The importance of networking is that it expands the reach of information and expands the network of experience among many organizations so that poor women have broader access to meet multiple kinds of needs.

Twelve of the NGOs under study were involved in 'fifth generation' type of activities, which include researching and documenting problems encountered by the poor and low-caste women, and using that research to recommend and evaluate policy changes. Some of the specific activities we found among our NGOs included: compiling data to show the incompatibility of women's educational programs and their daily lives, advocating for important policy changes, providing translations of laws and regulation into local languages, and publishing information and reports for use by clients and the public to increase knowledge and understanding of issues important to women, children, and families.

It is evident in Table 3.3 that our NGOs have traveled far on the empowerment continuum that starts with the immediate relief of basic needs, stretches to the development of community capacity, and finally to influencing policy and conducting research. Like other scholars, our findings manifest the synergies between direct and indirect activities. We note that organizations tend to start at the first and second generational levels (direct activities) and advance into third, fourth, and fifth generational levels (indirect activities) once they have successfully established themselves. Fourteen of the nineteen NGOs started at the first and second generational levels of activity and over time moved on to higher generational activities.

We further examine our data to draw a connection between the age of the organization and its generational activity level. As suggested by NGO literature, our data did not yield any clear pattern between the age of the NGO and the kinds of activities that it provides (See Table 3.3). The two oldest NGOs are involved in 'fourth' and 'fifth' generational type of activities, as expected; however, the younger NGOs are also involved in higher level activities. In fact one of our youngest NGOs is also involved in 'fifth generation' strategies such as advocacy undertaken for helping lower-caste women gain access to education. Hence the choice of the services provided are not based on any life cycle effects but are deliberate choices made by the founders, which are based on community needs and their passions.

Number of Integrated Services

When we examine the types of services that our NGOs offered over the five to six year period between 1995–2001, we note that there is an increase in the number of services offered in nearly all cases. We list these services by program type in Table 3.4. Women's health, for example, may include a variety of generational activities ranging from direct services to advocacy and research. In this analysis, we are interested in examining the vertical link between services, as defined by Uvin et al. By vertical link we mean that one service enhances another service because the second service is complementary to the first. For example, if education of teens is combined with vocational guidance, the two services complement each other; and taken together they enable a student to progress more rapidly than if only one of the two services was offered.

We do not observe any downsizing of activities, nor the concentration on a few programs as was observed in the NGO literature. Almost all the NGOs in our study have increased the number of their activities (with the exception of one, which maintained the same status throughout).

We find that there is a trend among our NGOs towards vertical integration of services. In other words, our NGOs offer services that complement each other and serve as either upstream or downstream activities. These services are generally targeted at one population and not diversified. Our data reveals that NGOs with higher vertical integration among their services also show a higher impact, as defined using the measures by Korten (1987) and Uvin et al. (2000). We find

TABLE 3.4
Services

	Change in number of services (1995–2001)	Types of services in 1995	Types of services in 2001	Vertical integration of services*
1	2 to 3	Resource and library	Resource and video library, photocopying, leadership training, election campaigning, political consciousness	High
2	2 to 3	Microcredit/networking	Microcredit/networking, training programs	High
3	1 to 5	Counseling	Counseling, health services, personal development, community development, scholarships	Medium
4	5 to 7	Promotion of SHGs, health awareness, group training, vocational guidance, publication	Promotion of SHGs, health awareness, group training, vocational guidance, publication, networking	High
5	5 to 7	Vocational training/tutoring, pre to primary school, health/addiction services	Vocational training, tutoring, pre to primary school, health, addiction services, medical services, SHG for political awareness	Medium
6	1 to 4	Awareness program	SHG for political awareness and microcredit, programs for income generation	High
7	4 to 6	Education counseling, library, training programs	Education counseling, library, training programs, children's programs and journals, scholarships	High

(contd.)

TABLE 3.4 (contd.)

	Change in number of services (1995–2001)	Types of services in 1995	Types of services in 2001	Vertical integration of services*
8	2 to 3	Helped poor Helped poor children	Helped poor, helped poor children, savings groups	Medium
9	2 to 4	Home for girls, orphanage	Home for girls, orphanage, family planning, AIDS awareness	High
10	2 to 6	Health resource development	Health services, resource development, SHG, community development, tribal empowerment, education, savings, SHG for political awareness	Medium
11	2 to 7	Counseling, shelter	Counseling, shelter, health services, leadership training, violence prevention, SHGs for microcredit, and political awareness	High
12	4 (no change)	Library, learning center, orphanage, home for street children	Library, learning center, orphanage, home for street children	Medium
13	6 to 8	Blood donation, center for the deaf, health clinic, short-term crisis/ adoption center, mental therapy	Blood donation, center for the deaf, health clinic, short-term crisis, adoption center, mental therapy, research and development, networking	High
14	1 to 3	Vocational guidance	Education for girls, aid to street children, children programs	Medium

15	5 to 11	Legal aid, counseling, political training, leadership, education	Legal aid, counseling, political training, leadership, education, income generation, international networking, SHG for saving, political consciousness and microcredit, leadership training	High
16	2 to 4	Research and document films produced	Research and document films produced, rural services, SHGs for political consciousness	Medium
17	2 to 4	Family/marital counseling	Family/marital counseling, adolescent counseling and SHG for political consciousness	High
18	3 to 7	Aid for destitutes, vocational training, financial guidance	Aid for destitute, vocational training, financial guidance, school for migrant children, family counseling, SHG for political consciousness	High
19	4 to 5	Hostel, tutoring, nursery school, family counseling	Hostel, tutoring, nursery school, family counseling, vocational training for the handicapped	High

Note: * Linkage of services: high: >70%
medium: 50–70%
low: <50%

that all eleven NGOs which rate 'high' vertical integration also rate 'high' on impact. We would expect this to happen as a result of the synergies at work in vertically-linked services.

For example, one NGO offers interlinked services that facilitate each other in assuaging female illiteracy. They offer tutoring for women, counseling, and a hostel providing accommodation, as well as a nursery school for their children. Another offers library books, videos, and photocopying facilities, as well as reading and writing programs to counteract illiteracy. In both cases, vertically-integrated services not only facilitate literacy but also enhance the impact of each of the activities because of their synergetic relationship.

This positive relationship between vertically-linked services and impact suggests that vertically-integrated services may be a better measure of the impact of an NGO than a simple increase in horizontal integration. An increase in vertical integration may also have a higher long-term impact on social problems, as it takes a multifaceted approach when dealing with serious multidimensional social problems. However, what our findings do not ascertain is whether higher generational strategies encourage the offering of vertically-linked services, or vice versa.

Organizational Sustainability

Using the measures of sustainability defined through organizational stages, structure, and existence of paid staff, Table 3.5 lists these characteristics for the NGOs in our study. Most of our organizations (sixteen out of nineteen) are at the third organizational stage—project implementation—using the criteria developed by Uvin et al. (2000) discussed earlier. There are only three NGOs still at the second stage of organizational sustainability of task teams.

It is interesting to note how NGOs in our study actually moved up the organizational stage. One example may illustrate just how this NGO progressed from the first to the second organizational stage. The NGO is collectivist in structure and started without any operating budget or paid staff. The founder, her husband, and a few volunteers began their services to help distressed women. Since then, the founder received funds from a local fellowship program and now has three paid staff and four part-time volunteers. This NGO now offers a 'savings' program that provides financial guidance to a larger group of women.

TABLE 3.5

Factors Contributing to Impact

	Impact	Age (years)	Funding[a]	Vertical integration of services	Organizational stage[b]	Organizational structure	Change in paid staff and full-time employees
1	High	12	FF	High	3	Hybrid	3.5 to 7.5
2	High	8	LF	High	3	Hybrid	2 to 10
3	Medium	8	LF	Medium	3	Bureaucratic	10 (no change)
4	High	6	LF, FF	High	3	Hybrid	21 to 61
5	Medium	6	M	Medium	2	Hybrid	2.5 to 8
6	High	9	FF	High	3	Bureaucratic	1.5 to 6
7	High	5	LF	High	3	Hybrid	2 to 12.5
8	Medium	5	M	Medium	2	Collectivist	0 to 1.5
9	Medium	6	LF	Medium	3	Collectivist	40.5 to 61
10	High	14	M, LF and FF	Medium	3	Hybrid	28 to 51
11	High	19	FF	High	3	Hybrid	2 to 20
12	Medium	15	LF	Medium	2	Collectivist	0 to 7
13	High	37	LF and FF	High	3	Bureaucratic	49 to 74
14	Medium	11	M and FF	Medium	3	Collectivist	0 (no change)
15	High	10	FF	High	3	Hybrid	10 to 29
16	High	19	FF	Medium	3	Hybrid	7 to 10
17	High	6	LF and FF	High	3	Hybrid	0 to 7
18	High	7	LF and FF	High	3	Hybrid	1 to 2.5
19	High	52	LF and FF	High	3	Bureaucratic	8 to 10.5

Vertical Integration of Services

High, Medium, Low

Notes: [a] Funding: LF = local sources of funding, private and public; M = membership and other income; FF = foreign funding

[b] Organizational stages: 1 = entrepreneurial; 2 = task teams; 3 = project implementation; 4 = program institutions

Thus it started at the entrepreneurial stage and has now moved to the task teams which are organized around saving programs. This NGO has yet to develop a long-term plan for funding for future services.

Another example is about a hybrid NGO at the second stage of development. The NGO has no full-time paid staff to deliver its services; instead it relies on part-time paid staff and volunteer professionals on an ad hoc basis depending on the availability of resources. The founder volunteers her services along with a team of professionals who volunteer their time and often donate money to hire part-time paid staff. The founder and her team of professional volunteers are able to complete the short-term tasks they set for themselves; however, they are aware that they require stable funding to implement long-term projects.

A third NGO at the second stage of development is collectivist in structure and is not a typical NGO. It lacks traditional structure and planning and seems to continue in an organic and spontaneous mode. Everytime the funds that are required to run the services get low, the charismatic founder goes out and solicits funding. To her credit, she has always been able to raise funds to give the services required for continuity. However, she is aware of the risks involved and is in the process of designing a project that will allow for greater predictability and stability. When that happens it is likely to advance this organization to the third generational stage.

Of the four organizations that are collectivist, two are relatively young organizations and all collectivist NGOs have a rating of 'medium' for the impact of their services. Furthermore, in terms of organizational sustainability, fifteen of the sixteen NGOs rated at higher levels of organizational sustainability are found to be either bureaucracies or hybrids. Eleven NGOs rated at high levels of impact, all of which are either bureaucracies or hybrids. These findings may reflect life cycle effects as two of the four collectivists are young and measures of organizational sustainability and impact may be skewed due to age.

Role of NGOs in Microcredit Financing and Political Empowerment

We now direct our attention to what is being done by our NGOs in two important areas of NGO activities: microfinance and political empowerment. With regard to microcredit financing, we note in Table 3.6 that seven out of nineteen NGOs are involved in some form of microcredit financing through SHGs. Self-help groups are a popular approach to microcredit financing that occurs in different states and regions of India.

Of seven NGOs, one has a savings group modeled on the Grameen structure, while others are hybrids of sorts. These differences are not significant and easily fall within the plurality of microcredit approaches. The various stages that microcredit financing groups go through lie on a continuum from pure microcredit financing where the focus is on getting group members access to credit, to credit for empowerment where the focus is on getting the poor to mobilize their own funds, building their capacities, and empowering them to leverage external credit. After group credibility is established by successfully completing a few cycles of mutual savings and credit, an external agency, like a bank, can be approached for additional capital (Gopalan, 2001). In some cases, the NGO functions as a bank to make additional capital available, or is willing to post collateral for the loan. In other cases, SHGs come together in a larger collective and assist each other with additional capital. Savings groups that fall under the Grameen model, however, follow an institutional route through which savings groups access more conventional bank loans.

Self-help groups, on the other hand, rely on many indigenous ways of establishing a savings and credit system. The SHG model is made up of autonomous groups that are able to gain access to large lending institutions by first capitalizing on group savings, each group making their own decisions on savings, loans, and other systemic policies. The informal modes of savings and credit systems become more formalized over time, especially when they link up with government organizations like NABARD (National Bank for Agriculture and Rural Development) (Fisher and Sriram, 2002: 107–109).

Despite the popularity of microcredit programs, only seven out of the nineteen NGOs were interested in providing programs related to microfinancing and credit for empowerment. Of these, five also promoted other forms of empowerment, such as political empowerment, which often took the form of educational programs for leadership training and campaigning for political office. Another five NGOs that did not involve themselves with microcredit were involved in political empowerment also using SHGs to promote awareness and leadership.

TABLE 3.6

NGOs Offering Microfinance and Political Empowerment

	Age (years)	Microfinance and other programs for financial independence	Services[a] political consciousness (PC), leadership training (LT), and election campaigning (EC)	Funding[b] membership (M); local funding (LF); foreign funding (FF)	Vertical integration of services	Impact
1	12	None	PC, LT and EC	FF	High	High
2	8	SHG for MC	None	LF	High	High
3	8	None	None	LF	Medium	Medium
4	6	SHG for MC	SHGs for PC	LF & FF	High	High
5	6	None	SHGs for PC	M	Medium	Medium
6	9	SHG for MC	SHGs for PC	FF	High	High
7	5	None	None	LF	High	High
8	5	Savings	None	M	Medium	Medium
9	6	None	None	LF	Medium	Medium
10	14	Saving groups	SHGs for PC	M, LF & FF	Medium	High
11	19	SHG for MC	PC, LT and EC	FF	High	High
12	15	None	None	M	Medium	Medium
13	37	None	None	LF & FF	High	High
14	11	None	None	M & FF	Medium	Medium
15	10	SHG for MC	PC, LT and EC	FF	High	High
16	19	None	SHGs for PC	FF	Medium	High
17	6	None	SHGs for PC	LF & FF	High	High
18	7	None	SHGs for PC	LF & FF	High	High
19	52	None	None	LF & FF	High	High

Notes: [a] Services: PC = political consciousness; LT = leadership training; EC = election campaigning
[b] Funding: M = membership dues; LF = local funding; FF = foreign funding

Thus, in all, just over half of the NGOs provided political empowerment through programs that used SHGs as a mechanism to raise awareness among women of their political rights and their opportunities to pursue those rights through elective office at the local level. One of the narratives that follow this chapter illustrates this: the story of Rahibai, who despite her lack of education, received help from an NGO to hone her leadership skills and consequently campaigned successfully to win a seat on the local panchayat.

What is interesting to note is that only half of the NGOs involved in SHGs for political empowerment were also participating in SHGs for microcredit financing. If SHGs have the structural formation that facilitates political empowerment, then why is this structure not used to facilitate women's economic well-being through gaining financial independence with microcredit and savings groups? It is likely that the risk involved in financial matters is a risk some NGOs do not wish to undertake. Furthermore, all saving groups and microcredit programs require extensive bookkeeping, collateral, and capital (financial and reputation), and NGOs may not have the capacity to invest in such efforts.

We have suggested that the adoption of a holistic perspective in the choice of programs serves to cater to the continued well-being of women in a community. The holistic approach addresses the needs of women on many fronts and helps them to develop themselves, gain self-confidence, and ultimately take more control of their lives. When programs that are pertinent to the social, economic, and political issues affecting women's lives can be offered simultaneously, women can build new competencies for best meeting a variety of their needs. For example, while a woman may first take advantage of a health program, she may soon be ready to move on to a microfinancing program, after which literacy may become relevant as she tries to work with institutions providing credit or merchandise.

We argue that the presence of SHGs for women's financial needs and political consciousness is an effective approach because it encompasses two key areas, financial and political, where women have been marginalized in comparison to their male counterparts. These two areas are by no means the holistic change we are arguing for, but are two instances of change that we consider important for women.

Self-help groups, in the process of helping women gain financial independence through a grass-roots approach, have succeeded in empowering women by building leadership skills and self-esteem that usually results from a successful financial enterprise. We do not believe that there are strong reasons that argue for women's financial independence to precede or follow political awareness. Some scholars argue that financial independence must precede other kinds of autonomy, and others argue that only after a woman is politically aware will she demand and gain financial independence (Goetz and Gupta, 1996; Hashemi et al., 1996; Rogaly, 1996). However, as stated earlier, financial and political empowerment are only two parts of an integrated approach that links other forms of empowerment through the availability of a variety of social programs such as literacy, gender programs, and health programs including reproductive health.

Proponents of programs limited to microcredit overlook components such as social and political consciousness-raising, literacy training, and skill development, and suggest that credit programs automatically empower women by strengthening their economic roles. By acting as catalysts in transforming the lives of women, minimalist microcredit programs are deemed sufficient enough to enhance the status of women and decrease their vulnerability to family violence and other domestic issues (Hashemi et al., 1996). Furthermore, minimalists suggest that even if women simply function as conduits to loan funds, a substantial effect on women's empowerment is achieved. Hashemi et al. (ibid.) present their findings on indices of empowerment for two such microfinanciers to prove the minimalist case. In this respect, microcredit purists argue that once the poor have cash, they can buy all the services they require (Rogaly, 1996).

Critics of minimalist programs have argued that holistic approaches involving strategies such as non-formal education as well as social and political consciousness-raising are necessary if women are to confront traditional patriarchal social structures. Furthermore, they say that programs simply offering credit cannot achieve this goal (Ahmed, 1982; Casper, 1994; Goetz and Gupta, 1996; Hasan, 1985; Nijera Kori, 1990; Rahman, 1986). Development practitioners, on the other hand, contend that the benefits derived from microcredit have been exaggerated, and many question the effectiveness of microcredit as a tool for sustained empowerment of women (Gopalan, 2001). In fact, much recent development literature suggests that the reverential attention paid to the 'sacred cow' of microcredit, the Grameen Bank, is a development mythology (Fisher and Sriram, 2002; Gopalan, 2001; Samuel, 1999).

We have tried to assess the viability of programs for financial empowerment, as well as programs for political autonomy, as if these programs were mutually exclusive. We have also tried to examine whether the presence of both programs allows for vertical integration, which in turn allows for a holistic perspective with greater impact. The reality is more nuanced. The manner in which microcredit is delivered through programs delimits what can be achieved. When the strategy stops at microcredit, then the focus is on delivering financial services to groups of poor women who tend to be good credit risks. Of course, the women learn to save and gain access to finance that was hitherto unavailable. However, the benefits to the women clientele often stop there and are sometimes dissipated through the patriarchal system wherein the male members of the family take advantage of a new found access to capital. When NGOs are involved in 'credit for empowerment', where the members of the group take the responsibilities and challenges of running their own programs, then this very process leads to autonomy, which the purely microcredit programs do not proffer. In addition, when a group of marginalized women get together and learn to mobilize their income, manage money, and rotate funds, they build their competencies and their opportunity to exercise control on their own behalf. These new skills and competencies can also be extended and applied to other areas of their lives. 'The capacities to manage financial resources and the confidence acquired through such activities become the basis for women's participation in numerous village development activities...they voice priorities in village assembly meetings and participate in village committees...' (Gopalan, 2001: 15).

Notwithstanding the debate in the literature regarding which should come first, financial or political empowerment, we believe that when microcredit is based on the model of 'credit for empowerment', then political and financial empowerment are mutually reinforcing . This results in a holistic approach that develops the capacities of women to exercise control over the economic, political, and social conditions of their lives.

Impact on Organizational Choices from a Gendered Perspective

Figure 3.1 explains how a gendered perspective gives rise to NGOs with a high-impact. To illustrate the relevance of this model we examined our data to see if organizational choices made on service delivery, choice of services, size of the organization or any other organizational characteristics that influence the impact of the NGO, is a function of the feminist ideology claimed by all of the founders in our study.

FIGURE 3.1

Model of NGOs with High Impact

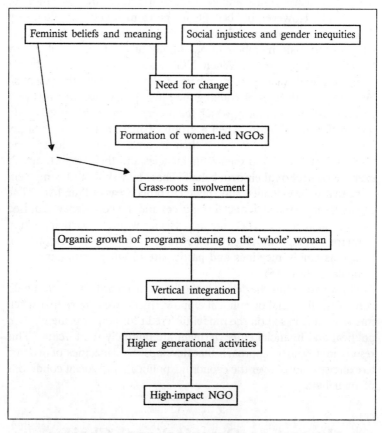

As we saw in the survey of the literature, female leadership is grounded in a gendered perspective. Women can easily empathize with the needs, spoken and unspoken, of other women. As many of our founders had come from family backgrounds where dinner table talk of social justice issues revolved around the injustices faced by women and other minorities, the understanding of the social and cultural realities their clients faced was not new. In fact, they were pursing their passion to bring social justice when they founded the NGOs. They were not government officials interested in development, nor were they outsiders or foreigners just trying 'to do good' in India. They felt connected to their 'sisters' and could fully empathize with the many injustices they experienced in their lives—poverty, domestic violence, subjugation—because of caste and male domination.

As one founder indicated, the reason for being in this 'business' is because she could feel the pain of her 'sisters'. Knowing the cultural and social backgrounds in which these injustices could flourish, she felt the urge to bring about change. She knew she was capable of initiating changes and could overcome traditional norms of patriarchy because she was a well-respected member of society with access to many resources. Our story about Sindhutai, the founder of the orphanage (discussed in Chapter One), is a case in point. Sindhutai had personally experienced many of the same injustices and could relate to the needs of women and understand the need for a variety of complementary services to be provided to children and mothers. Other founders said that their previous work with women had shown them that it was very important to provide an enabling environment if women were to make lasting changes in their lives.

In all the cases of the NGOs with vertically integrated services, the founders first started small, with one or two programs. Then in conversations with their clients, listening to their stories, and often seeking ideas from them at the grass-roots level, they were able to come up with other programs that enhanced their services to women. Most of these programs were structured in ways that provided easy access to local women. The NGO Annapurna is a case in point. Annapurna's founder insisted on it being located in the slums, amongst the women it served. In this way the organization, its director, staff and volunteers could tap into the pulse of daily life and thus better understand the needs and constraints of the local slum culture.

This also made it easier for the women they served to have access to their facilities. Medha Samant, the founder, also encouraged women from the slums to come to the NGO with their own ideas to further the work of the NGO. The founder made sure that she knew the people in the slums. On her way to work she would meet with the local business people to understand how they interacted with the slum women. She did this so she could find ways to ameliorate some structural inequities she encountered by providing women with loans at rates far below what local vendors charged. By approaching local businesses, Medha Samant was instrumental in not only helping the slum women but changing the attitudes of the mainstream businesses in the neighborhood.

At another NGO, we were told that when women came to health clinics for their children they were also interested in getting help with issues of family planning. As their husbands were not willing to encourage their wives in participating in issues related to family planning, women were able to access reproductive health clinics when combined with clinics for vaccination and other child-related health programs. As the founder of this NGO put it, there was no point in only helping with the health of children if the mothers were anxious about impending pregnancies and abortions. She understood how closely these issues were related being a mother herself. She was fortunate to have had support from her husband and other family members when making decisions about family planning. She also understood how a mother's health and psychological conditions are impacted with the uncertainty of unwanted pregnancies. This NGO went on to offer other related services for women and children, such as childcare, women's literacy, domestic abuse, spousal alcoholism, and awareness of their rights and protections. The NGO also later organized SHGs to help with women's economic independence.

Relative material deprivation occurs as a result of structural inequality and subordination, thus gender subordination and poverty are continuously reinforcing each other (Mayoux, 1995). By allowing women to access education related to their own health as well their rights and strategies in dealing with abuse, one other founder has leveraged the impact of the initial program on safeguarding children's mental health. She has also set up programs offering personality development, educational counseling, library facilities, as well as training programs that aimed to help children break the cycle of deprivation and poverty.

Another founder started a women's shelter after she encountered a single mother with children who sought help from an understanding family then experienced attempted molestation by the man of the house. Realizing that there must be other vulnerable women in this predicament she started a shelter for single mothers with children. Building on the needs of the women in the shelter this NGO went on to offer programs on violence prevention, health, and leadership training. We found that our women-led NGOs provided a bundle of integrated services to their clients as they found additional needs related to their experience of abuse, poverty, and subjugation.

We encountered a number of integrated services developed by NGOs that were not planned at the outset. Though these new services may appear to be ad hoc they are not. The concept of planned growth derives from the male model we have come to know as 'strategic planning' that is not necessarily embraced by women. Thus although the growth may appear ad hoc and not a result of formal planning, the women founder said that they relied on organic growth that came from participating and observing the field. This did not necessarily happen during planning meetings but often arose from conversations with clients and staff.

Furthermore, the founders were able to take their own experiences as women and relate it to their clients. This ability allowed them to know intuitively what the next service should be. Their intention was to leverage the existing programs and create new programs with better access to meet other critical needs of these women. Although it all happened organically, the underlying and overarching goal was that of empowering women.

Although this was not articulated as such, it was evident that many decisions on new services were made due to shared experiences of the women founders with their largely women staff. In many cases, the decisions were made by consulting women clients and listening to their stories of what was missing in their lives. Then they would ask them what was needed to enhance the initial benefits they were receiving. In one case, women were simply not able to access literacy classes because they had no access to childcare. It was not surprising that when the founders considered the childcare issue, many of them also had similar challenges in coming to work. It did not take long before they established a 'balwadi' (childcare facility set up to help the clients as well as the staff).

Conclusion

In our study of successful women-led NGOs, we examined whether certain patterns of impact, based on models proposed by Korten (1987) and Uvin et al. (2000), were exhibited. We found that the models proposed by both authors hold well. Services performed by the NGO follow the 'scaling up' of activities, which was reflected in their moving up the ladder of generational activities. Furthermore, the experience of the NGOs in our study also suggests an evolutionary scaling up through an increase in size, scope, and spatial coverage. Thus, we found a progressive trajectory of increasing social impact as NGOs moved from a lower level of generational activities to higher levels. This is achieved through moving from direct services that cater to immediate needs and empowering women, to advocacy aimed at the social development of women and the dissemination of new ideas through research and publications.

We note one important factor, 'vertical integration', that is evident in the NGOs that exhibit high levels of social impact. According to the models of 'scaling up' and 'generational activities', we should expect a change in the type of services, or an increase in the number of services provided, or the numbers of people served. While our data shows that this holds true, we also find that the services provided are vertically linked as well. There is a higher level of vertical integration among the NGOs that have increased their services, resulting in a higher impact. Vertical integration, we believe, contributes to the increasing effectiveness and impact of the range of services by using the synergies implicit in vertically-linked services. More importantly, we found that the provision of vertically-integrated services may reflect a gender bias. We posit this is true because feminist tendencies for social justice encompass all aspects of women leaders' lives. For example, they are not interested in seeing a woman become literate if she still faces domestic violence or vice versa. Thus, not surprisingly feminist women founders who firmly believe in social justice for women have provided services that cater to the 'whole woman'. More importantly, the programs chosen often complement each other so as take into consideration both forms of 'enabling environments'.

Our findings also suggest that the type of funding received by the NGO plays a role in scaling up and, therefore, increases the impact of the NGO on social development. Foreign funding has indirectly influenced the activities of the NGOs. Foreign funding sources that have been relatively stable have made it possible for NGOs to scale up the generational activity ladder, moving beyond the provision of direct services to activities such as networking, advocacy, and research.

In terms of organizational sustainability, we find that all NGOs with high levels of impact are at the third stage of organizational sustainability, none reaching the ultimate fourth stage. All the NGOs showing 'high' impact are either bureaucratic or hybrid, suggesting that the bureaucratic characteristics may help in achieving sustainability, and hence, impact. However, it is likely that bureaucratic features may develop in response to receiving foreign funding and increasing numbers of paid staff. These elements tend to make it possible to respond to needs characteristic of higher generational activity.

Increases in paid staff are seen in all but one of the NGOs; this may be a factor of growth in the number of services or the size of the clientele. However, we see no clear relation between levels of impact and the existence of paid staff, although the data do not rule out the possibility that NGOs with a 'high' impact have higher increases in paid staff than those with a 'medium' impact.

Finally, we find that our women-led NGOs are indeed sensitive to issues of power differentials amongst the workers and clients. To provide an enabling environment for their rural clients they include client participation in identifying their needs and suggesting solutions that work well for them. In the process, they are often able to encourage entire communities to participate and in that way take ownership of the new strategies or programs. As a matter of fact, one of the NGOs has wonderful documentation, both in English and Marathi, of efforts of tribal communities fostering grass-roots approaches to further women's education. Along the way they have compiled films, photographs of the process, and a resource booklet of the successful grass-roots strategies for functional literacy. They have been able to promote their approaches to education among other communities and NGOs. This facilitates the move from meeting the immediate needs of literacy to a higher level of generational activities, that is, networking and advocacy.

We find that our women-led NGOs are adopting a paradigm that encourages participation from the ground level. By allowing women at the grass roots to identify their own needs, these NGOs encourage and invite whole communities to participate in the ownership of programs that involve women suggesting ways in which they hope to meet their needs. In several of the NGOs, the founders remarked that all their efforts in dealing with women would come to naught unless their clients' spouses and other family members were involved. Especially in extended families, it was important that family members gave support to women's efforts to achieve financial and social independence. However, they also recognized that this would be difficult given the cultural and social norms. As a first step one of the NGOs invited husbands to programs that were family focused. Another NGO decided to help women by dealing with the prevalent alcoholism in the community by starting men's groups that focused on unemployment as well as alcoholism.

These and other programs helped to bring in other members of the community, hitherto excluded. One example illustrates the cooperation of men and women facilitated by the NGO that was very positive. In one village women complained that men were harassing and assaulting them as they went about their morning business in the fields. Several women, with the help of some workers from the NGO, went and complained to the police and did the same at town meetings. Because they went as a group and were accompanied by workers from the NGO, it was difficult to ignore their complaints. This resulted in a village-wide action in which men and women banded together to 'shame' men who had been assaulting and harassing women. With their support, women adorned the accused men with garlands of old shoes while the rest of the village jeered. This soon put a stop to the daily assaults and harassment.

In summary, we find that successful NGOs in our sample exhibit all of the features predicted in the literature. In addition, we find that the vertical integration of services, type of funding, and organizational structure are all features that are contributors to successful, high-impact NGOs. We also find that by adopting grass-roots approaches and including clients in searching for solutions, the NGOs follow the feminist principles of inclusion and equity. We posit this result may be particular to women-led NGOs which try to provide multidimensional strategies in providing enabling environments for women. Similarly, NGOs with access to stable sources of funding should show greater social impact as they proceed along the generational level activities with some security that their lower level generational activities are not at risk. Finally, the findings on the relationship of organizational sustainability through programmatic choices and deliberate organizational structures elaborated in Chapter Two give rise to NGOs that have the potential for sustained impact over the long run.

We conclude with a note of caution. With the current decline in foreign funding available to NGOs, the possibility of scaling up may be jeopardized, or at least compromised. Some see this change as a good thing (Edwards and Sen, 2000) because it may well herald the rise of genuine international cooperation and the decline of power inequities between the Northern and Southern NGOs. This seems to be a real possibility as we move away from the resource transfer paradigm. We wonder, however, if new patterns of resource transfer may expedite or impede the scaling up of NGOs. It is too early to tell and further research is needed as the typical patterns of funding from the North change.

The new patterns of resource transfer, advocated by Edwards and Sen (2000) as well as by Malhotra (2000), may bring about a climate of social justice, especially with careful attention to the financial stability of NGOs in the South. This could cultivate the benefits of the old paradigm within the new. A deliberate thrust to ensure that NGOs vertically integrate their services as they scale up, adding services such as credit for empowerment through SHGs to their range, will further increase the impact on social development.

Involving women at the grass-roots level not only leads to community involvement but it also allows NGOs to encourage women at the grass roots to identify their own needs and develop their own solutions. When such women are involved they take ownership of the process and this reinforces the need to stay involved. Moreover, it also allows for finding solutions that are grounded in the realities of the lives of poor women. This makes the solutions both cost effective and more acceptable. Policy makers in both donor and recipient countries can further aid in this by making certain that resource transfers are made with this in mind.

Narratives

Off the Beaten Path: Chaitanya

You would hardly imagine today that Sudha Kothari was once a rebellious adolescent. She comes from a well-to-do traditional Jain family in Pune. She was independent both in her thinking and spirit from a very early age. When she was thirteen years-old Sudha was concerned about what she saw as a significant contradiction between what religion taught her about life and what the societal norms seemed to be. She noticed that religion taught simplicity in all things. Society, on the other hand, taught that 'more is better'. She wondered why this was so. She felt peer pressure pushing her to conform to societal norms. This was particularly the case in what she was not allowed to do because she was a female. Why could she not participate in protest marches? Why could she not stand for election in college? Attend meetings that were held overnight and out of town? Why did she have to get married and not stay single?

Sudha rebelled in little ways at first, marching alone in a public demonstration at the age of sixteen. Then, when she was twenty, she was elected as a student representative at her college and wanted to organize a two-day program that involved an overnight stay. Her parents objected, as most traditional conservative Indian families would. It was simply not acceptable for her to be away overnight without an escort. Sudha was so angry about the injustice of this that she went on a fast until they relented. They finally did. Not long after that she also announced she would not marry, and she never did.

How did Sudha come by all of this strength and courage to stand up for herself and her beliefs at such a young age? She grew up in a strong spiritual environment and was troubled by society's rampant materialism and acquisitiveness even as a young girl. She joined an academy for education and youth services based on Gandhian principles, drawn to it for its beliefs in simplicity, social justice, and the equality of all people. She was drawn towards social action and the pursuit of social justice. Pursuing a Masters degree in Social Work at the Karve Institute seemed a natural choice after she finished college. Part of her degree program included a requirement for a field internship. She was thrilled as she was eager to learn how social needs in rural villages differed from those in cities. Her internship focused on youth and development with one of her projects helping to organize youth work camps.

She was surprised to discover she had a knack for organizing. As a result of her internship experience, Sudha later enrolled in a doctoral program to study more about youth and development, eventually changing her focus from youth to women. A few years later she made her own commitment to rural women's development and founded 'Chaitanya' with the assistance of Surekha Shrotriya.

During her work in the villages, Sudha became acquainted with women's associations—*mahila mandals*—that had been developed by the government. She, however, was disappointed to discover that these associations were largely inactive. The village women did not really understand their purpose and, therefore, had little incentive to attend the meetings. Sudha, on the other hand, saw them as potential foundations for empowerment. If there was a way to activate the *mahila mandals*, what would motivate the women to keep coming back and meeting on a regular basis? She realized the following:

(a) if the need is very great, people will come together to solve their problems;

(b) if people are provided opportunities and given positive feedback, their confidence will grow;

(c) if strong role models are provided, people will be moved to action; and

(d) if women are encouraged to decide for themselves and not ask permission from their husbands, their self-respect and self-confidence will grow.

These ideas, coupled with new opportunities created a fortuitous synchronicity for her. Sudha was a member of a local group that was concerned about a common action program among voluntary associations providing her with a chance to meet many people who were working in rural development across India. They inspired her to get more directly involved in rural development, especially women's development. She was invited to travel to other states, especially Andhra Pradesh, to see women's thrift groups, thrift cooperatives (essentially SHGs). These, Sudha could see, were the embryos of a women's empowerment movement. She wondered whether the floundering mahila mandals could become SHGs in rural Maharashtra. Could not a credit program provide the motivation for women to come together and keep coming together?

In 1989, she helped organize fourteen SHGs involving over 700 women in a savings project in the Chad District of Maharashtra. There had always been such groups for men, particularly through farm clubs, but there had never been any credit or bank programs available to women. When Sudha organized the SHGs, she started a thrift program hoping to create savings habits among the women. She encouraged them to save at least Rs 1 per week. After a year they had saved more than Rs 100,000. They were astounded at their own success and developed a new-found confidence in themselves. After this success, Sudha founded the NGO 'Chaitanya' because she realized that SHGs could be effective instruments of empowerment, which is what she wanted to focus on.

Chaitanya began building other programs that would use the SHGs for building trust among the women, teaching them the discipline of attending regular meetings, and helping them become effective decision makers. Chaitanya also taught SHG members the rules of credit processes so they could manage their savings and loans by themselves. As Chaitanya had hoped, SHG members began meeting on a regular basis and used meetings to talk about women's issues as well as credit. Often these discussions were about alcohol and domestic violence. They had never had a forum to discuss such issues together before. Their successes with coming together through micro savings programs made them realize that if they became powerful in one area of their lives, it was possible to become powerful in others as well. They began solving their family and village problems with collective confidence.

From knowledge about coming together through the savings processes, Chaitanya next began introducing SHG members to government officials at the panchayat, district, and state levels. They visited government offices, met and talked with the police and found out how political and judicial processes worked inside the villages and the district. The women continued to develop confidence because they began to understand how systems worked and how to use public channels for solving some of their problems.

The microfinance program[3] was an important building block for the fledgling Chaitanya, which formally registered in 1993 after four years of involvement with SHGs. In 1993, Chaitanya also helped build and register a federation, the Gramin Mahila Swayamsiddha Sangha (GMSS), to act as the Microfinance Organization (MFO) for the savings and credit program. It was an important step for Chaitanya to discover the power of microfinance to influence development through the establishment of SHGs. Sudha's purpose, however, was never to focus on a microfinance program for its own sake, but to use it as an instrument for empowerment. After the credit program came under the authority of the GMSS, she could focus on developing other programs that would build on the credit successes of the SHGs and empower women in other kinds of ways.

---

[3] For a more detailed account of microfinance projects, please see the microfinance cases discussed in the case studies on Chaitanya and the Annapurna Mahila Mandal.

Unleashing Resources:
Building Programs

Chaitanya developed its programs in a very deliberate way, beginning with helping organize SHGs. Chaitanya realized that while their primary focus was women's empowerment, SHGs might be the best vehicle for doing so. They knew that they had to tie economic development to women's social development in order to be successful. They used SHGs as their strategic approach to building women's emancipation. Once the GMSS was created and spun off, it provided Chaitanya the opportunity to build programs that would take advantage of the microfinance projects but not make microfinance their central concern. However, they have remained the principal promoter and trainer of the leaders of members of SHGs, but focused their efforts on the development of leadership and management skills, building legal and political literacy for women, offering health services, and training women to do sustainable organic farming.

Their three foundational strategies, which have been the basis of all program development, are helping groups organize (including other NGOs and grass-roots organizations as well as SHGs), providing graduated training programs, and creating collaborations and networks to build capacity. These foundational strategies have been assisted by their commitment to conducting research and applying their findings to practice and creating educational programs that are accessible to SHGs and NGOs working in rural areas. They do the latter through correspondence courses, which has been a recent development, with the collaboration of training institutes and colleges and universities.

With so many stable programs in place, with new additional programs simply building on existing ones, Chaitanya has progressed up the generational scale and is now involved in political advocacy. Chaitanya uses its own memberships on committees and organizations to create awareness and support for SHGs—and women's empowerment—in the public arena. Finally, Chaitanya is constantly finding ways to involve new groups in its work, groups who provide new capacity and groups that will eventually be in a position to carry out the work themselves.

For example, Chaitanya had established an internship program with the University of Minnesota in which undergraduate students come to India to work in Chaitanya's rural village programs. They also work with the University of Australia and are continuing to reach out to other colleges and universities whose students can benefit from their learning opportunities as well as contribute their ideas and volunteer activities to help Chaitanya accomplish its ambitious agenda. This is another example of its efforts to build and strengthen connections to resources.

In 2003, Chaitanya had a Women's Training Center on its agenda, as well as a new information center that would assist organizations and SHGs learn how to access the information they need from a distance. All of these programs were designed to enhance knowledge, understanding, build confidence, and independence.

Connecting Resources: Networks and Collaborations

Chaitanya's principal strategy for building women's empowerment is by creating and connecting resources. Its approach is to build strength in existing programs rather than create new ones. This is consistent with their basic philosophy to make existing groups work and to maintain simplicity. That is why, in the beginning, Sudha felt so strongly about using existing *mahila mandals* to form new SHGs. Using existing resources Chaitanya works to connect successful groups with NGOs so both benefit from sharing resources with each other. Creating networks and collaborations is the hallmark of Chaitanya's strategy for furthering women's empowerment. This approach is illustrated by the story of Ziya Sayyed and her organization SATH.

Ziya is a social worker from the Tata Institute who had just finished four years of relief and development work in Latur when she approached Chaitanya for assistance. She had been part of a large cadre of women's groups, grass-roots organizations, and NGOs that had come together to rebuild village communities after the Latur earthquake in 1993. She had experienced the effectiveness of capacity building through networks and collaborations and experienced the power of women working together in rebuilding Latur.

In 1997, she and a group of professionals, volunteers, NGOs, and grass-roots organizations came together to see if there was a way to pool and consolidate their resources and create a more permanent organization. They called it SATH (Social Action for Transformation and Harmony). By the time Ziya approached Chaitanya, SATH had already finished a process of identifying possible collaborators that focused on women and children. Finally eight NGOs, with experience in microfinance, formed the SATH collaborative and Ziya became its executive director. She approached Chaitanya for advice about how to work together most effectively for the empowerment of children and women. The SATH collaborative wanted to be self-sufficient and not dependent on other organizations. Chaitanya helped SATH get linked to UNICEF for funding. As a result of Chaitanya's intervention, SATH received a grant for community action projects that helped them to establish more grass-roots organizations in remote villages of Maharashtra.

By 2003, SATH had helped start 300 SHGs with 6,000 members and returned to Chaitanya to ask for assistance in training their 300 SHG group leaders. Chaitanya has been providing that program, including training on leadership, community worker education, and management training. They have also helped SHG group members with job training, mentoring, and employment skills that promote their economic independence.

Chaitanya, however, is not just the provider of services in this relationship; it also receives benefits making it a win-win relationship. Chaitanya benefits because it is able to extend its reach into new communities, and SATH helps them to recruit new grass-roots workers for those communities. SATH clearly benefits from the relationship not only because Chaitanya provides it with training and information, but Chaitanya also connects SATH with its own network of resources, including funders and educational institutions. SATH also extends its expertise in microplanning in the field area served by Chaitanya.

The story of SATH is just one illustration of the many ways in which Chaitanya builds networks and connections. In addition, Chaitanya distributes monthly bulletins on the work it is doing throughout the state so that all the organizations and groups in its network can benefit from each others work. It shares its research, manuals, and publications, teaching videos and other educational materials through the networks as well. Finally, Chaitanya has built networks of connections with government agencies, policy makers, major funders, universities, training institutes, and advocacy organizations that can become resources to share with other network members.

Chaitanya believes that its mission is to build a network that helps rural grass-roots organizations gain social recognition, credibility and status that can position them for financial support. Organizations like SATH also receive training and training materials because of Chaitanya's extensive training resources. For Chaitanya, collaborating with organizations like SATH means that they empower and strengthen other organizations that are working directly with rural villagers on women's empowerment.

Creating New Knowledge

Chaitanya is always discovering and implementing new ways to strengthen women's development programs. In addition to their on-going creation and revision of training programs, they currently plan to create a new women's health program, providing education through the existing SHGs. They are developing an information counseling center that will teach women, grass-roots organizations, and other NGOs in their network to learn how to access information sources that will contribute to their continuing development.

We asked Sudha if this meant that Chaitanya was becoming a behemoth as it continued to create new programs and broadening its own reach. Was this expansion contradicting its basic philosophy about simplicity, flexibility, and responsiveness? How could Chaitanya avoid getting bogged down in its own growth? She replied, 'We will not get too big because we continue to work primarily through our networks and balance how much we do. We will always do training and continue to build relevant and responsive training programs. But most of our work is about helping others strengthen themselves and build their capacity to be effective. We do that through our networks and collaborations. Our job is to be effective catalysts, facilitators, promoters and connectors and to stay as simple and lean as we can'.

Sudha feels that Chaitanya has a full future agenda. There is much more to do. 'Sometimes I wonder if Chaitanya has focused too many years on the SHGs and microfinance and not enough time with other programs of empowerment. On the other hand, I also know that social development goes hand in hand with economic development. Our philosophy and beliefs have always shaped both our direction and actions. We plan to build—and build on the strengths of others to accomplish our goals. We are not led by programs but rather by our commitment to developing people'.

Commentary

Chaitanya, a Sanskrit word for 'consciousness and life bubbling with spirit and energy', could not be a more apt descriptor of Chaitanya, its managing trustee, Dr Sudha Kothari, and the staff. Chaitanya is a powerful platform for social change and the economic independence of women. Their work is already highly visible and respected for the gains made in removing the power imbalance of women in their families, households, and villages. Always looking to the future, Chaitanya continues to build training programs that build capacity in the SHGs and the organizations that work with them. They plan to develop a women's resource and training center in the near future. They are expanding their research agenda to include monitoring and evaluation of all of their programs for continuous program improvement. As Sudha has indicated, on more than one occasion, Chaitanya works very hard at being a learning organization. As part of that 'continuous improvement' agenda, Chaitanya is committed to what it calls the 'convergence of various services' through people's institutions to ensure integrated development.

In some ways, Chaitanya is different from the other organizations and case studies we have included in this research. Chaitanya is less about delivering direct services to clients than it is about acting as a catalyst, connector, facilitator, teacher, promoter, and supporter of organizations that are providing direct services. The context for measuring its social impact is to consider the audience it serves, which are organizations and groups who are collaborators or members of its vast network. Chaitanya provides education, training, and counseling through its networks. All of its programs fall in the category of generational level two, four, and five. It helps develop the capacity of SHGs and NGOs in its network to develop their own capacity so they are more capable to look after their group or organizational needs. Theirs is a formation of a complex web of organizations and resources. It includes SHGs, cluster groups, grass-roots organizations, and NGOs as well as funders, universities, elected officials, and governmental agencies.

Finally, they are actively engaged in research and its application to practice. Their research findings are made available through monthly bulletins, training manuals, curricula, and audio-visual materials as well as through articles and books. Their research is used to monitor and evaluate the effectiveness of all of their programs providing them continuous feedback and the opportunity to make improvements on an ongoing basis. This is testimony to their performance at high levels of generational activity.

Since 1989, Chaitanya has significantly increased the numbers and types of programs and activities it engages in. It has extended its spatial reach to eight districts in the state. This growth is consistent with the measures of scaling up in our research. Because their principal strategy is to work through collaborations and networks, they have been able to broaden their indirect impact as well. Another dimension reflecting scaling up is an organization's financial stability and its participation in foreign funding schemes. On this dimension Chaitanya also receives high marks. More than 49 per cent of its revenues now come from its training programs and publications. Other support comes from local corporations and individual donors, government support, and from international funders.

Finally, there is considerable evidence when we take a look at the number and kind of programs that Chaitanya has built over the years, that their programs are vertically rather than horizontally connected. Each of Chaitanya's programs is designed to build on the success of the ones that have come before, providing the opportunity for SHGs and other organizations in its network to continue to develop themselves. For example, Chaitanya began its programs with a simple thrift program offered through SHGs. Then it built on the success of that program to include other microfinancing schemes. As those successes resulted in SHG members developing greater confidence in themselves, Chaitanya began introducing other training and skill development that would build their capacity for taking charge of their lives. A case in point is their work to introduce SHG members to government officials and politicians so that they could better understand the public systems that so affected their lives in their villages. They learned about their local and district governments and what they needed to know in order to stand for election to the panchayat raj.

In more recent years, Chaitanya has expanded its training programs to include reproductive health and nutrition education through helping women establish kitchen gardens and develop skills in organic farming. Chaitanya has consistently used a thoughtful and deliberate 'building block' approach to program development and expansion, a strong measure of high vertical integration and a significant predictor of high social impact. While Chaitanya clearly offers programs, they fall in the category of supportive group development, NGO development, institutional development and are available to all who can benefit and who are interested and involved in issues of women's empowerment in rural communities.

Chaitanya acts as a network creator and a facilitator of collaborations, thereby building the capacity of networked organizations to be effective in building strength in their own organizations as well as in their work with SHGs.

Chaitanya is now 15-years-old and has expanded the reach of its programs and influence. It has religiously stuck to its founding principles to maintain a simple structure and has not unnecessarily duplicated the programs of others. It has also adhered to its original strategies to improve women's development. They have provided opportunities for women to develop confidence with positive feedback; they have provided strong role models who can motivate women and organizations to move forward and take action; and they have created programs that have helped women and organizations develop confidence and the means to take charge of their lives.

Harmonious Communication: Susamvad

Social Equality in Families: A Prevention Approach

From the beginning the founders of Susamvad, Prasanna Invally and Sadhana Khati, had a vision and a dream for a new approach to building harmony in families. Their vision, even before they had a specific program in mind, was to create a prevention program, one that anticipated gender inequality in families before problems became crises. That prevention program, they dreamed, would build more democratic and harmonious relationships in families and society.

Both founders came from professional upper middle-income families. Prasanna's mother was a doctor and she often accompanied her to work as a child and noticed her mother's dedication to her patients. Prasanna thought about becoming a doctor after she saw poor patients having trouble finding doctors. However, she also became acquainted with young slum children and developed a compassion for the poor and that motivated her to go into social work, a decision strongly supported by her parents. She earned her Masters degree in social work from Nirmala Niketan, Mumbai, and stayed on to work in Mumbai for eight years, seven of those as the founder of a children's pre-school. She then moved to Pune and joined the Karve Institute as a marriage and family counselor.

Susamvad's other founder, Sadhana Khati, came from a family of social activists. She participated in public demonstrations or 'morchas' even as a pre-teen. She was 15-years-old when she participated in a Nari Samata Manch-organized 'morcha' to protest for justice. Then as an undergraduate college student, she met and worked with Vidya Bal,[4] who at that time was an editor of *Stree*, a women's magazine. Sadhana pursued her own interest in social justice issues by enrolling in a Master's degree in social work program as well. Both she and Prasanna worked at the same social organization and there developed a close friendship. They had hoped to put their academic theories to work in practice but became disappointed when that did not happen. They simply could not meet their clients' needs in a timely way. There were too many policies, procedures, and rules in government agencies and large social organizations that stood in the way of providing important assistance to people when they needed it most. People's crises became case files that gathered dust on desks and in file cabinets. By the time they received attention, the crises had long since occurred.

Prasanna and Sadhana especially objected to responding to crises using strategies aimed at fixing or repairing situations already gone badly. They dreamed of solving issues before they became major problems and people suffered. They were interested in prevention not intervention. This prompted them to leave their positions and establish their own organization in 1996, dedicated to creating peace and

---

[4] Vidya Bal later became a founder of the Nari Samata Manch (See Chapter Two).

harmony in families and society. They wanted their organization to be small and flexible. They wanted to prevent crises from happening by providing front-end services, through dialogue, education, counseling, and training programs.

Aspirations Without a Plan

They chose the name Susamvad as the name of their organization. It means 'harmonious communication'. They began without any funds but with the support of family and friends. They formally registered Susamvad in 1996 with a mission of peace and harmony. Their mission was based on principles of democracy, equality for all, fraternity, and freedom in society. Its goal was to promote and enhance democratic relationships and ensure non-violation of human rights by way of dialogue, confrontation, and social action. When they started Susamvad, the two founders had a long list of objectives:

(a) to organize, conduct, promote, assist, sponsor, and understand programs for the welfare of all sectors of society, for the purpose of enhancing the quality of marital, parental, and human democratic relationships;

(b) to undertake and promote activities for gender justice;

(c) to conduct and organize training, research, counseling, and other demonstration activities that would increase understanding of human democratic relationships;

(d) to collect, compile, and publish data, reports, and books as well as develop audio-visual aids, materials, and other media to publicize and promote other issues that influence human behavior and relationships;

(e) to liaison with policy makers, the government, NGOs, and national and international bodies in order to streamline and strengthen existing programs as well as financial and material resources; and

(f) to promote value systems essential for humane, equitable, and sustainable development of society.

These were lofty objectives for an organization that had neither funding nor outside support to initiate any programs. They and members of the board, however, shared common values, understood the needs of society, and had a commitment. They moved forward despite these obstacles. They knew what to do.

Creating Programs

Their first program was called a 'Dialogue for Harmony.'[5] This was a natural beginning for Susamvad because it aimed to promote democratic, humane, and egalitarian relationships through communication. Prasanna and Sadhana hoped this program would be a platform for people to discuss and debate the democratic elements of various kinds of relationships, especially within marriage and family. It was also a difficult way to begin. How do you build a generalized educational forum not targeted to any specific audience and make it work? Developing a more democratic and humanistic society through educational dialogue was a difficult—and perhaps a naive first step. It seemed replete with a generational idealism not grounded in reality. Somehow their doggedness to move forward—and identify individuals, groups, businesses, government agencies, and community organizations to participate in their forums—worked over time. It took a full year for them to get started.

Eventually, community centers, colleges, grass-roots NGOs, government training institutes and others began calling them to put on customized dialogue sessions and issue-focused trainings for their students, members, and clients. Eight years later, they have been widely recognized and respected for their Dialogue for Harmony program. It is their foundational program to create awareness about human rights and rights of the marginalized, backward, suppressed, and vulnerable sections of the society (Susamvad, 2002: 8). Through Samvaad (Dialogue for Harmony), Susamvad has offered a wide range of topics and training on issues, including building healthy pre-marital and marital relationships, the role of professional counselors in discord and domestic violence cases, family health and nutrition, law and human rights, responsible parenthood, and adolescent education.

The Dialogue for Harmony program has been successful, and in retrospect, was a good way for Susamvad to try out its ideas and

---

[5] This program is called Samvaadaatun Susamvaad (harmonious dialogue in Marathi).

become visible in the community. Since 1997, the Dialogue for Harmony program has served more than 2,100 women and men. It is still offered in Pune and eight other localities. Susamvad has created three additional major programs that have become umbrellas for a host of projects that continue to multiply, not only in Pune but many rural areas as well.

In 1998–99, they started the 'Dialogue' program[6] that provides face-to-face professional counseling on relational issues involving marriage, in-laws as well as domestic violence, legal, and women's rights issues. This program is not provided by Susamvad alone, but rather by a multidisciplinary network that supports it and provides a channel for women to seek their rights and ask for justice. The Dialogue program provides both preventive as well as remedial counseling. As this program has continued to grow, it offers legal and psychological counseling through professional networks. Between its inception and 2002, Samvaad has handled 250 cases (Susamvad, 2002: 10).

Susamvad established a 'Child and Adolescent' program—also known as the 'Experiential Learning'[7] program from 1999–2000. There are eight different projects under this umbrella that include both prevention and intervention programs. Using experiential learning as a strategy to create learning opportunities, it targets underprivileged and vulnerable groups of children including adolescent school drop-outs from low socio-economic communities. They started this program with the 'Pragati Group', a project serving adolescent girls in a slum area. Because these girls showed a high dropout rate in school, Susamvad created the project to help them develop psychologically and socially, and acquire vocational and literacy skills. Susamvad wanted to prepare these adolescent girls with the means to generate independent incomes for themselves.

The child and adolescent program also addresses a number of other critical issues including child rights, the empowerment of girls and adolescents, and education completion. In the future they intend to create adolescent SHGs and children's clubs in order to make this program self-sustaining.

In 1999–2000, Susamvad created its fourth major program, 'Journey Towards Lifelong Companionship'.[8] This is also a youth program

---

[6] The program is known as Samvaad (literally dialogue) in Marathi.

[7] This program is known as Swaanubhav (literally experiential learning) in Marathi.

[8] This program is called Pravaas Sahajeevanaacha (literally journey towards lifelong companionship) in Marathi.

that helps prepare young people for marriage. As Susamvad describes it in their five-year report, 'Journey' is designed to create an inquiry and dialogue around the concept of marriage. Aimed at people of marriageable age, the program addresses issues about self, role stereotypes, expectations, partnerships, and sexuality. It also includes legal education concerning marriage registration, child marriages, and forced marriages. More than 1,800 young people have participated in this program since it was started in 1999 (Susamvad, 2002).

In the beginning, Susamvad said it was committed to prevention rather than intervention. The development of these major programs reflects that commitment. At the same time, when crises happen Susamvad has not sidestepped undertaking the necessary intervention. They have developed a counseling center both for prevention and intervention and staffed it with professionals. Furthermore, they have developed a broad network of professionals with a range of specializations in order to be able to help their clients with their particular needs.

Sakhi: A Telephone Helpline

In 2000, Prasanna applied for and received a two-year leadership development grant from the John T. and Catherine D. MacArthur Foundation to initiate a telephone helpline[9] on a pilot basis. This project has provided access to counseling for women, including crisis counseling for women who wish to remain anonymous. As a result of the provision for anonymity, the helpline has opened up counseling to the upper and middle classes as well as to the poor. During the two-year pilot period, many callers have needed only one call. Others have had an ongoing telephone counseling relationship with Susamvad, some never revealing their identities.

The statistics that Susamvad has been keeping along with their case notes suggest that the helpline has been very successful in meeting the needs of many callers and that it can prevent a crisis before it happens. Many callers have chosen to see a professional in Susamvad's counseling center, while others have taken advantage of the telephone referral service, connecting them to a host of other professionals. Over

---

[9] This project, known as Sakhi in Marathi, is part of the 'Dialogue' program.

the two years of the pilot project, Susamvad has recorded nearly 2,000 calls and has provided direct service to over 700 individuals.

One of those helped through the telephone helpline was Jai.[10] We had the opportunity to interview Jai and meet her five children. Her eldest daughter came in wearing the traditional dress of a new bride. Her hands still showed the henna designs from her recent wedding.

We learned that Jai first came to Susamvad through the helpline at the urging of her eldest daughter. She was married for twenty-four years, to a man who abused her almost from the beginning. He would disappear for a week at a time, gambling and drinking away all of his earnings. Jai had to rely on her parents to support her for seventeen years, covering the expenses of running her household and schooling her children. When her eldest daughter was 11-years-old she had to leave school because there was no more money to pay the fees. She stayed at home for a number of years caring for her younger siblings.

The situation with her father grew worse and worse as she witnessed him beating her mother, sometimes threatening her with a knife, and driving her away from home. All of the children saw this happening and were constantly afraid. When the eldest daughter reached a marriageable age, her young suitors would disappear after seeing that her father was an abusive alcoholic. She had no prospects of finding a husband as long as she lived at home. So she left and moved in with a kind family that provided her room and board. She began working as a housekeeper for four different families so that she could send money home to her mother and siblings. When the violence escalated to a dangerous level and her brothers and sisters were threatened, she was able to persuade her mother, Jai, to seek help from Susamvad through the telephone helpline.

When Jai finally developed the courage to contact Susamvad, she had already filed complaints with the police, but they took no action against her husband. She did not want him put in jail, which she could have done under a recent law, because that would mean her husband would lose his job and have no means to support her and the children. Susamvad helped her through counseling and also intervened with the police. They found her a temporary shelter at a short-stay home, so that she and the children would be safe from her husband. They continued to provide counseling and helped her develop self-confidence and find employment while the children were in school.

---

[10] Name changed to protect identity of the individual.

Jai now rents a small apartment and pays the rent with her earnings from household work. Her husband has also come in for counseling at Susamvad and no longer abuses Jai, but Jai does not plan on returning home with him. Jai says she feels more self-confident and is happy that she will be able to pay for her children to complete their education.

Our second story is about 'Rali',[11] a 35-years-old woman, who has been divorced for the last five years. Over that time she resided in a slum area with her three children. She made a living as a housemaid. She received no help from her family because she started living with a man out of wedlock and this was wholly unacceptable to her family. After she moved in with 'Yurii', she discovered that he was addicted to drugs and alcohol. He began to abuse her, especially if she did not give him money or refused to have sex with him. She finally left 'Yurii', but he found her and harassed and threatened her on a regular basis also causing problems for her neighbors. They were troubled by the shouting and quarreling and wanted Rali to move away. But she had nowhere to go and did not know how to get out of the abusive relationship.

Rali found Susamvad's helpline phone number and called for help. She wanted to stop the abuse, she did not want to move, and she did not know what to do. Susamvad helped her figure out her options and provided support and encouragement, working with her over the phone to identify her own strengths and attributes that would help her have the courage to escape the situation. Rali was scared, ashamed, and consumed by guilt for living in this illicit relationship. She thought that this abuse was what she deserved. It took her some time, using only the helpline, to develop the courage and resolve to go to her employer, the neighbors, and the police to help her. She finally confronted Yurii and forbade him to come to her house. Her neighbors began helping her, realizing that she did not want to be in this relationship. They no longer asked her to leave. The police also helped. They found and arrested Yurii. Now Rali feels that she can take charge of her life and turn it around. She is confident that she now has got out of a cycle of abuse that began with Yurii and move on with her life. Now she is even helping her sister recover from a crisis of her own, having referred her to Susamvad as well.

Rali was one of Susamvad's anonymous callers. She never revealed her identity and never came in for counseling. Susamvad counselors

[11] Names have been changed to protect the identity of the individuals.

helped her to solve her own problems by working with her over the phone. This took eight sessions. It is unlikely that Rali would have sought any help at all had she not been able to access these services anonymously.

The story of Susamvad goes on. While the founders remain idealistic, they have taken pains to plan their future in strategic ways. They know what they want to do and they learn how to get there. They are applying for and receiving many grants to support a thoughtful expansion, all the while mindful of maintaining their flexibility and responsiveness to changing needs and new opportunities.

Commentary

Susamvad is a young organization (only 8-years-old in 2003), with young and idealistic founders. Susamvad developed very organically as did many of the other NGOs in our study. But what is particularly interesting, among other things, is that the founders took an idea and a very lofty set of objectives without a specific long-range plan and have quite systematically put their ideas in place. Susamvad now has four principal umbrella programs with multiple projects under each of them. They operate in multiple sites in Pune as well as in rural areas.

If we trace its program development, Susamvad has put into place all of the key elements that ultimately contribute to an organization having a high social impact. Beginning with Dialogue for Harmony, its very first program, Susamvad has been successful in reaching more than 2,000 people through public platform discussions. It has created a program that prods individuals and groups in corporations, schools, training institutes, and universities to reflect and change their thinking and behavior about equal rights of women and men. Unlike many NGOs in our study, Susamvad started with a broad awareness program rather than a specific service program, which is common among start-up NGOs. The awareness program is an educational one, a level three activity on the generational scale. If high generational activity is about having far-reaching effects in promoting social change and development, Susamvad launched its efforts at a high level from the very beginning.

Another characteristic of high social impact relates to scaling up. As Susamvad began developing its programs and projects, it expanded

them to multiple sites, both inside and outside Pune. It also increased
the kind and number of activities it was involved in, including both
direct and indirect services, but it has intentionally avoided putting too
many direct service projects in place. By direct service we mean
providing immediate welfare relief. We might say that their face to
face counseling service is direct as well as their provision of short-stay
shelters, but the latter is accomplished through their referral program.

For the most part, Susamvad has focused on programs that provide
education and training. It has created a broadbased network of professional services, linking people to important resources they might
need to address family problems. This not only keeps Susamvad from
replicating services provided by other NGOs, it has provided its clients
with the power to access what they need on their own. The network,
therefore, has become a tool of empowerment for its users.

In addition to its education, training, counseling, and referral programs, Susamvad is conducting research and disseminating results,
making them widely available to public educators, counselors, students, professionals, and volunteers. From the beginning Prasanna
and Sadhana had a commitment to research of a specific kind. They
were interested in research that applied theory to practice. So Susamvad
publishes its findings mostly in the form of articles, new curricula,
training material, manuals and practical books. While they disseminate their publications broadly, they are especially helpful to the staff
and volunteers who work in its many projects.

The stories we have included here provide evidence of the impact
of Susamvad's programs at an individual level. In the story of Jai,
Susamvad helped her through several programs, each building on new
needs as they emerged through their hotline and counseling sessions.
In addition to the helpline and counseling, Jai took advantage of
Susamvad's legal assistance project and network referral system. The
latter led to her securing short-term shelter for herself and her two
youngest children.

All of these services have helped Jai create a new, safe, and hopeful
future for herself and her children. She now enjoys new confidence
and has experienced freedom for the first time in twenty-four years.
Looking back at the important factors that contribute to high social
impact in NGOs, Susamvad's counseling, referral, and advocacy programs have clearly contributed to Jai's empowerment.

According to its 2002 report, Susamvad is moving into the future
with an ambitious agenda. That agenda, while it will result in adding

new programs, has been conceived and designed for high social impact. In its recent five year report (Susamvad, 2002), Susamvad decribed its plan for creating a comprehensive pre-marriage education program. They would include all of the following projects: counseling; group education for parents; handling issues and advocacy; workshops for training and dissemination, enhancement of expertise; documentation, research, publications, and manuals, linking and establishing nodal centers at the community level; and group education of youth.

This vast network of interconnecting activities reflects the essential elements of high social impact as reported in our research. These programs are vertically integrated and scaled up. They include all five levels of generational activity. The pre-marriage education program is just one of several future projects that Susamvad has on its drawing board. Others include the development of a crisis intervention and therapy center, a short-stay shelter, children's clubs, and adolescent resource centers. They are also clear about wanting to become more involved in direct advocacy work in the near future.

Armed with a vision and inspirational objectives, Susamvad has continued over time to develop programs for high social impact. It seems to have done so intuitively, organically, and with careful planning. While Susamvad has expanded its number of programs and has become involved with foreign funders, it has still avoided building up a large staff and a bureaucratic structure. It continues to operate as a collective pragmatic organization motivated by high commitment to shared beliefs and values. And its sustainability does not seem to be in question.

Microfinancing: Chaitanya

Organizing, Activating, and Empowering

Alkabai is 53-years-old and beginning to grey. She is a widow who single-handedly brought up four children. She assumed all of the duties and responsibilities of the household, providing financial support and making all of the decisions about the children's schooling, care, and family life in the village. These are traditionally roles and activities of husbands and fathers. She had no choice, of course. Nonetheless she wears her independence as if it had come as a birthright.

In order to support her extended family, including the in-laws of one of her married children, Alkabai works hard from 6 am until 11 pm. In the early morning she tends the farm animals and then prepares the food for the entire family for the day ahead. Then she goes off to work as an anganwadi[12] until mid-afternoon, returning home to once again care for the farm animals and prepare the evening meal, which normally begins around 9:30 pm. Alkabai usually retires at 11 pm and then starts all over again early the next morning.

While Alkabai's life might differ from other women living in the village of Akarwadi, she shares their concerns and their position within the community because she is a woman. She wanted the opportunity to participate in a group of women from her own village who gathered on a regular basis. They met to talk about family issues. Therefore, when she met Dr. Sudha Kothari, founder of the NGO Chaitanya, in 1986, and heard about the SHG movement she wanted to organize one for her own village. She found out that Dr. Kothari was the leader of the movement that introduced SHGs in the state of Maharashtra. Could Dr. Kothari and Chaitanya help her to organize an SHG in her own village? With Chaitanya's help, she was able to do so in 1993. Alkabai has remained the leader and organizer of the SHG 'Amar'[13] in her village of Akarwadi ever since.

The primary thrust of the SHG movement all over India was to create women's savings through a microfinance program that encouraged women to save their money in a systematic way. If successful, the women would have more funds available to meet the needs of their families. In the beginning, Amar members, like other SHGs, were asked to save Rs 1 a week. Alkabai felt this was not very significant. How could Rs 1 a week make a difference in anyone's life? However, when Amar's members began saving Rs 10 a month, members found that the amount really did make a difference in meeting family needs, especially for school tuition and health services. An important side

---

[12] A person responsible for providing prenatal and postnatal education to women, and preschool education to children under a central government scheme for rural areas.

[13] Amar means 'to live forever' in Marathi.

benefit of the savings program, just as Chaitanya and Alkabai had hoped, was that women came together on a regular basis and discussed other issues of concern besides financial ones.

From its modest but successful beginning, Amar began increasing its savings so that it could begin to use the group's accumulating capital for intra-group loans. The members developed rules for lending with assistance from Chaitanya fieldworkers who also helped them understand the important elements of a lending program: Chaitanya also provided help in answering some of the difficult questions members would have to answer in making lending decisions. For example, (i) how would members decide if the requests were reasonable and the amounts acceptable? (ii) how would the group decide, with limited capital, who most needed the loan? (iii) who would keep track of the amount of money that they would be able to loan to other members? (iv) how would they make a decision to say *yes* or *no* to the loan requests? and, (v) what if there were a number of reasonable and acceptable requests but they did not have enough money to meet all the requests of their members? Through a carefully designed training program, Chaitanya provided education and information in microfinance matters to help Amar and many other SHGs in Maharashtra. Locally-based fieldworkers from Chaitanya remained close to the SHGs to help them become successful and build the self-confidence of SHG members.

As their SHG became more successful in its savings program, Amar heard about the GMSS federation in Rajgurunager. The GMSS federation acted as a financial intermediary for SHGs providing financial leverage to their modest capital assets. Self-help groups could increase their lending capacity 700 times if they borrowed through the federation. This made it possible for Amar and other SHGs to meet larger needs among families and within their villages as well. When Amar was six-months-old, it was eligible to become a member of the GMSS federation. It was a big step. Members of Amar were skeptical about the federation's trustworthiness, just as they had been initially skeptical about their own members' trustworthiness. How did Amar know if its own members would repay their loans? How did they know if GMSS would not somehow cheat them or charge them unreasonable fees for borrowing? Of course, GMSS might have had the same questions and misgivings about Amar's creditworthiness. One of the hallmarks of GMSS, however, was that it was governed by SHG members through their cluster groups.

It is not surprising that issues of trust came up within SHGs themselves as they took on this new enterprise. They knew and understood so little about it. Would everyone pay back her loan? This was a shared concern within and across SHGs as they initiated lending programs for the first time. Amar, like other groups, need not have worried since they found that peer pressure, peer support, and peer solidarity were strong forces that could be counted on to guarantee that all members—and Amar itself—would always repay their loans. It was a matter of honor and self-respect.

Using Amar as an example of the success of SHGs, the story of Amar's enterprises has been impressive. Members of Amar have benefited in many ways because of the possibilities presented by their SHG program. They have borrowed money for seeds, grains, maintaining cows as well as for paying wages to farm worker, whom they often needed to provide additional help for managing their farms. On a different front, they used SHG funds to pay college admissions fees for their children—higher education had become a new priority in their villages as well as across India.

As Chaitanya and other SHG supporters hoped, SHG members have gone beyond meeting personal and family needs. Amar members, for example, have helped construct a new road in Akarwadi. They have financially supported a latrine project in partnership with the village. This has had a broad community impact. While men in Akarwadi still have some resentment about the power of Amar as well as the members' new-found independence, their attitudes have moderated somewhat because they and their village have benefited in so many ways. Families have additional disposable income and the village has begun to develop more infrastructure.

The leadership of Amar, however, has not changed. Alkabai has continued to be the one responsible for keeping the SHG going. Members still meet at her home. As organizer and leader she is the one who shoulders the burden of keeping the accounts, ensuring meeting attendance, and monitoring compliance with GMSS procedures and regulations. Sometimes she is resented for her power, however, no one else is willing to assume the group's leadership. Alkabai feels Amar is so important to the village—and to her personally—that she is willing to endure criticism from time to time. One source of resentment towards Alkabai is due to the perception that she has personally benefited a lot due to her leadership of Amar. Since 1993, for example, Alkabai has increased her own family's income from Rs 4000 to more than Rs 10,000 a year. However, Alkabai says that with her growing family and farm expenses, even Rs 10,000 is not enough. She also plans to start a new family enterprise and will need to borrow through Amar and GMSS to finance it.

There have been other benefits besides financial ones since Alkabai helped organize Amar. As the leader of Amar she speaks at the cluster meetings; she attends village council meetings; she speaks at quarterly school board meetings; and she frequently travels outside her village—alone—to conduct Amar's business matters. There is local resentment about that. Women still encounter resistance to attending meetings at night so for a woman to travel outside the village without the escort of a man—son, brother, husband, father, or uncle—is especially frowned upon. After the loss of her husband, Alkabai had to become independent in order to take care of her family. Nevertheless, her independence was certainly atypical in Akarwadi. Until she helped organize Amar, however, she had no opportunity to increase her family's income, obtain education and training, or develop her leadership skills to assist her family and village. Alkabai is grateful for all of these opportunities. As she says, to use a familiar Marathi expression, 'depending on the size of the blanket, you extend your legs'. Alkabai has made that blanket bigger not only for herself, but also for Amar and Akarwadi.

Chaitanya's Role as Promoter, Supporter, and Trainer

In the last ten years, Chaitanya has been recognized as one of the most outstanding agencies in Maharashtra for its role in organizing and promoting the SHG movement. When it began its work in the late 1980s, Chaitanya saw SHGs as a vehicle for bringing women together, providing them with an opportunity to taste success, and to use that success as a building block towards their empowerment. Chaitanya, and particularly its founder Dr Sudha Kothari, felt that women's economic success, derived from their participation in SHGs, could be the foundation for empowerment in other areas of their lives. The story of Alkabai is testimony to that.

The promotion and organization of SHGs has always been an instrumental goal for Chaitanya, the ultimate objective being women's development. That said, Chaitanya has done more than any other NGO in the state to ensure that the SHG movement spreads extensively across Maharashtra. Chaitanya has sponsored the formation of more than 300 SHGs, with members numbering more than 6000.[14] Chaitanya also helped found GMSS as the financial intermediary that could leverage the savings of women, thus increasing their access to credit. Some of Chaitanya's roles and accomplishments include:

(a) being the primary promoter of SHGs, cluster associations, and the federation;

(b) being the promoter of SHG linkages with banks;

(c) being the promoter of federation linkages to financial institutions and foundations; and

(d) being both a supporter and provider of training services to SHG members in microfinance and other development related topics.

It is important to understand the role of the federation, GMSS, and why Chaitanya stepped away from taking a primary role in its operation, even though GMSS has been the propeller for the formation of SHGs. The federation was an important creation for promoting the SHG movement. The GMSS became the base and source of energy for SHGs in order for them to get a strong foothold throughout Maharashtra. The federation is a separately registered society and a trust.[15] Its governing structure is democratic. It is made up of a variety of members, including representatives of SHGs and cluster groups. Apart from its financial services: savings, credit, audits, GMSS is also involved in non-financial activities that include: child adoption, legal aid, the kitchen garden and nursery programs, entrepreneurial development camps, and even animal husbandry projects.

Since its founding as an autonomous institution in 1993, the federation has established linkages to other agencies, most of them through Chaitanya. So while Chaitanya helped organize the GMSS, it deliberately stepped away from the business of the Federation as it saw its mission as promoting and supporting the formation of SHGs rather than serving as the financial agent or intermediary for SHGs.

Chaitanya, as described in an earlier case study, has played a central role in creating networks of resources to support the expansion

---

[14] Self-help groups are typically limited to twenty members each.

[15] As a registered society and a trust, the GMSS follows the structure prescribed by the Societies Registration Act, 1860, and the Bombay Public Trust Act, 1950.

of SHGs in eight regions in the state of Maharashtra. It continues to provide training for group organizers and cluster groups as well, but its relationship with SHGs is more that of a third party than that of a first party. Chaitanya facilitates the work of others rather than acting as a direct service provider. In that respect, Chaitanya is best described as a resource node; it develops the kinds of expertise that makes it possible for SHGs to grow, experience success, and develop their own social capital within local villages. Because it has the expertise, Chaitanya serves a major role in conducting research to determine how successfully the SHG movement has been in using credit programs for women's empowerment.

Microfinancing: Annapurna Mahila Mandal

Banks, Markets, and Moneylenders

She was a banker and she was the daughter of a banker. Everyday on her way home from the bank, Medha Samant walked through the market to buy her vegetables. Unlike most she did not bargain for them. In return, the women vendors selected the best of their produce for her. It was not long before they began telling her their woes about exploitive moneylenders. The women explained that the moneylenders provided them loans for Rs 1000 but they only received Rs 950, because the moneylenders kept Rs 50 as a service fee. Everyday the women were expected to pay the moneylenders Rs 25 towards their loans and do so for fifty straight days. If the vegetable vendors could pay that daily sum, they would have paid Rs 1250 in fifty days, giving the moneylenders a profit of Rs 300. Most of the time, however, the marketplace vendors could not pay, thus increasing the debt they owed.

'I can do better than this', Medha thought. So she offered nine of the market women the same loan with no upfront service fee. 'But how will you repay', she asked? They offered to pay her the same rate that they paid the moneylenders, Rs 25 per day. In fifty days, all nine women had repaid Medha Samant Rs 1250. But unlike the money-lender, Medha had put all of their money into a small child's saving box. At the end of fifty days she had put aside Rs 200 as savings for each of them, retaining a Rs 50 service fee for each loan. In using this method of credit and savings, Medha was able to show them how they could build savings for themselves and their families. The market women were surprised and delighted. As a result they gained confidence about their potential to be able to save money and improve conditions for their families. Medha was gratified because the scheme worked. If it worked for this group of nine, perhaps she could reach out and help other women in the slums.

Medha conducted this experimental credit project while she was still working at the bank. She was hoping to take this success back to her bank and set up a lending program for other poor women. The bank turned her down. Even though the law required banks to reserve 1 per cent of loans for the poor, the banks had experienced a high default rate and determined that service costs were also too high so they refused to lend. There had been clever but corrupt money dealers who had indulged themselves at the expense of the poorest of the poor. As a result the intended beneficiaries of the program, the kind of women Medha had just had such success with, were profiled as 'defaulters' and a big risk. What had looked like a new opportunity to benefit the poor had resulted in their further marginalization. The poor had once again become the victims of others' greed and manipulation. The banks went back to 'class' lending rather than 'mass' lending. Medha was disheartened because she knew that loan programs for the poor could work. She had the proof, didn't she?

If the bank would not help her, Medha felt she could find a way to help slum women on her own. Since her mother, Prematai Purao, had established a successful microfinance program in Mumbai, the Annapurna Mahila Mandal, Medha went to her for assistance. She obtained an agreement from the managing committee in Mumbai to establish a branch in Pune. Then she quit her job at the bank.

While her first success resulted in her gaining the trust of the nine women in the vegetable market, Medha had no widespread reputation among women in the other slums of Pune. She was convinced that the only way to build this reputation was to start the program with loans, just as she had done with the marketplace vendors. Once the women discovered that the loan program actually resulted in savings they could claim, they might see other opportunities for developing more economic independence through bank accounts. Eventually Medha hoped they would be able to obtain insurance for themselves and their families.

Understanding Annapurna's Approach to Microfinance

Not unlike other microfinance schemes, Annapurna (Pune) initiated its program by developing women's credit groups. Medha called these groups Common Goal Groups (CGGs) to distinguish them from SHGs that were also involved in microfinance. Common Goal Groups differed from SHGs in several ways. First they were about half of the size, numbering five to ten members rather than twenty members. The CGGs operated as collectives in that all members of each group guaranteed each other's loans. In other words, if someone in a CGG defaulted on a loan, no other loans were given until that loan was repaid. Another distinguishing characteristic of CGGs was that they did not use their own group's capital for loans as the SHGs did. They borrowed money from the Microfinance Organization (MFO) that Medha, using her banking acumen, had created in Annapurna.

The MFO capitalized loans to the CGGs by borrowing funds from Annapurna, Mumbai. The MFO also received money from outside funders to build their lending capacity. All CGG members borrowed from the MFO rather than from their own savings programs. Members of SHGs, by contrast, used their own savings capital as the source for intra-group lending until that capital was insufficient to meet their needs. If one SHG had too little in their savings, they would engage in inter-group borrowing. Thus the SHG program, by contrast to the CGG program, was an elaborate system of intra- and inter-group funding until they became members of the federation and were eligible to borrow from it.

As the number of CGGs increased, Annapurna organized Saturday group meetings—cluster meetings—in eighteen different locations throughout Pune. They met in clusters to discuss issues of loan recovery, the rules of loans programs, and any internal problems women were experiencing in the CGGs. It was not compulsory for each member of the CGG to attend the weekly meetings; however, each CGG had to provide a representative for each meeting. In addition to credit issues, the CGGs also discussed at least one social issue per week that was of particular interest to the women.

Medha hoped that the CGGs and the cluster meetings would become an effective vehicle for developing social capital in the various slum areas as well as greater economic independence. That happened. Common Goal Group members grew to trust and help one another, thus creating social capital within their own slums. Women came to understand that as individuals they had no power, but as a collective they did. Their success in obtaining loans to build their businesses as well as take care of their family's needs for health, education, and building assets brought them new respect and a more independent standing in the family.

The CGGs have continued to meet regularly in clusters and with Annapurna. They report their needs and ideas for new programs that are frequently adopted by Annapurna to build new schemes for economic independence within the slum areas. Many of the women have suggested programs for men and children. Medha is supportive of these schemes because she believes that without the support of men, women will never be fully empowered. Programs for women and men, she believes, change the way the family works together. Programs that include adolescent girls and boys also have the potential to change the traditional view of women as being subordinate to men.

Commentary

The model used by Annapurna shares some similarities with the Grameen Bank model, that is, 'implementation is largely driven from the top, with systems laid out well in advance and with little scope for variation'. (Fisher and Sriram, 2002). Members do not participate in the design and management of the MFO in the Grameen model. They do not develop the rules for the loans or set the interest rates or establish fees. Thus Annapurna might best be described as a hybrid model, one that includes some characteristics of the Grameen model and some characteristics of the SHG model. While Annapurna, as an MFO is the bank that establishes rules, fees, and fixed interest rates, it also incorporates the use of groups to act as collectives in its microfinance scheme. They require CGG members to guarantee each other's loans.

As Medha Samant is a businesswoman and believes that economic problems are the chief barriers to empowerment, she focuses on economic problems before social ones. Annapurna's microfinance program is available only to the self-employed. Annapurna's approach to microfinance is based on a belief that if slum dwellers can be successful in savings and credit programs, they are on their way to building economic independence. Economic self-reliance is the first and most important step in the empowerment of women; Medha believes other forms of empowerment would follow economic empowerment.

If we consider the substantial literature on microfinance in India, we find that it is organized and practiced in a variety of ways. Much of that literature compares and contrasts the microfinance schemes developed by the Grameen Bank in Bangladesh with SHGs that have developed elsewhere in India. It is not our purpose to support a particular microfinance scheme but rather to describe how microfinance has been a tool for enhanced social impact.

In the case of Chaitanya and Annapurna, as reported here, each has approached microfinance differently, both in terms of purpose and method. In spite of their differences, both organizations have developed microfinance programs that have contributed to women's empowerment. This we saw in the story of Alkabai and the marketplace vendors (Reference: Microfinancing case number 1, Chaitanya organizing, activating and empowering).

Dr Sudha Kothari, founder of both the GMSS (Gramin Mahila Swayamsiddha Sangha, a registered federation created by Chaitanya) and Chaitanya, organized SHGs beginning in the late 1980s as a way to re-energize the *mahila mandals*, first created by the central government. Dr Kothari found that while such women's groups were established in rural villages, they really had little purpose or drive to meet on a regular basis. She believed that if women came together on a regular basis, they would develop trust and find a forum to share their concerns about their individual lives, their families, and their villages.

Once she witnessed the successes of SHGs in other states of India, she felt that the lure of economic opportunity and independence might be the motivation that would keep women coming back together and meeting on a regular basis, so she supported their development. And it worked. But her real purpose was using SHGs as instruments of empowerment and hoped that once women experienced some success with savings programs—and later credit programs—that they would develop self-confidence and independence and be willing to push boundaries for greater empowerment. She believed that women acting as collectives could substantially increase their power and affect systemic change for the betterment of women in rural India.

Annapurna, on the other hand, was founded by a banker with a great deal of experience in the financial world. Medha Samant believed that the root cause of the oppression of people living in slums was economic. If slum dwellers, especially the self-employed, could gain access to financial resources and learn how to manage and make money, they could overcome poverty and social marginalization. The central focus of Annapurna's program was to alleviate poverty. Medha Samant also believed in the power of women's collectives and so designed the CCG program to bring women together once a week, to discuss economic as well as social issues. The differences between the approach of Chaitanya and those of Annapurna, however, were more in method and structure than in purpose. Both use microfinance for women's development.

The differences that stand out between the two programs are straightforward:

(a) Chaitanya serves rural village women; Annapurna serves slum women.
(b) Chaitanya is based on thrift first, credit second; Annapurna's is the opposite.
(c) Chaitanya uses a federation as the lender; Annapurna has created its own financial institution.
(d) SHGs act as lenders based on savings assets; CGGs borrow from banks, but members guarantee the loans.
(e) SHGs are for everyone; CGGs are only for the self-employed.
(f) SHGs have twenty members; CGGs have five–ten members.
(g) Chaitanya acts as a support and promoter of SHGs; Annapurna creates CGGs and serves them directly.

While these approaches are different from each other, and are driven by a different set of financial principles, ultimately they have produced similar social outcomes. Women have learned how to save, how to take responsibility for borrowing, how to leverage savings and earnings, and how to develop responsible plans for borrowing and managing their money. In addition, they have begun to address issues beyond their own immediate needs by reaching out to their communities and enacting programs that help the entire community. Many have learned new job skills and have new jobs; others have learned how to grow gardens, stand for election, and make independent health decisions.

Political Empowerment: Influence, Independence, and Courage

> *I am now the sarpanch and am treated badly by many, but I will not quit! And I will stand for election again (Rahibai Khandu Unde, 2003).*

Rahibai Khandu Unde

We sat in the upstairs office of the Nari Samata Manch (NSM) in the early summer's heat waiting for the arrival of a village woman, Rahibai Khandu Unde. We were anxious to hear her story as she was a woman who had successfully stood for election for a seat on the seven-member panchayat in her village of Rajpur. She was coming to talk with us about her experiences as an elected official. We did not realize until later that she had to travel three hours by bus one-way to meet with us. This extraordinary effort to share her story provided us with some insight about the woman who would sit with us for three hours and then return to Rajpur, riding a bus without air conditioning for another three hours. And then prepare food for her family.

Rahibai is a woman in her late fifties or early sixties with a quiet energy that cannot be missed. As she began telling her story she became more and more animated, leaning forward in her chair gesturing as if to punctuate her words with exclamation marks. While Rahibai told of the many challenges she was facing in her small village of forty households and 100 villagers, she was clearly proud and honored to be serving her village as an elected member of the panchayat.

Influences

There are often shared testimonies in the lives of leaders, women and men. Rahibai is no exception. She was strongly influenced early in life by her father, and later by her husband, her brother, her women friends, and the NSM, dedicated to eradicating violence against women.

To go back to the beginning, however, Rahibai was profoundly influenced by her family, especially her father. While her father was both a social worker and a land owner, Rahibai knew him best as a person who modeled kindness, caring, even-handedness, and generosity. She noticed that he regularly assisted needy villagers in obtaining food when they did not have enough. He provided local villagers with continuous employment and maintained their employment from planting through harvest. He frequently loaned money to the needy but never charged interest. If a borrower could not repay a loan, he provided a work opportunity to remove the debt. In this way he was able to preserve the pride and dignity of the borrower. He also helped mediate family and village altercations, asking for nothing in return.

One of her father's strongest values, apart from helping others in direct ways, was education. He had a strong belief that education provided a way out of poverty. He was always encouraging young people to acquire as much education as they could. In one case he paid for the education of a young man who was orphaned at an early age. This young man, convinced of his patron's wisdom that education was a way out of poverty, swept the floors of the local school to earn money to further his education and eventually became a school teacher. Her father's generosity of spirit and his belief in the power of education as a way to a better life did not escape Rahibai's notice. In many ways, she has followed in his footsteps.

It is a puzzle why Rahibai's own learning stopped at the third standard given her father's strong belief in the power of education. This was an anomaly, as most girls in her village typically finished the seventh standard. While Rahibai did not have much formal education, her hunger for knowledge took her to lectures, presentations, and trainings whenever possible. When the NSM began giving lectures in neighboring villages, Rahibai was usually there.

Her second significant influence was her husband. She married a school teacher—the orphan boy whom her father had helped educate at the age of seventeen. They lived apart until she was eighteen when she was legally eligible to marry under the new law in India. After finishing his education, her husband found a teaching position in the distant village of Ratnagiri. He and Rahibai lived together there for several years and had two of their five children. After a few years, Rahibai's parents needed someone to look after them and tend the land. By mutual agreement Rahibai and her husband decided that she should return to her home village to help her parents. Her husband was fond of his in-laws and grateful for all that they had done for him, so he was not only supportive of her return but encouraging as well. For most of the next fourteen years they lived apart. Her husband would join her in Rajpur for a month every year during the school vacations. Over those fourteen years they had three more children.

With elderly parents and young children to care for, Rahibai became more independent than most village women. She made decisions usually left to men. Naturally she made domestic decisions like those about the education of her children and obtaining medical treatment for the family. She also managed the farm. She was the head of the household. Through all of this she was supported and encouraged by her husband.

A Leader in the Community

After her children had grown up and her husband had retired and moved back to Rajpur, Rahibai had time to become more involved in the community. Like her father, she wanted to improve life in her village. She did social work, helping her neighbors with their troubles, and trained and worked with the NGO, Stree Adhar Kendra, on issues regarding family violence. She sat on the dak shaketya (police) committee as a representative of the villagers. She worked hard to provide advice to families with domestic difficulties, mediating problems to avoid the police having to get involved. With the assistance of the NSM she also learned how to apply for funds for village projects and was able to get funds that provided employment opportunities for villagers to make physical improvements to the village. Her principal motive was always about helping others improve their lives. She felt that the happiness and standard of living that she experienced could also be achieved by others.

As a participant in the work of the Stree Adhar Kendra and the NSM, she became more aware of women's issues and rights and became a regular participant in the programs offered by the NSM. She wanted to take on bigger issues that would improve life in the community such as alcoholism, which had become a serious problem in the village. And she did. However, there would be consequences that she could not imagine at the time.

Rahibai was convinced that overcoming alcohol abuse would make everyone's lives better. She was pretty sure that others in the community would also want to help overcome this problem. Families could meet their basic needs if the problem of alcohol was tackled. This could reduce domestic violence caused by alcoholic spouses. The NSM helped her gather women together and educate them about how to go about getting a ban on alcohol.

Thirty of the forty households supported a ban, while ten opposed it. The ban succeeded and for four years there was no production or sale of alcohol in Rajpur. Life in the village improved. Families had more money to spend on their other needs. Personal and family attitudes and behavior improved. However, power struggles emerged among the households which supported and those which opposed the ban. The latter had suffered economically during the four-year ban because it curtailed their business of producing and selling alcohol. This created a rift in the community. Eventually the power of the ten families triumphed and the ban ended; the villagers returned to their old habits and alcoholism and domestic violence resumed.

It was not long after the ban had ended that Rahibai's brother suggested she stand for election to the panchayat. Her entire family was supportive of this and encouraged her. Other people in the village also felt she would be a good candidate and do good work. They found her to be liberal and independent, not under the control of any political party. With the new 'reservation' law that ensured the election of women to the panchayat, she could run for one of the three seats reserved for women. Until that point no woman had served on the panchayat in this village. Without knowing very much about what her duties or responsibilities would be, Rahibai stood for election and won, fifty-seven to forty-five.

Local Control through the Panchayat

In order to understand what makes the story of Rahibai remarkable requires some knowledge about just what a village panchayat is and what it does. Long before India's Independence in 1947, the panchayat was the traditional system of local rule. It was only after Independence that this form of local government disappeared. In an effort to create a strong and unified country after Independence, the new national government centralized all government functions in Delhi. It expected that continuing rural development would radiate out to the villages from Delhi. Ten to twelve years after Independence it became clear that development in rural villages was not taking place.

The centralized national government approach was not working. As a result, in the late 1950s, the national government returned development to the people. They reactivated the panchayat and established a new three-tiered system that included village-level government, as well as a block-level (panchayat samiti) and district-level (zila parishad) government.

This system also did not seem to work well and by the 1980s the panchayat directive from central government was weak, corrupt, and floundering. The laws governing meetings, elections, and management of funds were not monitored. There was little representation of villagers in the election of panchayat members. All over India panchayats were perceived as corrupt, controlled by a few elite who did not have to be accountable for the funds earmarked for public goods and services.

In 1992, the national government once again took up the issue of local village government by passing an amendment to the Constitution—the 73rd Amendment. This amendment made it compulsory for all states to support panchayats. It also required 33 per cent of the seats to be reserved for women. It further stipulated that elections must be held every five years. Finally the 73rd Amendment enhanced the powers of the panchayats by transferring to them authority and responsibility for: land improvement and conservation; watershed development; animal husbandry; social forestry and minor forest produce; cottage industry; rural housing; roads; electrification and communication; health; education—both primary and secondary; the public distribution system; poverty alleviation; and women and development.

The central government's devolution of these responsibilities was so broad that nearly all projects and issues facing a village had to be handled through the panchayat. Elected panchayat members, therefore, had significant power, authority, and responsibility for almost every local village concern. As a result, villager participation and representation in elections took on a whole new significance. The panchayat had suddenly become, at least on paper, the principal venue for development in rural India. (Crowell, 2003)

The 73rd Amendment clearly provided new opportunities for village women. While many won their seats because they were assertive and dynamic women, others stood for election as the puppets of powerful men. Some men stood behind a woman's election because they felt they could control her. This was particularly possible when illiterate or low-caste women were elected.

Now to return to the story of Rahibai and her election to the panchayat. She was already a leader in her community and her election was supported by most in the community, with the exception of the ten families who opposed the ban on alcohol that she had instigated. Most families, however, felt she would be a strong leader and that she understood the important issues facing the community. Because she stood for office as an independent and not a member of a party, villagers felt she would be impartial. They also considered Rahibai to be a liberal thinker. She was the only woman on the seven-member panchayat. Four of the members supported her and two did not.

Rahibai did not realize what she was getting into. She did not know her duties or responsibilities except for what her brother, a former sarpanch (member and head of the panchayat) had told her. The NSM, which was working in her community already, provided guidance and training. They taught her the laws she needed to know; they taught her how to approach government offices. She had been uneasy about facing government officers because she felt she lacked information and knowledge—and an education. She relied heavily on the help from the NSM and her brother who had served on the panchayat before her.

Rahibai was also somewhat shy and fearful about making speeches or making protocol mistakes. At the NSM meetings in Rajpur, they urged her to get up and speak and gain confidence in stating her opinions and thoughts about village issues before the panchayat. She worked hard to improve the employment conditions in the village and she focused considerable attention on water management rights, making proposals to the panchayat for improvements.

At the time of our meeting in May of 2003, Rahibai had served for one-and-a-half years as an elected official, with three-and-a-half years to go. While she had already accomplished a good deal for her village, she had also experienced a great deal of strife. Two of the panchayat members resented her for the alcohol ban she championed before standing for office. Some in the village resented that her family had become too powerful in public matters because her brother had also been a sarpanch. These kinds of attitudes became unpleasant obstacles for Rahibai because they became very personal. She told us about a recent experience during the celebration of Independence Day. As a member of the panchayat she was asked to unfurl the flag. This was considered an honor and one that was reserved for a community leader. But the ten households who opposed her refused to attend the celebrations and held their own separate flag-raising ceremony. She felt they were trying to malign her.

She drove the point home about how personal the attacks on her became. In 2003, at a wedding she attended, the ten opposing households beat up two of her sons, aged thirty-three and thirty-five. Both sons suffered broken bones. When a village woman there tried to intervene, she was also beaten up. This village woman went to the police with evidence of the attack but the local police did nothing. The villagers called in senior officers to investigate the beating. The end of that story is unknown.

Rahibai was troubled by the escalating aggressiveness towards her and her family and considered stepping down. She felt that her opposition had mostly to do with being a woman, and an independent woman willing to stand up for what she believed to be right. At the time of our interview, Rahibai was meeting every two weeks with other women members of panchayats in neighboring villages to share their experiences.

Other women panchayat members also complained that most of the obstacles they encountered were really about the fact that they were women and unafraid of using their voices in support of community needs. Sometimes they questioned whether they had done the right thing by sitting on the panchayat. But mostly they agreed that they would complete what they started.

Rahibai did not waver for long, even in the face of violence. Her family believed that she won the election on her own and she must not be intimidated by village bullies. The family wanted her to keep her position and to continue to fight for the rights of women and the villagers. With continuing help from the NSM in providing education, training, and personal support, she has grown in confidence and determination. Her children continue to help and support her. All of them had been educated to the tenth or twelfth standard and were able to explain budgets, assist her with evaluating proposals, and advise her about what she should and should not sign. What about the future? In her own words, Rahibai said: 'I am now the sarpanch and am treated badly, but I will not quit! And, I will stand for election again'.

Commentary

This case, perhaps like the earlier one about 'Sindhutai and the Cow', concerns the achievements of a village woman who has shown extraordinary courage and commitment in the face of challenging obstacles. Rahibai, like Aie, has very little education. Unlike Aie, Rahibai comes from an educated family that provides support and encouragement. They inspire her with a commitment to community betterment. They also encourage her independence.

This kind of family support provides fertile ground for her to become more politically empowered. If we consider the measures of political empowerment as reported in the research, we know that women's independent decision making is its hallmark. Such independence plays itself out in home and family environments as well as in the political arena.

In the context of an Indian woman's home and family environment, this empowerment includes making decisions about purchasing durable goods, children's education, and family health treatment. It also means that women can, independently, make visits to parents, visit the hospital, assist relatives with financial needs and maintain separate bank accounts. Other family examples of women's growing empowerment include mutually deciding family size, entertaining guests, deciding day-to-day family expenditures, and traveling independently—without an accompanying brother, father, husband, or son.

Outside of the family, politically-empowered women make their own decisions about political issues. They vote and they vote according to their own preferences. Politically-empowered women are aware of the political environment and current issues. Empowered women can participate in public protests and freely represent their own interests. And now they also stand for election.

Prior to the 73rd Amendment, such political opportunities were uncommon, particularly for village women and others with little education. The 73rd Amendment along with many other recent laws addressing women's rights, have facilitated women's empowerment. These laws have helped women achieve their rights in public and political arenas. Rahibai's story is about a woman's achievement as well as her persistence to remove public and family obstacles to women's full participation in society.

In the matter of family influence, Rahibai's background seems atypical. She had a strong father who encouraged her and acted as a role model for her developing social consciousness. Her husband, from the beginning, respected and honored her when he lived apart from her until her eighteenth birthday. The two of them made mutual decisions concerning her return to her family to take care of aging parents and independently rearing their children. These were extraordinary circumstances that fostered an unusual independence for a rural village woman.

Early on, in the footsteps of her father, she ministered to the village and gained a reputation for trying to improve other people's lives. This was also a mark of her independence and self-assurance. When the Stree Adhar Kendra came to her village to help villagers deal with family violence, Rahibai got involved. She already knew something about how to work with the police and mediate within families as a result of her representing her village on the police committee. When the NSM began to visit rural villages offering education and training to women, Rahibai was an enthusiastic participant. She was hungry to learn. She was hungry to help. The NSM preached and taught about gender equality, secularism, social justice, friendship, and service. These were core values in Rahibai's life. What the NSM did was add a new and more public dimension to Rahibai's community involvement. The NSM felt that education and training were fundamental to women's empowerment. As a first step, the NSM organized women's groups in seven or eight rural villages to address women's issues at home and in the community. First, women needed to be aware of their shared circumstances and their rights to better treatment under the law. After 1992 and the passage of the 73rd Amendment, the NSM stepped up their activities and began identifying village leaders for further development. They began one of their four leadership development programs.

In Rahibai's case, the NSM helped by introducing her to government officials at the panchayat and district levels. They provided training and practice in public speaking within the local women's support group—the *bachat gat*. The NSM provided education and training in public laws as well as how to work effectively within the panchayat. Rahibai learned how to review budgets, create correct documents, and develop proposals for public goods and services. The NSM provided an ongoing vehicle for her personal and professional growth and support.

Political empowerment, for whatever its measures, is not a private and solitary achievement. Nor does political empowerment in itself guarantee women's general empowerment because that is a multifaceted issue involving literacy, finance, general and reproductive health, and so on. Rahibai's family life helped her develop confidence, self-reliance, and commitment to village improvement. Village support, the *bachat gat*, and ongoing education from the NSM provided her with the strength and tools to stand for election and win a seat on the panchayat. These elements of empowerment—to give authority sufficient purpose as well as the means to take action—are what keep Rahibai 'standing' in the face of vicious personal and public attacks. She knows this and is determined to keep on with her work.

Conclusion

Much has happened since we began this book. The tsunami devastated parts of Indonesia, Thailand, Sri Lanka, and India. Although the world's response to the Asian tsunami was as one experienced aid worker put it, 'magnificent' (Reynolds, World Affairs correspondent, BBC News website, 26 June 2005), the response to the grand gesture was not uniform. The Indian government politely refused all international aid claiming that it was capable of handling its own affairs.

It has been speculated that India's stance is consistent with its efforts to portray itself as a self-reliant nation. With India campaigning for a permanent seat on the UN Security Council, it needed to show greater confidence in its own capability. On one hand, India displays all the indicators of a regional power, a space program, a nuclear bomb, and a thriving software industry. On the other hand, India still has one of the world's largest populations living in poverty, with over a third of the population living on less than $1 a day.

The grim reality is that millions live in poverty. In the last two decades, the government has legislated and implemented many policies of affirmative action to better the lot of the lowercastes and improve the status of women. However, many of those affected remain ignorant or unable to access the benefits because of cultural and social barriers. Non-governmental organizations in India have achieved commendable success in putting into action affirmative action legislation and advocated for social justice for women. Much has been written about their efforts, especially about the larger NGOs that have made significant changes in the lives of women. They have been justly celebrated. Little, however, is known of the myriad of small grass-roots NGOs that work locally and improve the lot of women and children in their communities. Their reach is small, their goals are laudable, and their achievements admirable. Collectively they have made an impact in both rural and urban settings throughout India.

From our study we believe these small NGOs are the important engines behind development efforts both in urban slums and rural areas. Although we concentrate in one geographical area, these NGOs exist everywhere, slowly but surely changing the lives of women in India. We found the twenty women-led NGOs we studied to be effective and successful organizations helping empower women and children in innumerable ways. They are successful NGOs in that they have been around for an average of fourteen years and continue to serve an ever-expanding base of women.

These organizations have been founded by unsung heroes, women who are committed to ambitious social goals and persevere in the face of meager resources and little support from mainstream organizations. They advocate for change and challenge mainstream service organizations to acknowledge traditional gender inequities that result in the disenfranchisement of women.

Our twenty women entrepreneurs have been strongly influenced by women's role in social movements and feminist ideology. Most of them had previous experience working for social justice either through their workplaces or as volunteers. They were disillusioned by the large mainstream organizations in which they worked that tended to be bureaucratic, hierarchical, and often promoted social attitudes and norms that were at the root of the problems of the disenfranchisement of women. By starting their own NGOs, these women entrepreneurs believed they could be innovative, flexible, and responsive in raising consciousness in women about their rights and other issues of social justice. In addition, they wanted to meet the unfulfilled daily needs of poor women in the local and rural communities. They believed that they were best able to empathize with women and understand the cultural and traditional barriers they face.

With scarce resources and growing needs it is crucial to understand and replicate strategies that make these women-led NGOs successful in mobilizing people and transforming communities. In this concluding chapter we summarize the lessons that emerge from our analysis of the twenty successful women-led NGOs that cater to women.

All our women entrepreneurs shared a feminist ideology and an overwhelming desire to help others and promote social justice. In addition, they were disillusioned with current efforts at meeting the needs of women. The existence of social injustices compelled them to act, and they did so by forming NGOs that would further the cause of women, help them achieve certain basic needs, and empower them to be self-reliant.

Motivation and ideology give women the impetus to start NGOs and dictate to a large extent the organizational nature of the NGO.

Other enabling factors that were common to the majority of the entrepreneurs were higher education, prior work or volunteer experience in social services, a supportive family system, family role models, and social capital. The overwhelming majority of our women entrepreneurs came from middle to upper class and high castes, which is consistent with the indicators of socioeconomic status. Our findings also show the capacity of women entrepreneurs to generate social capital that is crucial and is often more difficult to generate than financial capital, especially when organizations take on issues that go against the prevailing social norms.

Our case studies of women entrepreneurs in Chapter One portray two successful women: Medha Samant who fits the typical model and Sindhutai who does not. Sindhutai is from a poor, low-caste family; she does not have formal education, no family support, and no prior work experience in the field of social work. As a matter of fact, she herself was a victim of injustice. However, what Sindhutai does have in common with Medha Samant is the keen motivation to serve others and make their lives better coupled with a strong feminist ideology. They also both possess characteristics common to all entrepreneurs such as self-confidence, risk taking, the ability to persevere and work hard. Their stories illustrate that it is possible to come to NGO entrepreneurship from very divergent paths.

We find that our NGO founders are feminists (although a few did not particularly like the feminist label but described themselves as espousing feminist goals). Most of the organizations reflect their feminist philosophy and are collective, inclusive, and build on consensus. Feminists claim that a collective form of organization is congruent with their ideology and belief system. We found that as organizations grow and increase in size and complexity, some of the NGOs pragmatically adopt bureaucratic features to meet organizational goals, thereby transforming their structures from a pure collectivist form to a collectivist pragmatic structure. Others either chose to stay collectivists or adopt the bureaucratic form. In the latter case, we find that adopting bureaucratic features did not necessarily mean that feminist principles were abandoned.

Indeed, growth did not imply that the founders were willing to compromise on the quality of their work, their commitment to empowering women, and other important issues related to their core mission. Their own feminist ideologies did not prevent them from making tradeoffs to compromise on the organizational processes to increase their output and impact. The leadership in the NGOs that had adopted bureaucratic features was very different from the leadership in traditional patriarchal bureaucracies. The women founders retained leadership characteristics of inclusiveness, egalitarianism, and participatory democracy.

In general, leaders who claimed a feminist organizational philosophy always identified their organizations as collectivist ones despite the reality of organizational structure. However, we find that neither feminist principles nor the goals of the organization are displaced due to choices of any particular organizational structure. The NGOs we studied are distinctive in that they are led by women who pioneered new ways of organizing and were successful in building ownership among the stakeholders hence ensuring sustainability. These women were able to find creative ways to meet the practical constraints of the external environments and not function like traditional bureaucracies even though they adopted features characteristic of bureaucracies. Our findings from two case studies discussed in Chapter Two elaborate this further.

The NSM is a typical collectivist NGO started by two feminists. Their program, Speak Out, provides a space for women to share their experiences. The other programs grew organically from the needs expressed by the clients and staff of Speak Out. For example, the counseling center added vocational guidance and educational programs, with a safe house for women being added later on. As the programs grew in number and complexity, the founder applied for and received international funding. Professionals were hired to staff the new centers and also meet the accountability demands of the funders and the government. Given the increasing presence of professional staff, formal structures, material incentives, and formal decision-making criteria, the NSM adopted several features of a bureaucratic organization. Despite their move towards growth and professionalization, the NSM founders did not compromise feminist collectivist ideals of participatory leadership and grass-roots involvement. The overall organization is egalitarian, decision making is participative, and it devolves authority and responsibility to the lowest level, including staff, members, and clients.

Swadhar found itself in a similar dilemma. After initiating several programs rapidly in response to perceived needs, some paid professionals were hired for service delivery, and to meet administrative needs. The founders were worried that the young professionals they hired did not have experience in social movements and, therefore, did not share similar normative beliefs. In addition, moving from volunteer labor to paid labor could signal a shift from normative to material incentives. These important concerns were uppermost in the minds of the two founders of Swadhar as it began to grow in size and complexity. The founders strategized to find ways to keep their organization functioning as a collective by bringing on younger members to the management committee and passing on the beliefs that guided the organization since its inception.

The founders of both NGOs paid close attention to maintaining a non-hierarchical organizational structure as a close examination of the NSM and Swadhar reveals. We find that their overarching goal remains essentially feminist—to empower women and redress injustices, using a broad-based leadership and inclusive management style. The founders insist, and we concede, that the overall organizational structure at the macro level is still collectivist while the micro level of service delivery increasingly adopts certain bureaucratic features. They retained their feminist values, where the ethos of care and inclusion permeates the organizational structure.

We find that our women-led NGOs espouse a paradigm that promotes input from the ground level. The NGOs encourage and invite whole communities to participate and thereby share in the ownership of programs. Programs are initiated by clients' needs and build on each other organically to take into consideration women's ways of multitasking. Their role, especially in rural settings as cultivators, managers of livestock, suppliers of water and fuel often allows the family to subsist in rural India. Alongside, they bear children, look after their needs, cook and clean, and contribute to daily life and living. When development agencies offer one or two main programs to help women they must take into account the invisible demands that constrain women from doing more.

The NGOs in our study, being led by women are sensitive to these issues and offer integrated programs that take into consideration the practical aspects of enabling women to access the programs as well providing services that take into account the social, psychological, political, and economic dimensions necessary for the sustainable development of women.

We find that the choices of programs and services offered in the natural evolutionary process of successful NGOs are suited to women's holistic development. New programs and services are often chosen deliberately to complement existing services to form a series of integrated services which have a multiplier effect on women's lives. Women leaders provide a multidimensional range of vertically-integrated programs that cater to the whole woman and enable her to become independent.

The judicious mix of programs offered by our NGOs often includes SHGs that provide microcredit services and political empowerment which coincides with the Maharashtra government's policies from 1994–2001 that emphasized women's empowerment through SHGs (Datar, 2003). As we saw, SHGs provide an effective instrument through which women can build economic self-reliance, solidarity, and self-confidence. This often has a domino effect in the overall development of their families and communities. Belonging to a group gives many women self-identity, status, and security. When SHGs get involved in microcredit financing and politics we find that women get access not only to the means to control their own lives but to implement change in society. Most importantly SHGs give women a platform on which to bring together common concerns and use the power of the collective to negotiate in ways that would be closed to the individual.

That our NGOs had more SHGs organized for political empowerment than microcredit does not imply that our women founders believed that one kind of SHG was better than the other. Indeed, political and financial empowerment are mutually reinforcing. When women earn economic resources through microcredit financing, these gains are sometimes dissipated through the patriarchal system wherein the male members of the family take advantage of a new found access to capital and earnings. However, such abuses may not result if women are more aware of their rights and have broken through the traditional patriarchal controls.

We put forward an explanation on how a gendered perspective gives rise to high-impact NGOs. Essentially, we find that a female leadership which is grounded in a gendered perspective can easily empathize with the needs, spoken and unspoken, of other women. Our entrepreneurs are not development professionals with the aim of meeting certain proscribed goals; rather they are women with passion, dedication, and the ability to deal with the many injustices due to class, caste, and male domination. In general, the founders started small, with one or two programs, relying on a grass-roots approach they were able to come up with vertically-integrated services that leveraged existing programs so as to acknowledge a holistic approach to women's empowerment.

Despite the limitations due to the small size of the sample and one geographic locale, we can make a few policy proposals of interest to governments and donors. Governments in many countries cannot provide various social services for the disadvantaged due to poverty (or ideology). They may see NGOs as substitute providers of public services and support such activity through tax subsidies and other ways. Thus, it is rational to assume, from a public policy perspective, the need to encourage the founding of such NGOs and to make certain that those founded are sustainable and efficient.

Furthermore, local and international donors, who are keen to sponsor women's issues and want to encourage start-ups, need to make certain that the NGOs they fund will be successful. Thus, from the donor and government perspectives, this research provides some insights on how to support NGO growth and success.

As early volunteer experiences in social service agencies seem to be catalytic in exposing the social injustices women confront as well as the potential to help, policies that get more young women to volunteer may increase the number who may eventually start social service organizations. For example, domestic and foreign donors can help existing NGOs to recruit more volunteers and offer them training in the different skills—interpersonal skills, negotiating bureaucracies, legal and administrative aspects of starting, managing, and running an NGO.

Governments can make volunteering part of educational training so as to expose youth to social problems and thereby increase the pool of likely entrepreneurs. Volunteering may also give women a chance to expand their social connections, which is crucial in recruiting volunteers and collecting donations necessary for starting NGOs.

Although existing affirmative action programs help many women of lower-castes achieve social and financial status in India by providing entry into elite professions and the political arena, more attention should be paid to the education and empowerment of lower-caste women in rural areas. Non-governmental organizations that help empower women should seek out women who have the potential to become leaders and interest them in dealing with social injustices. By offering training and relevant experiences they can provide fertile ground for new NGO leaders. Such leaders prove to be very capable in bringing about change by being a positive role model.

Governments and donors can make an effort to make sure that more women, especially of lower-castes, receive higher education, training in interpersonal skills and opportunities to work and volunteer in NGOs. This may help reduce the trend for only upper-caste women to start NGOs. Furthermore, there is a need to enable a wider dissemination of some of the perspectives that are part of the feminist ideology, specifically the concern for equity and social justice. If more people (men and women) are exposed to feminist ideology, more may take part by starting NGOs or support the entrepreneurs who do.

It may be of value to target those involved in social work and in volunteering to receive resources, if they choose, to enable them to start new organizations. These resources include training programs given at local schools or colleges and mentoring at existing NGO services to facilitate the formation of new NGOs. If such programs can be made available to those who are contemplating starting NGOs, or who are in the process of doing so, they may be able to increase their chances of success. This study cannot, naturally, throw light on unsuccessful NGOs. However, it does suggest where to direct training resources and information so that the potential group of NGO founders is targeted early on, when it is critical to make good decisions.

Our findings on the structure and choice of programs suggest further policy implications for improving the impact of NGOs. It is helpful for those starting NGOs or running NGOs disseminating knowledge about successful models of governance and management in achieving greater impact. Management models embraced by our women-led NGOs show clearly how a grass-roots approach can be successful in ensuring that services and programs delivered are indeed what is required on the ground.

Such participatory and inclusive management styles would ensure that the communities in which the NGOs exist will be positioned to take ownership of the process. Taking ownership of the process would facilitate incorporating indigenous knowledge into solutions and the acceptance of programs. New programs could be designed to leverage existing programs for women and provide vertically-integrated services for greater impact.

As NGOs grow larger or intentionally remain the same size, if organizations are careful to retain their founding ideologies of collectivist principles, as did many of our NGOs, they will still be able to cultivate broad-based leadership despite judiciously adding bureaucratic features to meet with the pressures of the environment.

Efficiency for our NGOs stemmed not from adding bureaucratic features, but in getting a broad-based consensus among their stakeholders. Consensus building, which was part of the process, was empowering for women, the staff, and clients, thereby meeting a goal of the NGOs, as well as ensuring participation and cooperation to achieve other goals.

This book highlights the specific contributions of women-led organizations as they herald a new organizational structure that is efficient and successful. Pioneering new ways of successful organization, they remain efficient even as they grow. Thus women-led NGOs are setting essential precedents for how local, national, and global organizations should model themselves in the future.

References and
Select Bibliography

Aburdene, P. and J. Naisbitt. 1992. *Megatrends for Women*. New York, NY: Villard Books.

Acebo, S. 1994. 'A Paradigm Shift to Team Leadership in the Community College' in G. Baker (ed.), *Handbook on the Community College in America: Its History, Mission, and Management*, pp. 580–88. Westport, CT: Greenwood Press.

Ahmed, M. 1982. *Nijera Kori in Retrospect: In Search of an Organization of the Rural Poor*. Dhaka, Bangladesh: Nijera Kori.

Aital, V. 2004. *Women in India Struggle for Water and Social Transformation: Can the Subaltern Speak?* Konigstein, TS: Ulrike Helmer Verlag.

Allen, S. and C. Truman. 1993. *Women in Business: Perspectives on Women Entrepreneurs*. New York, NY: Routledge.

Assayag, J. 1995. *The Making of Democratic Inequality: Caste, Class, Lobbies and Politics in Contemporary India*. New York, NY: McGraw-Hill Higher Education.

Atack, I. 1999. 'Four Criteria of Development NGO Legitimacy', *World Development*, 27(5): 855–64.

Baron, R.A. 1998. 'Cognitive Mechanisms in Entrepreneurship: Why and When Entrepreneurs Think Differently Than Other People', *Journal of Business Venturing*, 13: 275–94.

Batliwala, S. 1996. *Training Grassroots Activists for Women's Empowerment: The Indian Experience*. Bangalore, India: National Institute of Advanced Studies, Women's Policy Reservation and Advocacy Unit.

Beegle, K., E. Frankenberg, and D. Thomas. 1998. 'Bargaining Power within Couples and Use of Prenatal and Delivery Care in Indonesia', *Studies in Family Planning*, 32(2): 130.

Berger, B. 1991. *The Culture of Entrepreneurship*. San Francisco, CA: ICS Press.

Billing, Y.D. and M. Alvesson. 1994. *Genders, Managers and Organizations*. Berlin, Germany: Walter de Gruyter.

Bilodeau, M. and A. Slivinski. 1996. 'Volunteering Non-profit Entrepreneurial Services', *Journal of Economic Behavior and Organization*, 31(1): 117–27.

Blanchflower, D.G. and A.J. Oswald. 1998. 'What Makes an Entrepreneur?', *Journal of Labor Economics*, 16(1): 26–60.

Bordt, R. 1997. *The Structure of Women Nonprofit Organizations*. Bloomington: Indiana University Press.

Bose, A. 1991. *Population of India: 1991 Results and Methodology*. New Delhi, India: D.K. Publishers.

Bourdieu, P. 1986. 'Forms of Capital' in J.G. Richardson (ed.), *Handbook of Theory and Research for the Sociology of Education*, pp. 241–58. New York, NY: Greenwood Press.

Brandstalter, H. 1997. 'Becoming an Entrepreneur—A Question of Personality Structure?', *Journal of Economic Psychology*, 18: 157–77.

Bratton, M. 1989. 'The Politics of Government NGO Relations in Africa', *World Development*, 17(4): 569–87.

Brett, E.A. 1993. 'Voluntary Agencies as Development Organizations: Theorizing the Problem of Efficiency and Accountability', *Development and Change*, 24: 269–303.

Brockhaus, R.H.S. and P.S. Horowitz. 1986. 'The Psychology of the Entrepreneur' in D. Sexton and R. Smilor (eds), *The Art and Science of the Entrepreneur*, pp. 25–48. Cambridge, MA: Ballinger.

Brown, E.A. 1991. 'Bridging Organizations and Sustainable Development', *Human Relations*, 44(8): 807–31.

Brush, C.G. 1992. 'Research of Women Business Owners: Past Trends, A New Perspective and Future Directions', *Entrepreneurship Theory and Practice*, 16(4): 6–30.

Brush, C.G. and Hisrich, R.D. 1991. 'Antecedent Influences on Women-owned Businesses', *Journal of Managerial Psychology*, 6(2): 9–16.

Bushley, D., S. Brockman, M. Ramsey, R. Saeed, and E. Berhane. 2003. *Integrated Reproductive Health Services: Evidence-Based Approaches.* Paper presented at the Caribbean Catalyst Consortium, May.

Campbell, D. 2003. 'The Keeper of the Co-Op Faith', *Rural Cooperations*, 70(2): 2.

Campbell, M. 2003. 'Dorothy Smith and Knowing the World We Live In', *Journal of Sociology and Social Welfare*, 30: 3–23.

Caputo, R. and A. Dolinsky. 1998. 'Women's Choice to Pursue Self-Employment: The Role of Financial and Human Capital of Household Members', *Journal of Small Business Management*, 36(3): 8–17.

Carr, M., M. Chen, and R. Jhabvala. 1996. *Speaking Out: Women's Economic Empowerment in South Asia.* London, UK: IT Publications.

Carrington, D. 2002. 'The Investor Approach: A Way Forward for the Community Fund?' Accessed 12 December 2005 at www.community-fund.org.uk.

Carter, S. and T. Cannon. 1992. *Women as Entrepreneurs.* London, UK: Academic Press.

Casper, K.L. 1994. *The Women's and Children's Health Programs and Gender Equity in Banchtie Shekha.* An Evaluation Report for Ford Foundation, NORAD.

Center for Development and Population Activities (CDPA). 1997. *Voices of Young Women.* Washington, DC: Center for Development and Population Activities.

Center for Development and Population Activities (CDPA). 2003. *Enabling Change for Women's Reproductive Health: Overview of the ENABLE Project.* Washington, DC: Center for Development and Population Activities.

Charlton, S.M. and J. Everett. 1998. *NGOs and Grassroots in Development Work in South India: Elizabeth Moen Mathiot.* Lanham, MD: University Press of America.

Chandra, K. Ravi. 1991. *Entrepreneurial Success: A Psychological Study.* Columbia, USA: South Asia Books.

Chattopadhyay, R. and E. Duflo. 2004. 'Women as Policy Makers: Evidence from a R 'omized Policy Experiment in India', *Econometrica*, 72(5): 1409–43.

Canadi ternational Development Agency (CIDA). 2001. *Gender Profile: India.* Available at, http://www.acdicida.gc.ca/cida_ind.nsf/0/9f7712d8a5bd9bf85256b1b0074259d.

Clark, J. 1991. *Democratizing Development: The Role of Voluntary Organizations.* West Hartford, CT: Kumarian Press.

Clary, E.G. and M. Snyder. 1999. 'The Motivations to Volunteer: Theoretical and Practical Considerations', *Current Directions in Psychological Science*, 8: 156–59.

Collins, O. and D.G. Moore. 1970. *The Organization Makers*. New York, NY: Appleton-Century Crofts.

Coltrane, S. 1996. *Family Man: Fatherhood, Housework and Gender Equity*. New York, NY: Oxford University Press.

Cooper, A.C., E.J. Gimeno-Garcon, and C.Y. Woo. 1994. 'Initial Human and Financial Capital Predictors for New Venture Performance', *Journal of Business Venturing*, 9: 371–95.

Crowell, D. 2003. *The SEWA Movement and Rural Development*. New Delhi, India: Sage Publications.

Datar, C. 2003. *Status of Women in Maharashtra: An Update*. Mumbai, India: Tata Institute of Social Sciences.

D'Cruz, N. 2003. *Constraints on Women Entrepreneurship Development in Kerala: An Analysis of Familial, Social and Psychological Dimensions*. Discussion Paper No. 53, Kerala Research Programme on Local Level Development. Ulloor, Kerala: Center for Development Studies.

Dhillon, P. 1998. *Women Entrepreneurs: Problems and Prospects*. New Delhi: Blaze Publishers and Distributors.

Divekar, V.D. 1991. 'Introduction' in V.D. Divekar, G.T. Kulkarni, and M.R. Kantak (eds), *Social Reform Movements in India*, pp. vii–xvi. Bombay, India: Popular Prakashan.

Eagly, A.H. and S.J. Karau. 1991. 'Gender and the Emergence of Leaders: A Meta-Analysis', *Journal of Personality and Social Psychology*, 6: 685–710.

Economic and Social Commission for Asia and the Pacific (ESCAP). 1997. *Women in India: A Country Profile: Biennial Report*. New York, NY: United Nations, UN Development Fund for Women, UNIFEM.

Edwards, M. and D. Hulme (eds), 1995. *Non-Governmental Organizations—Performance and Accountability: Beyond the Magic Bullet*. London, UK: Earthscan.

Edwards, M. and G. Sen. 2000. 'NGOs, Social Change and the Transformation of Human Relationships: A 21st Century Civic Agenda', *Third World Quarterly*, 21(4): 605–16.

Elliot, C. 1987. 'Some Aspects of Relations between North and South in the N.G.O. Sector', *World Development*, Supplement, 15: 57–68.

Ellis, S.J. and K.H. Noyes. 1990. *By the People: A History of Americans as Volunteers*. San Francisco, CA: Jossy-Bass.

Erkut, S. 2001. *Inside Women's Power: Learning from Leaders*. Wellesley Center for Research on Women, Wellesley, MA: Wellesley College.

Everingham, J.A. 2002. 'Mahila Sanghas as Feminist Groups: The Empowerment of Women in Coastal Orissa', *Indian Journal of Gender Studies*, 9(1): 43–60.

Ferguson, K. 1984. *The Feminist Case against Bureaucracy*. Philadelphia, PN: Temple University.

Ferree, M. and B. Hess. 1994. *Controversy and Conditions: The New Feminist Movement Across Decades of Change*. Toronto, ON: Maxwell Macmillan Publishers.

Fischer, E.M., A.R. Reuber, and L.S. Dyke. 1993. 'A Theoretical Overview and Extension of Research on Sex, Gender and Entrepreneurship', *Journal of Business Venturing*, 8: 151–68.

Fisher, J. 1988. *NGOs and the Political Development of the Third World*. Connecticut, CT: Kumarian Press.

Fisher, J. 1993. *The Road From Rio: Sustainable Development and Nongovernmental Movement in the Third World*. Westport, CT: Praeger.

Fisher, T. and M.S. Sriram. 2002. *Beyond Micro-Credit: Putting Development Back Into Micro-Finance*. New Delhi, India: Vistaar.

Fowler, A. 1985. 'NGOs in Africa: Naming Them By What They Are', in K. Kinyanjui (ed.), *Non-Government Organizations (NGOs): Contribution to Development*, pp. 7–30. Occasional Paper No. 50, Institute of Development Studies, Nairobi: University of Nairobi.

Frank, R.H. 1996. 'What Price the Moral High Ground', *Southern Economic Journal*, 63: 1–17.

Frye, M. 1983. 'Oppression' in M. Frye (ed.), *The Politics of Reality: Essays in Feminist Theory*. Trumansburg, NY: The Crossing Press.

Gedalof, I. 1999. *Against Purity: Rethinking Identity with Indian and Western Feminism*. London, UK: Routledge, Taylor and Francis.

Goetz, A.M. and R.S. Gupta. 1996. 'Who Takes Credit? Gender, Power and Control Over Loan Use in Rural Credit Programs in Bangladesh', *World Development*, 24(1): 45–63.

Goffee, R. and R. Scase. 1985. *Women in Charge*. London, UK: George Allen and Unwin.

Gonyea, J.G. 1999. 'The Non-Profit Sector's Responsiveness to Work Family Issues', *Annals of the American Academy of Political and Social Science*, 562: 127–43.

Gopalan, P. 2001. 'The Many Faces of Microcredit', *Humanscape*, 8(7): 1–7.

Gorkenker, L. and T.G. Weiss. 1995. 'Pluralizing Global Governance: Analytical Approaches and Dimensions', *Third World Quarterly*, 16(3): 357–87.

Grameen, Trust. 2000. *Grameen Trust Annual Report '99*. Dhaka, Bangladesh: Grameen Trust.

Griffith, G. 1994. *Poverty Alleviation for Rural Women: Indian Voluntary Organizations and Village Development*. Aldershot, Brookefield, VT: Avebury Publishers.

Gundry, L. and H. Welsch. 2001. 'The Ambitious Entrepreneur: High Growth Strategies of Women-Owned Enterprises', *Journal of Business Venturing*, 16: 453–70.

Gupta, A. 1991. 'Indian Entrepreneurial Culture: Bengal and Eastern India' in B. Berger (ed.), *The Culture of Entrepreneurship*, pp. 99–136. San Francisco, CA: ICS Press.

Handy, F. and M. Kassam. 2001. Non-Profit and For-Profit Entrepreneurship: More or Less of the Same? A Literature Review, Unpublished paper, York University.

Handy, F., M. Kassam, and S. Ranade. 2003. 'Factors Influencing Women Entrepreneurs of NGOs in India', *Nonprofit Management and Leadership*, 13(2): 139–54.

Hasan, F.R.M. 1985. *Process in Landless Mobilization in Bangladesh: Theory and Practice*. Dhaka, Bangladesh: Bangladesh Institute of Development Studies.

Hashemi, S., S.R. Schuler, and A. Riley. 1996. 'Rural Credit Programs and Women's Empowerment in Bangladesh', *World Development*, 24(4): 635–53.

Hines, R. 1992. 'Accounting: Filling the Negative Space', *Organization and Society*, 17(3/4): 314–41.

Hisrich, R.D. 1986. 'The Woman Entrepreneur: A Comparative Analysis', *Leadership and Organization Development Journal*, 7(2): 8–17.

Hisrich, R.D. and C.G. Brush. 1984. 'The Women Entrepreneurs: Management Skills and Business Problems', *Journal of Small Business Management*, 22(1): 31–36.

Hochschild, A.R. and A. Machung. 1990. *The Second Shift*. New York, NY: Avon Books.

Hughes, R.L., R.C. Ginnett, and G.J. Curphy. 2002. *Leadership: Enhancing the Lessons of Experience*. New York, NY: McGraw-Hill.

Ianello, K.P. 1992. *Decisions Without Hierarchy: Feminist Interventions in Organization Theory and Practice*. New York, NY: Routledge.

Independent Sector. 2001. 'The New Non-Profit Almanac in Brief: Facts and Figures on the Independent Sector 2001'. Washington, DC: Independent Sector.

Jacobson, D. and S. Wadley. 1977. *Women in India—Two Perspectives*. New Delhi, India: Manohar Book Service.

————. 2001. 'Advancing Government through Peer Learning and Networking: Lessons Learned from Grassroots Women', Huairou Commission: Our Best Practices Campaign.

Jaeckel, M. 2002. 'Mother Centers: Rebuilding Social Cohesion in a Fragmented World', *Habitat Debate*, 8(4): 17.

Jaeckel, M.and S. Purushothaman. 2000. 'Conclusions' in S. Purushothaman and M. Jaeckel (eds), *Challenging Development: A Grassroots Women's North-South Dialogue*, pp. 156–84. Bangalore. India: Books for Change.

Jain, P. September 1996. *Women Changing Governance, Gender in Development, Monograph Series No. 5*. United Nations Development Project (UNDP).

Jani, N. and M.N. Pedroni. 1997. 'Financing Women Entrepreneurs in South Asia: A Conversation with Nancy Barry', *Journal of International Affairs*, 51(1): 159–78.

John, M.E. 1998. 'Feminism in India and the West: Recasting the Relationship', *Cultural Dynamics*, 10(2): 197–209.

Karunanithi, G. 1991. *Caste and Class Organizations*. New Delhi, India: Commonwealth Publishers.

Kassam, M. and F. Handy. 2003. Practice What You Preach? Closing the Gap Between the Rhetoric and Reality of Female Empowerment. Paper presented at the ARNOVA Conference, Denver, CO, 20–22 November.

Kassam, M., F. Handy, and S. Ranade. 2000. 'Forms of Leadership and Organizational Structure of Non-Profits: A Study of Women's NGOs in India', *Chinmaya Management Journal*, 4(1): 30–40.

————. 2002a. 'Organizational Structures of Feminist Social Service Delivery in India', *Pakistan Journal of Women's Studies*, 9(1): 1–25.

————. 2002b. 'Understanding NGO Impact: The Case of Women NGOs in India', *Social Development Issues*, 23(3): 27–36.

Kaushik, S. 1999. 'Women's Movement in India' in S.K. Chaube and B. Chakraborty (eds), *Social Movements in Contemporary India*. Calcutta, India: K.P. Bagchi and Company.

Kishor, S. 1995. *Autonomy of Egyptian Women: Findings From the 1988 Egypt Demographic and Health Survey: Occasional Papers 2*. Calverton, MD: Macro International Inc.

————. 2000a. 'Empowerment of Women in Egypt and Links to Survival and Health of Their Infants' in H. Presser and G. Sen (eds), *Women's Empowerment and Demographic Processes Moving Beyond Cairo*. New York, NY: Oxford University Press.

————. 2000b. 'Women's Contraceptive Use in Egypt: What Do Direct Measures of Empowerment Tell Us?' Paper presented at the Annual Meeting of the Population Association of America, Los Angeles, CA, 23–25 March 2000.

Korten, D.C. 1987. 'Third Generation NGO Strategies: A Key to People-Centered Development', *World Development*, 15 (Supplemental): 145–59.

————. 1990. *Getting to the 21st Century*. West Hartford, CT: Kumarian Press.

Krueger, D. 2000. 'Characteristics of the Female Entrepreneur', *Journal of Business and Entrepreneurship*, 12(1): 87–93.

Kudva, N. 2003. 'Engineering Elections: The Experiences of Women in Panchayati Rajin Karnataka, India', *International Journal of Politics, Culture, and Society*, 16(3): 445–63.

Lakshmi, C.S. 1998. *Development of Women Entrepreneurship in India: Problems and Prospects*. New Delhi, India: Discovery Publishing House.

Leonard, A. 1989. *Seeds: Supporting Women's Work in the Third World*. New York, NY: Feminist Press.

————. 1995. *Seeds 2: Supporting Women's Work around the World*. New York, NY: Feminist Press.

Limaye, C. 1999. *Women: Power and Progress*. New Delhi, India: South Asia Books.

Lindenberg, M. and C. Bryant. 2002. *Going Global: Transforming Relief and Development NGOs*. Bloomfield, CT: Kumarian Press.

Lingham, L. 2002. 'Taking Stock: Women's Movement and the State' in G. Shah (ed.), *Social Movements and the State*. Thousand Oaks, CA: Sage Publications.

Loden, M. 1985. *Feminine Leadership or How to Succeed in Business Without Being One of the Boys*. New York, NY: Crown Publishers.

Malhotra, A. and M. Mather. 1997. 'Do Schooling and Work Empower Women in Developing Countries? Gender and Domestic Decisions in Sri Lanka', *Sociological Forum*, 12(4): 599–630.

Malhotra, K. 2000. 'NGOs Without Aid: Beyond the Global Soup Kitchen', *Third World Quarterly*, 21(4): 655–68.

Mansbridge, J. 1984. 'Feminism and Forms of Freedom' in F. Fischer and C. Sirianni (eds), *Critical Studies in Organization and Bureaucracy*. Philadelphia, PN: Temple.

Martin, J. 1990. 'Re-Reading Weber: Searching for Feminist Alternatives to Bureaucracy.' Paper presented at the Academy of Management Meeting, San Fransisco, 11–15 August.

Martin, P.Y. 1990. 'Rethinking Feminist Organizations', *Gender and Society*, 4(2): 182–206.

MASHAL. 1996. *First Annual Report on the States of the Environment*. Pune, India: Pune Municipal Corporation.

Mathiot, E.M., S.E.M. Charlton, J. Everett, and J.M. Everett. 1997. *NGOs and Grassroots in Development Work in South India*. New York, NY: University Press of America.

Matthews, N.A. 1994. *A Confronting Rape: The Feminist Anti-Rape Movement and the State*. New York, NY: Routledge.

Mawdsley, E., J. Townsend, G. Porter, and P. Oakley. 2002. *Knowledge, Power and Development Agendas: NGOs North and South*. Oxford, UK: INTRAC.

Mayoux, L. 1995. 'From Vicious Circle to Virtuous Circle? Gender and Micro-Enterprise Development', *The Social Effects of Globalization* Occasional Paper no. 3. Geneva, Switzerland: United Nations Research Institute for Social Development (UNRISD). Available at, http://www.unrisd.org.

McClelland, D.C. 1987. 'Characteristics of Successful Entrepreneurs', *The Journal of Creative Behavior*, 21(3): 219–33.

Metzendorf, D. 2005. *The Evolution of Feminist Organizations: An Organizational Study.* Lanham, MD: University of America Press.

Metzendorf, D. and R.A. Cnaan. 1992. 'Volunteers in Feminist Organizations', *Nonprofit Management and Leadership,* 2(3): 255–69.

Mills, A. 1988. 'Organization, Gender and Culture', *Organization Studies,* 9(3): 351–69.

Mishra, S.N. and S. Mishra. 1998. 'Good Governance, People's Participation and NGOs', *The Indian Journal of Public Administration,* 44(3): 439–53.

Moldt, E. May 1991. 'Men, Women and Leadership-Management Styles' in *Nation's Business.*

Moore, D. and E. Buttner. 1997. *Women Entrepreneurs: Moving Beyond the Glass Ceiling.* Thousand Oaks, CA: Sage.

Moser, C. 1991. 'Gender Planning in the Third World: Meeting Practical Needs and Strategic Needs' in *Changing Perceptions: Writing on Gender and Development.* Oxford, UK: Oxfam.

Naffziger, D.W., J.S. Hornsby, and D.F. Kuratko. 1994. 'A Proposed Research Model of Entrepreneurial Motivation', *Entrepreneurship Theory and Practice,* Spring: 29–42.

Naffziger, D.W. and D. Terrell. 1996. 'Entrepreneurial Human Capital and the Long-Run Survival of Firms in India', *World Development,* 24(4): 689–96.

Nanavatty, M.C. and P.D. Kulkarni. 1998. *NGOs in the Changing Scenario.* New Delhi, India: Uppal Publishing House.

Narasimhan, S. 1996. *Empowering Women: An Alternative Strategy from Rural India.* New Delhi, India: Sage Publications.

National Foundation of Women's Business Owners. 2002. Center for Women's Business Research. Accessed on 19 March 2003 at www.nfwbo.org/key.html.

Neft, N. and A.D. Levine. 1997. *Where Women Stand: An International Report on the Status of Women,* 1997–98. New York, NY: Random House.

Neilson, G.W. 1987. 'Information Needs of Female Entrepreneurs', *Journal of Small Business Management,* July: 38–44.

Nelton, S. 1991. 'Men, Women and Leadership—Management Styles, Cover Story' in *The Nation's Business,* 79(5): 16–23.

Nijera Kori. 1990. *Annual Report.* Dhaka, Bangladesh: Nijera Kori.

Niranjana, T. 1998. 'Feminism and the Translation in India: Contexts, Politics, Futures', *Cultural Dynamics,* 10(2): 133–46.

Overseas Development Institute. 1988. 'Development Efforts of NGOs', *Development,* 4: 41–46.

Paavo, A. 2002. 'Creating the Conditions for Democracy: Lessons from Feminist Organizations.' Paper presented at the OISE Conference, 30–31 May and 1 June, Toronto, ON.

Perkins, D., V. Nieva, and E. Lawler. 1983. *Managing Creation: The Challenge of Building a New Organization.* New York, NY: John Wiley.

Peters, T.J. and R.H. Waterman. 1985. *In Search of Excellence: Lessons from America's Best Run Companies.* Toronto, ON: HarperCollins Canada.

Pierce, J.L. and J.W. Newstrom. 2003. *Leadership and the Leadership Process: Readings, Self-Assessments and Applications.* New York, NY: McGraw-Hill Irwin.

Pilz, D.M. 1995. 'A Study of Characteristics and Start-Up Activities of Entrepreneurs in the Nonprofit (Non-Governmental) Organizations.' DBA dissertation, Nova South Eastern University.

Pore, K. 1991. 'Women and Social Reform Movements in India' in V.D. Divekar, G.T. Kulkarni, and M.R. Kantak (eds), *Social Reform Movements in India*, pp. 104–11. Bombay, India: Popular Prakashan.

Powell, G.N., A.D. Butterfield, and J.D. Parent. 2002. 'Gender and Managerial Stereotypes: Have the Times Changed?', *Journal of Management*, 28(2): 177–93.

Purushothaman, S. 1998. *The Empowerment of Women in India*. New Delhi, India: Sage Publications.

Purushothaman, S. and M. Jaeckel. 2000. *Challenging Development: A Grassroots Women's North–South Dialogue*. Bangalore, India: Books for Change.

———. 2001. *Huairou Commission Report*. Bangalore, India: Books for Change.

Puroshothaman, S. and S. Purohit. 2001. 'Introduction' in S. Puroshothaman and M. Jaekel (eds), *Engendering Governance and Development: Grassroots Women's Best Practices*. Bangalore, India.

Putnam, R. 1993. 'The Prosperous Community: Social Capital and Public Life', *American Prospect*, 13.

Quarter, J., L. Mook, and B.J. Richmond. 2003. *What Counts: Social Accounting for Nonprofits and Cooperatives*. Upper Saddle River, NJ: Prentice Hall.

Rahman, A. 1986. *Consciousness Raising Efforts of Grameen Bank*. Dhaka, Bangladesh: Bangladesh Institute of Development Studies, Agriculture and Rural Development Division.

Ray, R. 2000. *Fields of Protest: Women's Movements in India*. New Delhi, India: Sage Publications.

Rogaly, B. 1996. 'Micro-Finance Evangelism, Destitute Women and Hard Selling of a New Anti-Poverty Formula', *Development Practice*, 6(2): 100–12.

Rondstadt, R. 1984. *Entrepreneurship: Text, Cases and Notes*. Dover, MA: Lord Publishing.

Rosener, J.B. 1990. 'Ways Women Lead: The Command and Control Leadership Style Associated With Men Is Not the Only Way to Succeed', *Harvard Business Review*, November/December: 119–25.

Rosenfeld, J.M. 1997. 'Learning From Success: How to Develop User Friendly Social Work', *Society and Welfare*, 17: 361–78.

Rotschild, J. 1976. 'Taking Our Future Seriously', *Quest*, 2(3): 17–30.

Saadallah, S. 2002. 'Transcending Difference: The United Nations Role', *Women Watch—UN Chronicle*, 39(2): 48–50.

Sadik, N. 1988. 'Women, the Centre of Development', *Society for International Development*, 1: 30–31.

Salamon, L. and H. Anheier. 1997. *The Nonprofit Sector in the Developing World*. Manchester, England: Manchester University Press.

Salamon, L.M. and W.S. Sokolowski. 2004. *Global Civil Society: Dimensions of the Nonprofit Sector, Volume 2*. Bloomfield, CT: Kumarian Press.

Samuel, J. 1999. 'Straight Talk: The Holy Cow of Micro Credit; Why Its Difficult to Swallow the Development Mythology That Surrounds the Grameen Bank', *Humanscape*.

Sebstad, J. 1982. *Struggle and Development among Self-Employed Women*. Washington, DC: USAID.

Segal, A. 1996. 'Flowering Feminism: Conscious-raising at Work', *Journal of Organizational Change Management*, 9(5): 75–90.

Sexton, D.L. and N. Bowman-Upton. 1990. 'Female and Male Entrepreneurs: Psychological Characteristics and Their Role in Gender-Related Discrimination', *Journal of Business Venturing*, 5(1): 29–36.

Shabbir, A. and D.S.D. Gregorio. 1996. 'An Examination of the Relationship Between Women's Personal Goals and Structural Factors Influencing Their Decision to Start a Business: The Case of Pakistan', *Journal of Business Venturing*, 11: 507–29.

Sheilds, L.E. 1992. The Development of a Model of Empowerment with Women: Implications for Health Planning and Practice. Unpublished paper, University of Oregon.

Shelton, B.A. and D. John. 1996. 'The Division of Household Labor', *Annual Review of Sociology*, 22: 299–322.

Sinha, S. and C. Commuri. 2002. 'Success by Strategic Co-Optation: A Case Study from India.' Paper presented at the ARNOVA Conference, 5–7 November, Seattle, WA.

Sinha, S. and F. Sinha. 2002. 'Sustainability and Development: Evaluating the Performance of Indian Finance' in T. Fisher and M.S. Sriram (eds), *Beyond Micro-Credit: Putting Development Back Into Micro-Finance*, pp. 263–99. Oxford, UK: Oxfam in association with New Economics Foundation.

Smilie, I. 1995. *The Alms Bazaar: Altruism under Fire; Non-profit Organizations and International Development*. Ottawa, ON: IDRC.

Smith, D.H. 2000. *Grassroots Associations*. Thousand Oaks: Sage Publications.

Srilatha, B. 1996. 'Transforming Political Culture: Mahila Samakhya Experience', *Economic and Political Weekly*, 31(21): 1248–51.

Srivastava, S.S., R. Tandon, S.W. Sokolowski, and L.M. Salamon. 2004. 'India' in L.M. Salamon and S.W. Sokolowski (eds), *Global Civil Society: Dimensions of the Nonprofit Sector, Volume 2*, pp. 157–69. Bloomfield, CT: Kumarian Press.

Sunthankar, B.R. 1996. 'Social Reform Movement in the 19th Century Maharashtra' in V.D. Divekar, G.T. Kulkarni and M.R. Kantak (eds), *Social Reform Movements*, pp. 42–61. Bombay, India: Popular Prakashan.

Susamuad. 2002. *Five Year Reports*, 1991–2002.

Tata, S.L. 2002. *The Statistical Outline of India 2001–02*. Mumbai, India: Tata Services Ltd.

UNIFEM. 2000. Progress of the World's Women 2002, Volume 2. Accessed on 12 December, 2005 at http://www.unifem.org/resources/item_detail.php? ProductID=10

United Nations. 1995. Beijing Declaration Platform for Action (BPFA). Paper presented at The United Nations Fourth World Conference On Women, 4–15 September, Beijing, China.

————. 2000. 'The World's Women 2000: Trends and Statistics'. New York, NY: United Nations.

United Way. 6 October 1997. 'The Focus in On Outcomes', *News and Views: United Way of America's Executive Newsletter*, 2(7). Accessed on 12 December 2005, at http://national.unitedway.org/outcomes/library/nvfocus.cfm?&print=1national.

Uvin, P., P. Jain, and D. Brown. 2000. 'Think Large and Act Small: Toward a New Paradigm for NGO Scaling Up', *World Development*, 28(8): 1409–19.

Vakil, A.C. 1997. 'Confronting the Classification Problem: Toward a Taxonomy of NGOs', *World Development*, 25(12): 2057–70.

Verma, G.D. 2002. *Slumming India: A Chronicle of Slums and Their Saviours*. New Delhi, India: Penguin Books.

Vijayanthi, K.N. 2002. 'Women's Empowerment Through Self-Help Groups: A Participatory Approach', *Indian Journal of Gender Studies*, 9(3): 263–74.

Viswanath, V. 1991. *NGOs and Women's Development in Rural South India: A Comparative Analysis*. Boulder, CO: Westview Press.

Watkins, J.M. and D.S. Watkins. 1983. 'The Female Entrepreneur: Her Background and Determinants of Business Choice—Some British Data', *Frontiers of Entrepreneurship Research*: 271–88.

————. 1984. 'The Female Entrepreneur: Background and Determinants of Business Choice—Some British Data', *International Small Business Journal*, 2: 21–31.

Weber, M. 1930. *Protestant Ethic and the Spirit of Capitalism*. New York, NY: Scribner's.

————. 1968 (1921). *Economy and Society*. New York, NY: Bedminster Press.

Weisbrod, B.A. 1988. *The Nonprofit Economy*. Cambridge, MA: Harvard University Press.

Wilson, L.S. 1999. 'Technical Expertise and Indiginization' in K. Gupta (ed.), *Foreign Aid: New Perspective*. The Netherlands: Kluwer Academic Publishers.

Wolch, J. 1990. *Building the Shadow State*. New York, NY: Foundation Center.

Young, D.R. 1983. *If Not For Profit, For What?* Lexington, MA: Heath Books.

————. 1999. 'An Interview with John C. Whitehead', *Nonprofit Management and Leadership*, 9(3): 315–22.

Yudelman, S. 1987. *Hopeful Openings: A Study of Five Women's Development Organizations in Latin America and the Caribbean*. Hartford, CN: Kumarian Press.

Index

About the Authors

Femida Handy is Associate Professor at the School of Social Policy and Practice, University of Pennsylvania, and at the Faculty of Environmental Studies, York University. She was awarded the ARNOVA and Sage Publishers' Award for Outstanding Article in 1996 for her article that appeared in the *Nonprofit and Voluntary Sector Quarterly* as well as the award by ARNOVA for the Outstanding Doctoral Dissertation written in *Nonprofit and Voluntary Action Research*. Dr. Handy's research looks at various economic aspects of the nonprofit and voluntary sector and is published in journals such as *Social Development Issues, Nonprofit and Voluntary Sector Quarterly, Nonprofit Management and Leadership, Journal of Comparative Economics, Annals of Public and Cooperative Economics* and the *Journal of Community Practice*. She has also co-authored (with R.A. Cnaan, S.C. Boddie, G. Yarcey and R. Schneider), *The Invisible Caring Hand: Congregations and the Provisions of Welfare* (2002).

Meenaz Kassam is Assistant Professor, Ontario Institute for Studies in Education, University of Toronto and American University of Sharjah. She is also Director, Chinmaya Organization for Rural Development, Hamilton, Canada (in partnership with the Chinmaya Organization for Rural Development, Himachal Pradesh, India). Dr. Kassam has published articles in various journals such as *Nonprofit Management and Leadership, Social Development Issues, Pakistan Journal of Women's Studies* and *The Canadian Journal of Sociology*. She has authored *Immigrants from Pakistan: A Cultural Profile* (1998), part of a series commissioned by the Ministry of Immigration and Citizenship, Government of Canada.

Suzanne Feeney is Director, Institute for Nonprofit Management and an Associate Professor at the Hatfield School of Government, Portland State University. She is a past President of the Nonprofit ^cademic Centers Council (NACC) and past Vice President of the ~ciation for Research and Nonprofit Organizations and Voluntary ˙ɔns (ARNOVA). Dr. Feeney has been the recipient of two

Civic Engagement Awards from Portland State University and from the Albina Ministerial Alliance (an African-American community organization). She has published in many journals including the *Nonprofit and Voluntary Sector Quarterly* and the *Yale Case Study Series*.

Bhagyashree Ranade is CEO, Marketing & Market Research Consultants, Pune, India. She is also Founding Trustee of the Institute for Women Entrepreneurial Development and One Animal Life—both based in Pune, India. She has also published articles in various journals such as *Nonprofit Management and Leadership*, *Social Development Issues* and the *Pakistan Journal of Women's Studies*.